INTRODUCTION TO RISK MANAGEMENT AND INSURANCE

Brooke Grissom

TAP

Toronto Academic Press

INTRODUCTION TO RISK MANAGEMENT AND INSURANCE

Brooke Grissom

Toronto Academic Press
4164 Lakeshore Road
Burlington ON L7L 1A4
Canada
www.tap-books.com

Email: orders@arclereducation.com

ISBN: 978-1-77956-290-6

ABOUT THE AUTHOR

Brooke Grissom is a seasoned insurance agent with over seven years of experience in the industry. Currently working as an Insurance Agent, she specializes in providing comprehensive coverage solutions, guiding clients through the complexities of insurance policies, and ensuring their financial security. Previously, Brooke has developed a strong foundation in risk assessment and customer relationship management, which she applies in her daily interactions with clients. Brooke's professional journey includes extensive experience in personal and commercial insurance lines, where she has consistently delivered tailored advice to meet individual client needs. Committed to continuous professional development, she actively pursues industry certifications and training. Alongside her career, Brooke is passionate about community involvement and regularly volunteers with local organizations. Her dedication to the field and her clients makes her a trusted and reliable insurance professional.

Table of Contents

List of Figures

List of Tables

PREFACE

In an era characterized by an unprecedented interplay of economic dynamics and unforeseen challenges, the field of risk management and insurance stands as a linchpin in fortifying organizations against potential uncertainties. The landscape of financial risk mitigation and insurance strategies has evolved exponentially, presenting both remarkable opportunities and intricate challenges. The significance of safeguarding businesses and individuals against a myriad of risks cannot be overstated, and this book delves into the core principles, practices, and strategies that constitute the bedrock of effective risk management and insurance.

This book comprises eight chapters. Chapter 1 introduces the foundational concepts of risk management and insurance. Emphasizing the importance of a proactive approach to identifying and mitigating risks, this chapter sets the stage for the in-depth exploration of different aspects of risk management and insurance.

Chapter 2 delves into the principles and aims of risk management and insurance, unraveling the guiding philosophies that underpin effective risk management strategies. Chapter 3 focuses on risk assessment and identification strategies, shedding light on methodologies to discern and evaluate potential threats. Enterprise risk management, discussed in Chapter 4, provides insights into holistic approaches to managing risks across organizational structures.

Key drivers of risk management, discussed in Chapter 5, dissect the influential factors that shape risk landscapes and decision-making processes. Chapter 6 describes a critical link between insurance and mitigation to manage natural disaster risk, showcasing the symbiotic relationship between insurance mechanisms and proactive risk mitigation measures.

Chapter 7 explores diverse insurance products and provides a comprehensive view of the range of insurance instruments available for risk transfer. The final chapter on emerging trends and challenges in risk management and insurance navigates through the evolving landscape, addressing contemporary issues and forecasting future challenges.

This book has been specifically written for students and scholars to meet the knowledge needs of those seeking a profound understanding of risk management and insurance fundamentals. It aims to serve as a valuable tool for academics across various disciplines, offering clarity and insight to a diverse readership.

—Author

CHAPTER 1

Introduction to Risk Management and Insurance

LEARNING OBJECTIVES

After studying this chapter, you will be able to:

1. Understand the origins of risk management and its historical evolution in the insurance industry.
2. Identify the importance and scope of risk in various contexts, including personal, commercial, and systemic perspectives.
3. Classify risks into different categories, such as pure risk and speculative risk, diversifiable and non-diversifiable risk, and enterprise risk.
4. Define and explain the concept of systemic risk and its implications in risk management.
5. Differentiate between personal and commercial risks and recognize their distinct characteristics.
6. Analyze the characteristics of insurable risk, including multiple exposure units, unintentional and accidental loss, and economically feasible premiums.
7. Explore the role of insurance as a risk mitigation tool and its significance in transferring risk.
8. Identify various types of risks addressed by insurance and distinguish between private and government insurance.
9. Understand the objectives of risk management, both pre-loss and post-loss and their significance in risk mitigation.

INTRODUCTORY EXAMPLE

Let's consider a hypothetical manufacturing corporation named "General Electric" that operates in a turbulent international market. This business relies on a complex supply network involving multiple vendors and intricate logistical procedures. Given the interconnected nature of its operations, the company faces various concerns, including geopolitical risks, disruptions in the supply chain, and volatility in currency values.

Without a robust risk management plan, the business becomes more vulnerable to unforeseen events that could have a negative impact on its earnings, stability, and productivity. For instance, an abrupt interruption in the supply chain caused by natural disasters or geopolitical unrest could halt manufacturing operations, resulting in financial losses and damage to the company's reputation in the market.

This hypothetical situation emphasizes the importance of having insurance and effective risk management. A comprehensive risk management plan would involve recognizing and evaluating potential risks, implementing mitigation strategies, and obtaining insurance coverage to safeguard against financial losses. By understanding and mitigating these risks, the organization can enhance its resilience, ensure uninterrupted operations, and ultimately thrive in a volatile and unpredictable business environment. This initial example sets the foundation for the detailed exploration of insurance and risk management that will be presented in the following chapters.

UNIT INTRODUCTION

Historically, risk has been described in terms of the degree of uncertainty involved. Taking this idea into consideration, risk can be defined as the uncertainty that exists regarding the occurrence of a loss. An example of this would be the possibility of being involved in a fatal car accident, as there is a certain level of uncertainty. Smokers are at risk of developing lung cancer due to this uncertainty (Acharyya & Johnson, 2006).

In the insurance sector, employees often use the term "risk" in a different manner than usual when discussing the property or life that is being considered for insurance. For instance, it is common to hear phrases such as "That driver's life is at risk" or "Investing in that building is an intolerable risk" within the insurance sector (Feng, 2023).

According to the Oxford English Dictionary, risk is defined as "the likelihood or possibility of danger, loss, damage, or other undesirable consequences." The definition of "at risk" is "exposed to danger." Within the framework of this conversation, "risk" designates the unfavorable consequences. However, there is a chance that taking a risk will be profitable. Another possibility is that there is a connection between risk and uncertainty of results (Dionne, 2013).

For instance, owning a motor vehicle provides most individuals with the opportunity to increase their mobility and reap the benefits that come along with it. Nevertheless, there are a number of risks associated with the ownership of a motorcar, including the cost of maintenance and repairs. Furthermore, since automobiles can be involved in accidents, obviously undesirable outcomes can occur. The International Organization for Standardization (ISO) Guide 73 is the international guide on risk-related definitions. It defines risk as the "effect of uncertainty on objectives" (Eikenhout, 2015). This definition appears to encompass some knowledge about risk management, and its implementation in real-world scenarios may not be straightforward. Risk is defined by the Institute of Internal Auditors (IIA) as the uncertainty surrounding the occurrence of an event that could potentially impact the achievement of objectives. Additionally, according to the IIA, risk is assessed based on its potential consequences as well as its likelihood. Various disciplines have different definitions of what constitutes risk. Professionals in the field of health and safety define risk as the combination of an event's likelihood and magnitude; however, this definition may not be sufficient for more comprehensive risk management approaches (Liu et al., 2007).

Risk in the context of an organization is described as everything that has the potential to influence the accomplishment of corporate goals. However, the majority of firms do not often define their corporate objectives in their entirety. Where the objectives have been established, they tend to be stated as internal and annual objectives that can be changed over time. This is especially true with regard to the personal goals established for employees working for the businesses, which typically pertain to change or advancements, as opposed to the ongoing or ordinary activities of the organization (Hoyt & Liebenberg, 2008). There is not a single definition that can be applied to insurance. Insurance can be defined from the perspective of different fields, such as sociology, law, economics, history, actuarial science, and risk theory. However, we will not be looking into every possible definition. Instead, we will investigate the components that are typically present in any insurance policy. Before moving forward, it is necessary to construct a workable definition of insurance, one that encompasses the basic qualities of a true insurance plan (Briys et al., 1991).

The definition of insurance provided below was formulated by the Commission on Insurance Terminology of the American Risk and Insurance Association, following a thorough investigation and analysis. Insurance refers to the process of pooling catastrophic losses by transferring the associated risks to insurers. These insurers then agree to compensate insured individuals for these losses, offer financial benefits in the event of such losses, or provide services related to managing the risks. While this extensive explanation may not be satisfactory to every risk manager and insurance expert, it is valuable for evaluating the shared components of an insurance plan (Liu et al., 2007).

This chapter systematically dissects the concepts of risk management and insurance, providing a thorough examination of their constituent elements. Special attention is given to the historical origins and development of risk management, emphasizing its significant role in various contexts. The discussion underscores the importance of categorizing risks for informed decision-making and highlights the multifaceted nature of insurance, extending beyond financial considerations.

Throughout the chapter, readers delve into the workings of insurance as a mechanism for risk transfer and adaptation to challenges. The various types of insurance are explored, each with its own distinct features. Positive outcomes, such as financial stability and resilience, are consistently emphasized. In conclusion, the chapter revisits fundamental concepts, exploring the core meaning and objectives of risk management and establishing a framework for more in-depth discussions (Acharyya & Mutenga, 2013).

1.1. ORIGINS OF RISK MANAGEMENT

Learning Objectives

- Understand the historical context and early trade practices that gave rise to risk management.
- Identify key figures and events that played a pivotal role in shaping early risk management concepts.
- Recognize the impact of the Industrial Revolution in necessitating structured risk management approaches amid growing business complexities.

In the 1950s, the selection of insurance in the United States expanded to encompass corporate risk management. During the 1960s, corporations began to place greater importance on contingency planning. Alongside risk financing, loss prevention and safety management were also taken into account. In the 1970s, organizations started implementing risk retention and self-insurance. This period also witnessed the emergence of captive insurance businesses. Subsequently, contingency plans evolved into disaster recovery and business continuity plans. The 1960s and 1970s also marked a significant shift in the risk management approach adopted by occupational health and safety practitioners. The 1980s saw notable progress in the application of risk management techniques in project management. Financial institutions continued to refine their risk management techniques and procedures for credit and market risks during this decade. In the 1990s, financial institutions systematically expanded their risk management plans to include operational risks (Dickinson, 2001).

Additionally, treasury departments began developing a financial approach to risk management in the 1980s. Finance directors recognized the need for improved coordination between insurance risk management and financial risk management procedures. In the 1990s, derivatives, and insurance were integrated to create new risk-financing products. The appointment of the first chief risk officer (CRO) occurred during this period, and corporate governance and listing requirements prompted boards to prioritize enterprise risk management (ERM) even more (Covello & Mumpower, 1985).

During the 2000s, financial services companies were encouraged to establish internal risk management systems and capital models. The number of CRO roles in banks, insurance firms, and energy corporations has significantly increased. Due to the U.S. Sarbanes–Oxley Act of 2002, boards are increasingly focusing on ERM. Additional corporate governance regulations, such as more comprehensive risk reporting, have also been implemented. However, the 2008 financial crisis raised concerns about the role of risk management in promoting corporate success, especially in financial institutions.

Undoubtedly, the global financial crisis occurred as a result of an incorrect application of risk management processes and procedures (Weimer, 2017).

Did you know?

In ancient China, "bottomry" referred to a primitive method of risk management in which lenders provided financial support for nautical expeditions. They would cancel the loan if the ship encountered disasters, thus anticipating the fundamental status of contemporary insurance.

A broad spectrum of professionals practice risk management, which has many roots (Figure 1.1). The insurance management function in the United States was responsible for one of the earliest advancements in risk management. Because insurance had become prohibitively expensive and had limited coverage in the 1950s, risk management became a more common and well-coordinated process. Companies came to understand that insurance alone would not be sufficient if people and property were not given enough care. As a result, consumers of insurance started to worry about issues such as product liability, health and safety regulations, property protection quality, and other risk control concerns (Crockford, 1982).

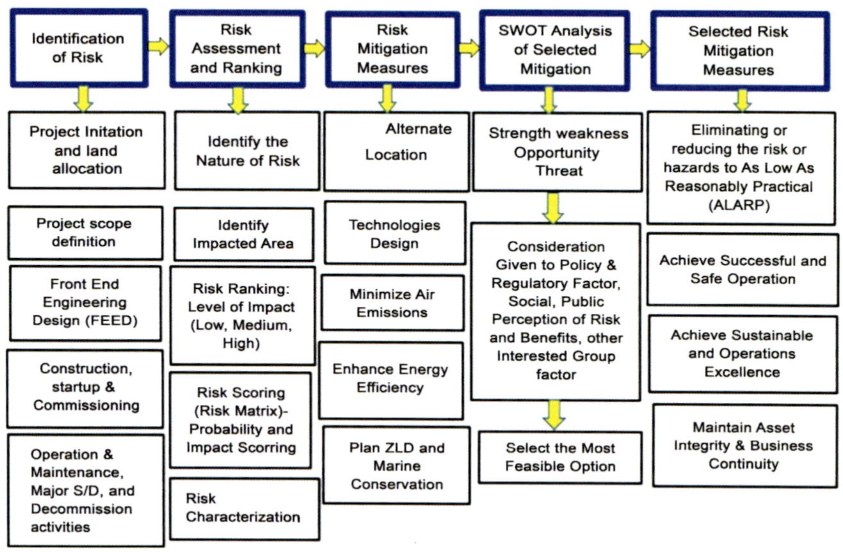

Figure 1.1. Diagram of risk management flowchart. (Source: Mohammed Albeldawi, Creative Commons License)

In Europe, a combined approach to risk financing and risk control evolved during the 1970s, and the concept of total cost of risk became increasingly important. As this approach gained popularity, it also became evident that businesses were exposed to a variety of risks that were not protected by insurance. The risk management techniques and tools were then applied by other disciplines. The risk management discipline has evolved to the point where there are now considerably weaker ties to insurance. Although insurance is only applicable to a subset of risks, it is currently regarded as one risk control approach. Although historically outside the purview of insurance, risks pertaining to finance, commerce, the marketplace, and reputational concerns are acknowledged as being quite significant. The risk management definitions in Table 1.1 provide a description of the variety of approaches to risk management (McShane, 2018).

Table 1.1. Definition of Risk Management

Organization	Definition of Risk Management
ISO Guide 73 BS 31100	Coordinating activities to effectively manage and oversee an organization's risk.
Institute of Risk Management (IRM)	Risk management is a systematic approach that assists businesses in comprehending, assessing, and addressing all potential risks in order to enhance the likelihood of success and minimize the likelihood of failure.
HM Treasury	Risk management is the entirety of the procedures encompassing the identification, evaluation, and determination of risks, allocation of responsibility, implementation of measures to reduce or predict them, and the ongoing observation and evaluation of progress.
London School of Economics	Risk management is the process involves identifying the risks that a firm should embrace and those that should be avoided or reduced, and thereafter implementing measures to prevent or minimize such risks.
Business Continuity Institute	Risk management encompasses the culture, processes, and structures that are established to efficiently handle both possible opportunities and negative consequences.

Source: Paul Hopkin, Creative Commons License.

1.2. HISTORICAL EVOLUTION OF THE INSURANCE INDUSTRY

Learning Objectives

- Investigate the historical origins of the insurance industry, examining its early practices and evolution.
- Recognize key moments and innovations that have shaped the development of the insurance sector over time.

The concept of insurance has existed since ancient times. Merchants in Babylon were familiar with bottomry contracts as early as 4000–3000 BCE. Bottomry was a common practice in ancient Greece as early as the 4th century BCE, and it was first documented by the Hindus around 600 BCE. Under a bottomry contract, merchants received loans with the understanding that they would not be repaid in the case of a loss at sea. The loan's interest accounted for the insurance risk. In ancient Rome, the bottomry contract was acknowledged as a legal transaction when a written document was created, and money was entrusted to a currency exchange agent. The development of marine insurance reached a high level of sophistication throughout the 15th century (Pearson, 1997). Rome also had burial organizations that covered funeral expenses for their members through monthly dues.

Early on, the insurance contract also came into existence. This information was widely known in ancient Greece and among other maritime nations that traded with Greece.

The concept of fire insurance emerged later, gaining momentum due to the Great Fire of London in 1666. Several insurance businesses were established in England after the year 1711, during the period commonly referred to as the Bubble Age. Many of these schemes were deceptive, with the primary objective being quick profit through the sale of securities to the public. Nevertheless, this period witnessed the establishment of the London Assurance Corporation and the Royal Exchange Assurance Corporation, two notable and successful English insurance companies. Their project marked the beginning of modern liability and property insurance (Njegomir & Marvoic, 2012).

A comprehensive analysis of the early development of insurance in Europe must acknowledge Lloyd's of London, the international insurance market. This coffee shop, which dates back to the 17th century, attracted customers who were bankers, insurance underwriters, and merchants. Over time, it became renowned as the premier destination to find underwriters specializing in maritime insurance. Edward Lloyd supplied his customers with marine information gathered from the docks and other sources, which eventually evolved into the continuous publication known as Lloyd's List (Manes, 1942).

Following a reform in 1769, Lloyd's became an official association of underwriters committed to assuming marine risks. The term "underwriter" is said to have originated from the practice of having each risk taker sign their name below the total amount of risk they were willing to accept at a specified premium. With the growth of British naval power, Lloyd's became the dominant insurer for risks associated with marine activities. Over time, they also began offering insurance for fire and other property risks. Presently, Lloyd's is a leading provider of reinsurance and primary insurance. It does not directly engage in insurance transactions. However, it is the member underwriters who bear this responsibility. They individually accept insurance on their own behalf and assume the full risk while competing (Martin et al., 2000).

Benjamin Franklin founded the Philadelphia Contributionship in 1752, establishing the first insurance company in America. The Presbyterian Ministers' Fund, founded in 1759, was the first life insurance institution in the American colonies. By 1820, there were precisely 17 stock life insurance companies in New York state. A significant proportion of the early property insurance companies faced collapse due to high-risk investments, ineffective management, and inadequate distribution networks. Following the Great Chicago Fire in 1871 and the San Francisco earthquake and fire of 1906, several individuals and organizations also experienced failure (Longnaker, 1962).

The difficulty in rate-making stemmed from inadequate regulation and the absence of cooperative endeavors to establish accurate statistics. The life insurance industry is also afflicted by several challenges. After the U.S. Civil War, certain detrimental practices arose. These factors encompassed the declaration of dividends that were not actually earned, inadequate reserves, inflated advertising claims, and the development of office buildings that sometimes surpassed the total assets of the companies. During the period from 1870 to 1872, a total of 33 life insurance companies were bankrupt, and an additional 48 failures occurred between 1873 and 1877 (Maurer & Somova, 2007).

Life insurance experienced consistent and continuous growth in the United States after 1910. From 1910 to 1990, the insurance experienced an annual growth rate of around 8.4%, resulting in a 626-fold rise over the span of 80 years. The increase in property-liability insurance was rather modest. In 1989, there were over 3,800 property-liability insurance companies and 2,270 life insurance companies operating, with a workforce of nearly two million employees. In 1987, insurers based in the United States accounted for around 37% of the total premiums collected globally (Hardwick & Guirguis, 2007).

The nationalization of insurance in Russia occurred following the Russian Revolution in 1917. In the Soviet Union, domestic insurance was provided exclusively by Gosstrakh, while insurance for foreign risks was handled by Ingosstrakh, a subsidiary business. Ingosstrakh maintains its insurance coverage for properties owned by foreigners in Russia, as well as properties owned by Russians in foreign countries. It engages in the practice of accepting reinsurance from insurers based in other countries. However, because of the transition to a free market economy (perestroika) that commenced in 1985 and the subsequent disintegration of the Soviet Union in 1991, over 230 new private insurance firms were established (Pearson, 2002).

Remember

Ancient Rome introduced the idea of "wagering contracts" or "aleatory contracts," in which the result is contingent on an unforeseen circumstance. Romans entered into agreements pertaining to maritime hazards through contracts known as "sponsio" and "stipulatio," which are similar to modern insurance. If the ship successfully completed its voyage, the insurer would compensate the insured. There are historical similarities between current insurance practices and this early form of contractual risk transfer.

Gosstrakh offers insurance policies that protect both property and personal insurance. Property insurance is required for government-owned property and specified property of communal farms. Voluntary property insurance provides coverage for privately held property. Furthermore, there are individual insurance plans, such as life and accident insurance, as well as annuities, that can be acquired through purchase (Jitschin, 2015).

Before 1991, insurance coverage for tort liability was not allowed because it was believed that it would allow negligent individuals to escape the financial consequences of their acts. However, the implementation of a free market economy in Russia is likely to make liability insurance available (Leonard, 2016).

After the Soviet Union disbanded, countries in Eastern Europe implemented a variety of insurance systems, ranging from highly centralized and state-regulated systems to systems like those found in Western countries. Given the recent political and economic disturbances in these nations, it is likely that there will be a move towards decentralized systems like those observed in the Western world (Scordis & Katrishen, 1997).

Several generalizations can be made regarding insurance in Eastern European countries. While state insurance monopolies are prevalent, they are seeing a decline in market share due to competition from private insurers. Insurance coverage for state-owned property, once deemed superfluous in socialist nations, has been implemented in various countries (Peters, 1993).

The global insurance market experienced significant growth in the 20th century, primarily driven by the substantial increase in international trade and the expansion of corporate investments abroad. As a result of this development, the establishment of a global network of offices became necessary to provide brokerage services, underwriting assistance, claims support, and other related services. The majority of the world's insurance industry is concentrated in Europe and North America, where these businesses must meet a significant share of the global insurance market. However, there are notable legal and regulatory obstacles that need to be overcome in order to achieve this (Grace & Klein, 2009).

In terms of the percentage of total premiums collected, the top ten insurance markets in the world in 1990 were the United States

(35.6%), Japan (20.5%), the United Kingdom (7.5%), Germany (6.8%), France (5.5%), the Soviet Union (2.6%), Canada (2.3%), Italy (2.2%), South Korea (2.0%), and Oceania (1.8%) (Schwartz et al., 2011).

Major world trends in insurance include a gradual movement away from the nationalism of insurance, the development of worldwide insurance programs to cover the operations of multinational corporations, increasing use of reinsurance, increasing use by corporations of self-insurance programs administered by wholly owned insurance subsidiaries (captive companies), and increasing use of mergers among both insurers and brokerage firms (Altuntas et al., 2021).

1.3. IMPORTANCE AND SCOPE OF RISK

Learning Objectives

- To understand the importance and scope of risk
- To highlight the integration of risk into decision-making

Since 2008, in the global financial system, risk and risk management have become more important to all firms. It is widely recognized that there are benefits of actively managing risks. Organizations can achieve improvements in three areas by adopting a proactive strategy towards risk and risk management:

a) Operations will become more efficient since events that could cause disruptions will be recognized in advance, and actions will be taken to reduce their likelihood, limit the harm they cause, and contain their costs. This will also enable regular, effective production operations to continue (Ewold, 1991).

b) Processes will be more effective because they will have been chosen with careful consideration of the risks associated with potential alternatives. Furthermore, process modifications implemented through projects will be executed more successfully and consistently.

c) Strategy will be more effective as it will thoroughly analyze the risks associated with various strategic possibilities, leading to better strategic decisions. The term "effective" refers to the ability of the planned strategy to produce the desired results.

Organizations can no longer afford to be in a situation where unforeseen events result in revenue loss, disruption of regular business operations, damage to their brand, and decline in market share. Stakeholders increasingly expect companies to fully consider the risks that could lead to operational disruptions, project delays, or strategy failures (Hellner, 1963). The likelihood of a risk materializing and the impact it may have can be used to determine the exposure presented by each individual risk.

Risk management's scope and significance are crucial factors to consider in both the personal and professional spheres. To put it simply, risk management encompasses various domains, including project management, business operations, healthcare, and finance. It functions as a systematic approach to identify, comprehend, and address potential concerns before they become significant ones (Lindsay, 1918). Risk management serves as a toolkit that organizations utilize to safeguard their assets and make well-informed decisions. It is not solely about avoiding issues; it also involves compliance with the law, fostering creativity, and being prepared to handle unforeseen challenges. By enhancing resilience and the ability to recover from unexpected circumstances, it contributes to the long-term success of a firm (Powers, 2006).

In the personal context, risk management often entails owning insurance policies such as life, health, or property insurance. These policies act as safety nets, assisting individuals and families in resolving unforeseen circumstances without incurring significant financial losses.

Risk management is important for both individuals and enterprises. It requires astuteness, organization, and resilience in the face of unexpected events. Whether in the corporate world or personal life, understanding and managing risks are crucial aspects of making informed and successful decisions (Williams, 1966).

1.4. CLASSIFICATION OF RISK

Learning Objectives

- To discuss the examples of types of risk classifications
- To highlight the several distinct classes of risk

There are various categories into which risk can be divided. The following are among the most significant:

a) Pure and speculative risk;

b) Diversifiable risk and non-diversifiable risk;

c) Enterprise risk;

d) Systemic risk.

PRACTICE PROBLEM

As a project manager, your responsibility is to identify and categorize risks associated with a software development project. Enumerate three prospective hazards, categorizing them according to their classification (e.g., financial, operational, strategic), and provide a concise account of the potential consequences each hazard could have on the project.

SOLUTIONS TO PRACTICE PROBLEM (1)

Operational Risk:

A key developer, responsible for a critical component, resigns abruptly.

Classification: Operational risk

Impact: These circumstances may lead to delays in the project timetable, increased workload for other team members, and potential setbacks in meeting deliverables.

Financial Risk:

Currency exchange rate fluctuations affect project costs.

Classification: Financial Risk

Impact: Exchange rate fluctuations can impact budgeting and financial projections, potentially leading to exceeding estimated costs if not carefully managed.

Strategic Risk:

Changes in market trends render the developed software less competitive.

Classification: Strategic Risk

Impact: Changes in market dynamics may require modifications to the project's strategic objectives, which could affect the product's relevance and positioning in the market.

1.4.1. Pure Risk and Speculative Risk

Pure risk refers to a scenario where there are just two outcomes: either a loss occurs or no loss occurs. The only conceivable results are unfavorable (loss) and neutral (no loss). Examples of pure risks include premature death, job-related accidents, catastrophic medical expenses, and damage to property from fire, lightning, flood, or earthquake. In contrast, speculative risk is defined as a situation in which either profit or loss is possible. For instance, if you acquire 100 shares of ordinary stock, you will gain if the stock price rises but will incur a loss if the price decreases. Additional instances of speculative risks encompass wagering on a horse race, engaging in real estate investments, and embarking on entrepreneurial endeavors. Under such circumstances, the potential for both gain and loss exists (Ferrer & Mallari, 2011).

Differentiating between pure and speculative risks is crucial for three key reasons. Private insurers primarily focus on ensuring pure risks rather than speculative ones. However, there are instances that deviate from this norm. Some insurers provide coverage for institutional portfolio investments and municipal bonds to protect against potential losses. Moreover, corporate risk management is a notable example of how certain speculative risks can be insured. Additionally, the law of big numbers can be more readily applied to pure risks compared to speculative risks. The law of large numbers is significant as it allows insurers to forecast future loss experience (Kahane & Kroll, 1985).

Conversely, it is typically more challenging to utilize the law of large numbers to forecast future loss occurrences for speculative risks. One example of a speculative risk is gambling, where casino owners can effectively utilize the law of big numbers. Ultimately, society can benefit from taking a calculated risk, even if it results in a loss (Ben & Levy, 1980).

However, society is negatively affected when a speculative risk is present, even if a loss occurs. On the other hand, society is harmed if a pure risk is present and a loss occurs. For example, a company might innovate novel technologies aimed at manufacturing cost-effective computers. As a result, some competitors may be forced into bankruptcy. Despite the bankruptcy, society benefits because the computers are produced at a lower cost. Nevertheless, the overall welfare of society is typically not enhanced when a loss from a pure risk occurs, such as a devastating flood or earthquake that annihilates a town or region (Barth & So, 2014).

1.4.2. Diversifiable and Non-Diversifiable Risk

Diversifiable risk, also known as idiosyncratic risk, refers to the type of risk that is specific to certain individuals or small groups and does not have a widespread impact on the overall economy. Diversification can mitigate or eliminate this risk. For instance, a portfolio that includes a variety of stocks, bonds, and certificates of deposit (CDs) carries lower risk compared to a portfolio that is entirely invested in common stocks. Losses incurred from investing in equities can potentially be counterbalanced by gains derived from bonds and certificates of deposit (CDs). Similarly, the risk to a property and liability insurer is reduced when they underwrite different lines of insurance instead of just one line (Anyika, 2015).

Losses incurred in one line can be counterbalanced by profits generated in other lines. Illustrative examples of diversifiable risk encompass automobile thefts, burglaries, and residential conflagrations. Only individuals and commercial firms who incur such losses are impacted, rather than the entire economy (Chen et al., 2010).

In contrast, non-diversifiable risk is a risk that affects the entire economy or large numbers of persons or groups within the economy. It is a risk that cannot be eliminated or reduced by diversification. Examples include rapid inflation, cyclical unemployment, war, hurricanes, floods, and earthquakes because large numbers of individuals or groups are affected. Non-diversifiable risk, also known as fundamental risk, has a broad impact on the entire economy or a significant portion of the population (Nocco & Stulz, 2006).

The differentiation between diversifiable and non-diversifiable (fundamental) risk is significant, as government intervention may be required to provide insurance coverage for non-diversifiable risks. In the United States, certain risks that cannot be diversified may require the implementation of social insurance, government insurance programs, or government guarantees and subsidies. For example, the risks of insuring against widespread unemployment and floods are considerable, since these risks do not possess the features that make them easily insurable. Consequently, state unemployment compensation programs are essential for providing regular income to individuals who experience involuntary job loss. Similarly, the federal flood insurance program provides property insurance to people and businesses located in flood-prone areas (Bromiley et al., 2015).

1.4.3. Enterprise Risk

Enterprise risk refers to the entire range of significant risks encountered by a commercial organization (Figure 1.2). These risks include pure risk, speculative risk, strategic risk, operational risk, and financial risk. The definitions of pure and speculative risk have already been explained. Strategic risk relates to the uncertainty surrounding a company's financial goals and objectives. For instance, if a company enters a new business sector, there is a possibility that the sector may not generate profits. Operational risk arises from the activities and processes carried out by the company. For example, a financial institution that offers internet-based banking services may experience financial setbacks if unauthorized individuals gain unauthorized access to the institution's computer system (Hiles, 2012).

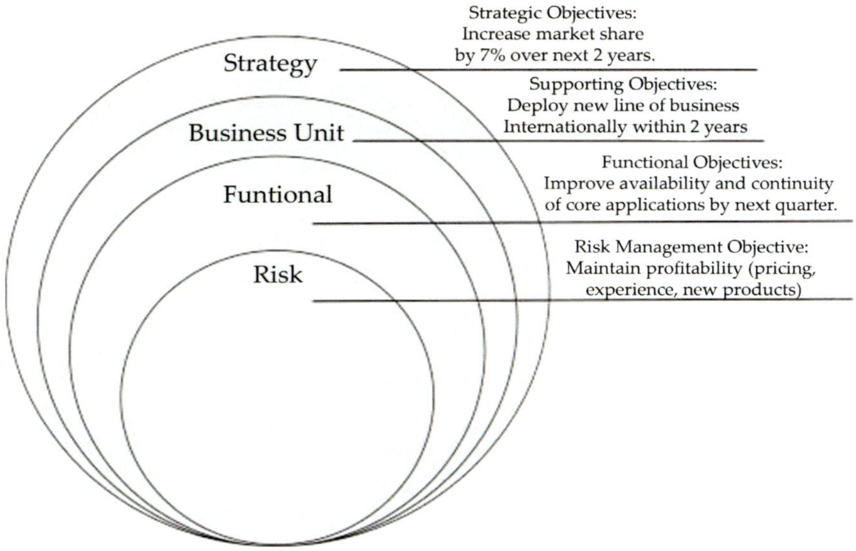

Figure 1.2. Image showing that risk assessments are linked to strategic objectives in an organization as a whole to allow a company to understand the risks in the organization, the company's risk appetite, and risk tolerance. (Source: Scott R. Ellis, Creative Commons License)

Enterprise risk encompasses financial risk, which is becoming increasingly important in a commercial risk management program. Financial risk relates to the uncertainty of potential losses resulting from unfavorable fluctuations in commodity prices, interest rates, foreign exchange rates, and currency value. For example, a food corporation that commits to supplying cereal to a retail chain at a certain cost within a 6-month period may incur financial losses if grain prices rise. If a bank holds a significant amount of Treasury bonds in its portfolio, it may experience financial losses in the event of an increase in interest rates. Similarly, an American corporation engaged in business activities in Japan may incur financial losses when converting Japanese yen into American dollars (Hoyt & Liebenberg, 2011).

Enterprise risk is increasingly important in the field of commercial risk management, which refers to the systematic approach used by firms to identify and mitigate significant and minor risks. Some risk managers are currently considering the inclusion of all categories of risk within a single program. Enterprise risk management integrates all significant risks faced by the company into a comprehensive and consistent treatment program (Acharya et al., 2017).

The corporation can mitigate one risk by combining multiple risks into a single program. Consequently, the overall level of risk can be diminished (Schwarcz, 2008). Managing financial risks often necessitates employing intricate hedging strategies, financial derivatives, futures contracts, options, and other financial instruments. Certain companies designate a chief risk officer (CRO), such as the treasurer, to oversee and handle the financial risks of the company.

1.4.4. Systemic Risk

Systemic risk is a substantial economic risk that has a significant impact on the interest rate decisions of the Federal Reserve, fiscal policies of the federal government, and government regulation of the economy. The failure of systemic risk is particularly crucial when it comes to prominent commercial banks and other financial institutions that are so large that their collapse would result in considerable financial harm to a substantial portion of the American economy (Smaga, 2014).

Systemic risk refers to the possibility of a complete collapse of a system or market due to the failure of a single corporation or group of companies, which can lead to the failure of the entire financial system. The economic recession that occurred in the United States from 2008 to 2009 was a profound decline and the second-most severe in the history of the country. The primary cause can be attributed to systemic risk. The economy experienced a significant financial crisis and a substantial downturn in the stock market, resulting in substantial losses for numerous Americans (Plomaritou & Nikolaides, 2016).

The national unemployment rate reached unprecedented levels. The housing market had a significant downturn, resulting in a surge in foreclosures. More than 100 commercial banks and financial institutions experienced failure or consolidation, leading to a credit crunch and a freezing of credit markets. Unregulated complex derivatives were marketed by commercial banks and certain insurers, leading to significant financial losses for investors on a global scale. The regulation of the financial services industry, both at the state and federal levels, was found to be inadequate and inefficient, particularly in relation to insurance businesses (Wu et al., 2019).

1.4.5. Personal and Commercial Risk

The previous discussion demonstrates many methods of categorizing risk. However, it is important to focus largely on the recognition and management of pure risk. Specific types of pure risks pose significant financial vulnerability for both individuals and families, as well as for commercial enterprises. Let's explore two categories of risks: significant personal risks that impact individuals and families, and large commercial risks that impact business enterprises (Elvik et al., 2009).

1.4.5.1. Personal Risks

Dangers that directly impact an individual or their family are referred to as personal risks. These circumstances carry the risk of further expenses, the depletion of financial resources, and a reduction or loss of earned income (Houston, 1964). The following are significant personal risks that can lead to substantial economic insecurity:

a) Premature death;
b) Poor health;
c) Insufficient income during retirement;
d) Unemployment.

1.4.5.2. Commercial Risk

One essential part of all-encompassing risk management plans for companies is commercial risk. These risks, which result from the dynamic and complex character of the business environment, cover a wide range of difficulties, such as supply chain interruptions, market volatility, regulatory changes, and technology uncertainties. A methodical and proactive approach is necessary for the effective management of commercial risks. Potential threats must first be identified, evaluated, and prioritized. Then, strategic countermeasures must be developed and implemented to mitigate or eliminate the threat. Strong risk management practices protect against negative effects and lay the groundwork for informed decisions and long-term growth. In the analysis, understanding, and enhancement of firms' resilience in a dynamic economic environment, the examination of commercial risk within the framework of risk management provides a crucial perspective.

1.5. CHARACTERISTICS OF INSURABLE RISK

Learning Objectives

- To define the insurable risk characteristics
- To apply these characteristics to differentiate between insurable and uninsurable risks for informed decision-making in risk assessment and insurance practices.

Private insurers typically provide coverage only for pure risks. However, there are many pure risks that private entities cannot cover. From the perspective of a private insurer, an insurable risk should ideally possess specific qualities. An insurable risk ideally possesses six distinct qualities:

a) A substantial quantity of exposure units is required.
b) The loss must be accidental and unintentional.
c) The loss must be measurable and determinable.
d) The loss should be non-catastrophic.
e) The probability of experiencing a loss must be quantifiable.
f) The premium must be financially viable.

1.5.1. Large Number of Exposure Units

An essential requirement for a risk to be insurable is the presence of a significant number of exposure units. Ideally, there should be a substantial collection of exposure units that are approximately comparable, if not necessarily identical, and are susceptible to the same danger or set of dangers. For instance, a large number of wood-frame dwellings in a city can be grouped together to provide property insurance on the dwellings (Fishcer, 1990).

The purpose of this initial requirement is to enable the insurer to predict losses based on the law of large numbers. Over time, loss data can be compiled, and losses for the group can be predicted with reasonable accuracy. The costs of these losses can then be spread across all insured individuals in the underwriting class (Ingram & Ostfeld, 1984).

1.5.2. Unintentional and Accidental Loss

A second requirement is that the loss must be unplanned, unexpected, and outside of the insured's control. For this reason, someone should not be compensated for a loss they purposefully caused (Shaik et al., 2006).

There are multiple justifications for this requirement. Initially, the loss should be accidental as the law of large numbers relies on the unpredictable nature of events. An intentionally induced loss is not a random event, as the insurance company is aware of the timing of the loss. Therefore, if there are several deliberate or nonrandom losses, the prediction of future experiences may be exceedingly unreliable. Furthermore, the presence of moral hazard is heightened when the insured purposefully seeks to bring about a loss. Allowing insured individuals to get compensation for intentional losses is ultimately detrimental to public policy (Prabhakar et al., 2015).

1.5.3. Measurable and Determinable Loss

The third requirement is that the loss must be determinable and measurable. This means that the cause, timing, location, and value of the loss must all be clearly specified. Life insurance typically suffices to cover this need. The cause and date of death are typically easily determined, and if the person is insured, the full life insurance policy amount is paid out (Ibragimov et al., 2009).

Some losses, on the other hand, present difficulties when it comes to determining and measuring them. Within a disability-income policy, the insurance company agrees to provide a monetary payment to the person who is disabled, but only if the specific conditions described in the policy's definition of disability are satisfied. Some deceitful individuals may deliberately claim a medical condition or physical harm with the objective of obtaining financial reimbursement from the insurance company. Irrespective of the claim's legality, the insurer must nevertheless evaluate whether the insured satisfies the disability conditions specified in the policy (Radu & Naghi, 2020).

1.5.4. No Catastrophic Loss

The fourth requirement states that it is more desirable for the loss to be non-catastrophic. This indicates that a significant proportion of exposed units should not encounter losses simultaneously. Pooling serves as the fundamental basis of insurance, as previously mentioned. If a substantial majority or all of the exposure units within a specific class experience a loss at the same time, the pooling strategy becomes ineffective and impractical. Raising premiums to exorbitant amounts becomes necessary, as the current insurance method of distributing losses across the entire group is no longer a feasible solution (Cevolini, 2016).

Insurers strive to completely prevent any catastrophic losses. However, this goal is unattainable due to the intermittent occurrence of catastrophic losses caused by floods, hurricanes, tornadoes, earthquakes, forest fires, and other natural calamities. Acts of terrorism can also lead to catastrophic losses (Martinez, 2012).

1.5.5. Calculable Chance of Loss

Additionally, it is necessary that the probability of experiencing a loss can be calculated. The insurer must possess the ability to accurately calculate both the mean occurrence rate and the mean magnitude of forthcoming losses. This condition is essential to ensure that an appropriate premium is assessed, which is adequate to cover all claims and expenses and generate a profit during the duration of the policy (Smith & Watts, 2019).

Some losses are challenging to insure due to the inability to precisely assess the likelihood of occurrence and the possibility of a severe loss. Instances such as floods, wars, and cyclical unemployment happen sporadically, making it challenging to forecast the typical occurrence and intensity of damage. Therefore, in the absence of government aid, private carriers find it challenging to provide insurance coverage for these losses (Akter et al., 2009).

1.5.6. Economically Feasible Premium

Finally, the premium must be financially viable. The insured must possess the financial means to cover the cost of the premium. Moreover, the premiums paid must be much less than the face value or amount of the policy for the insurance to be a desirable investment. A relatively small risk of suffering a loss is required for a premium to be economically feasible. From one angle, the cost of the insurance policy will exceed the amount that the insurer is required to pay under the terms of the contract if the likelihood of a loss is more than forty percent. As an illustration, an insurance company can provide a life insurance policy worth $1,000 to a 99-year-old man. However, the cost of the pure premium itself would be nearly equal to that amount, and an extra sum to cover expenses would also need to be included. The aggregate premium would surpass the nominal value of the insurance policy (Nieuwoudt, 2000).

It is often possible to obtain private insurance for personal risks, property risks, and liability risks, as these types of risks typically possess the necessary features to be insurable. However, private insurers find it challenging to provide insurance coverage for most market risks, financial risks, industrial risks, and political risks. The risks mentioned are speculative, and determining an accurate premium may be challenging due to the inability to precisely assess the probability of loss. Insurance coverage that safeguards a merchant from financial loss resulting from shifts in consumer preferences, such as changes in style, is typically unavailable (Fadun, 2013).

1.6. ROLE OF INSURANCE IN RISK MITIGATION

Learning Objectives

- To understand the concept of insurance in risk mitigation
- To discuss the types of risks addressed by insurance

Risk mitigation is a crucial element in managing uncertainties, and insurance plays a varied role in this process, serving as an essential component in protecting individuals and organizations.

1.6.1. Insurance as a Risk Transfer Tool

Essentially, insurance serves as a powerful mechanism for transferring risk. When individuals or organizations purchase insurance, they are simply shifting the financial responsibility of certain risks to the insurance provider. If a loss that is covered by the insurance policy occurs, the insurer will intervene to offer monetary compensation, thus reducing the immediate impact on the policyholder. This transfer mechanism plays a crucial role in spreading and controlling risks across a wider range, hence contributing to the general stability of the economy (Kling & Woltihuis, 1992).

1.6.2. Types of Risk Addressed by Insurance

Insurance reduces a wide range of hazards by providing safeguards and monetary assistance in different areas. The insurance addresses various categories of hazards.

1.6.2.1. Property Risks

Property insurance minimizes the potential hazards linked to the destruction or disappearance of real possessions, such as residences, structures, and personal items, resulting from occurrences like fire, theft, or natural calamities (Wagstaff & Lindelow, 2008).

1.6.2.2. Liability Risks

Liability insurance provides coverage for legal claims and the related expenses that result from injuries or losses for which the insured party is held accountable. It is essential for people and corporations to minimize future financial obligations.

1.6.2.3. Health Risks

Health insurance is crucial for reducing the financial risks linked with medical costs. It encompasses expenses associated with medical services, pharmaceuticals, and hospital stays, thereby mitigating the financial consequences of unforeseen health problems.

1.6.2.4. Life Risks

Life insurance offers monetary assistance to designated recipients in the event of the policyholder's demise. It reduces the economic consequences for the remaining relatives by covering the costs of the funeral and providing a cash cushion (Roll et al., 2012).

1.6.2.5. Business Risks

Company insurance comprises a range of products that mitigate the impact of risks related to company activities, such as property damage, liability claims, and disruptions to business operations. It ensures uninterrupted flow and economic security in the presence of unexpected circumstances.

1.6.2.6. Financial Risks

Certain insurance products, such as those related to investments or financial instruments, mitigate risks associated with market fluctuations, providing a degree of financial protection for investors (Pauly et al., 2006).

In essence, the role of insurance in risk mitigation is dynamic and expansive. It not only serves as a financial safety net but also contributes to broader risk management strategies, fostering resilience and stability in the face of diverse uncertainties. The diversity of risks addressed by insurance underscores its versatility as a risk mitigation tool in both personal and business contexts.

1.7. TYPES OF INSURANCE

Learning Objectives

- To define the types of insurance
- To discuss the private and government insurances

There are two types of insurance:

i. Public insurance; and

ii. Private insurance.

Life, health, property, and liability insurance are all included in private insurance (Figure 1.3). Social insurance plans and other government insurance policies are included in government insurance (Mantis & Farmer, 1968).

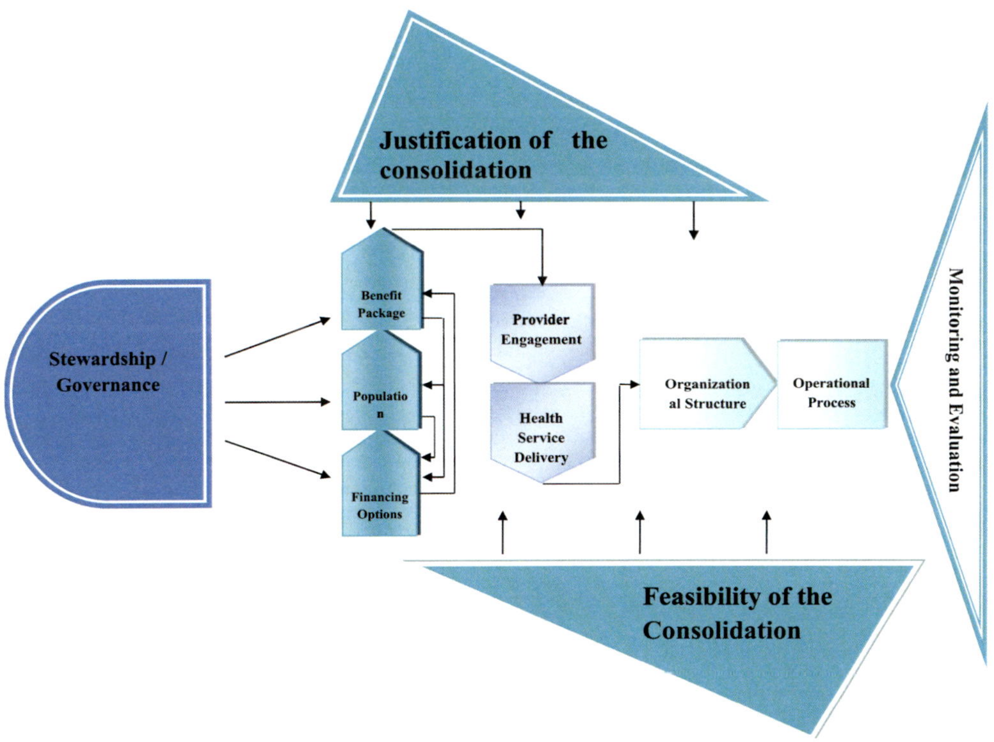

Figure 1.3. Illustration of design elements for a health insurance scheme (Source: M. Bazyar et al., Creative Commons License)

1.7.1. Private Insurance

The term "private insurance" describes insurance that is offered by companies that are not owned or run by the government. These companies provide financial protection against a variety of risks by offering a range of insurance products to individuals, businesses, and organizations. Government-sponsored or public insurance programs, like social security or government health insurance plans, are not the same as private insurance (Lewis, 1989) (Figure 1.4).

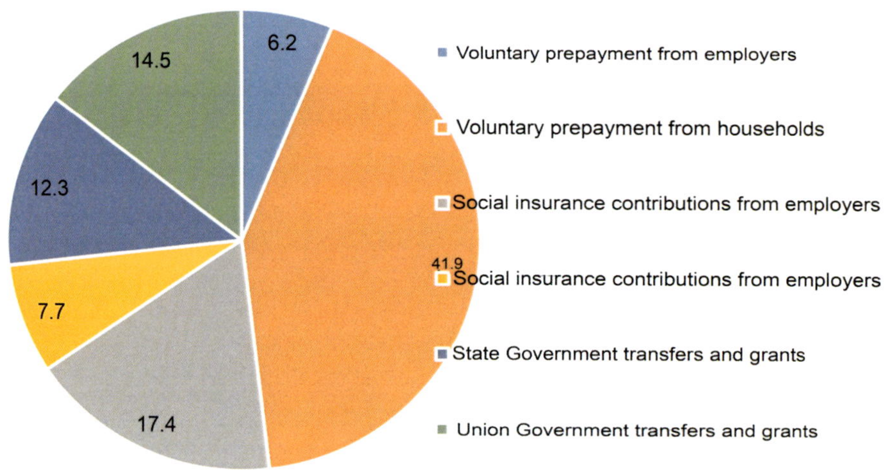

Figure 1.4. Diagram of the source of financing of health insurance (Source: Shailender Kumar, Creative Commons License)

Keyword

Insurance: Insurance is a contractual agreement in which a person or organization, referred to as the policyholder, remits regular payments to an insurance company in return for coverage against specific hazards. If there are any losses or damages that are included in the insurance coverage, the insurer promises to provide the policyholder with money or benefits. This helps to mitigate the financial impact and offers a form of financial protection. An insurance policy is a formal contract that outlines the terms and conditions of the insurance agreement.

1.7.1.1. Life Insurance

There were 850 life insurers operating in the US at the end of 2013, down from 2,343 at the peak in 1988. Mergers and consolidations aimed at reducing operational and general overhead expenses and enhancing efficiency are the primary factors behind this decline. When an insured individual passes away, life insurance provides death benefits to predetermined beneficiaries. These benefits cover burial expenses, uninsured medical bills, inheritance taxes, and other related costs (Gruber, 2000).

The death proceeds can also be utilized to provide regular payments to the beneficiary of the deceased. In addition to life insurance, these companies offer annuities, 401(k) plans, individual and company retirement plans, and individual retirement account (IRA) plans. Furthermore, some life insurance companies offer:

a) Health insurance policies, both for individuals and groups, that cover medical expenses associated with illness or injury,

b) Disability income plans that replace lost earnings during periods of disability and

c) Policies for long-term care that include coverage for nursing home care (Cutler & Zeckhauser, 2000).

1.7.1.2. Health Insurance

The health insurance market is highly specialized and dominated by a small number of insurers, even though many of the life insurers also offer individual or group health insurance plans. United Health Group, Well Point, AETNA, and Blue Cross Blue Shield Association are some of these businesses. Prescription medicines, hospital and surgery bills, doctor fees, and a variety of other additional medical costs are all covered by medical expense plans (Figure 1.5).

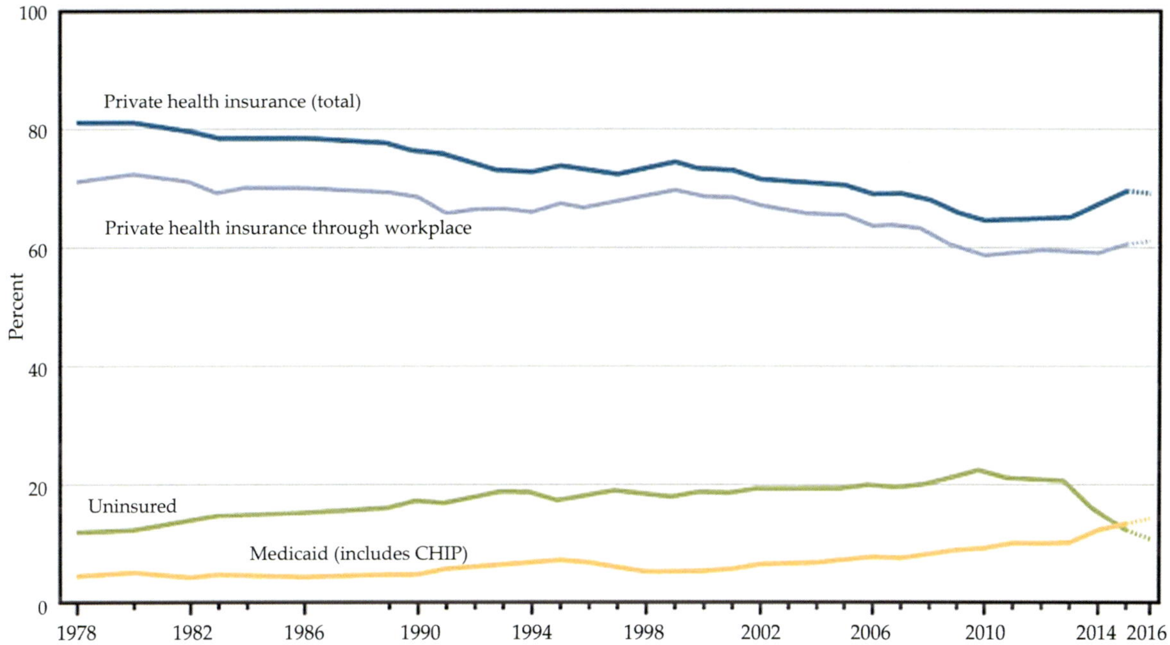

Figure 1.5. Illustration of health insurance coverage by age group in USA 2017–18 (Source: Theodore et al., Creative Commons License).

Health insurance is an essential financial tool for reducing the financial burden of medical costs on individuals. In consideration of periodic premium payments, policyholders are entitled to a wide range of healthcare benefits. This insurance model is essential in protecting people and families from the frequently crippling expenses of healthcare, which include hospital stays, prescription drugs, and preventative care (Stone, 1993).

Health insurance is important for reasons more than just money. It promotes routine health exams and preventive care, which improves people's general health. In addition to providing concrete advantages, health insurance gives people and families a sense of security by easing the financial burden of unanticipated medical costs. Having health insurance is required by law in many places, highlighting its critical role in guaranteeing that everyone has access to high-quality healthcare and fostering a better social environment (Aaron, 1966).

1.7.1.3 Liability and Property Insurance

Property and liability insurance are interchangeable with property and casualty insurance. When referring to the different coverages and operational results, nonlife insurers usually use the term property and casualty insurance rather than property and liability insurance. Casualty insurance is a broad field of insurance that covers whatever is not covered by fire, marine, and life insurance; casualty lines include auto, liability, burglary and theft, workers compensation, and health insurance (Woodard et al., 2012) (Figure 1.6).

Property and Casualty Insurance Coverages

1. Personal lines
   - Private passenger auto insurance
   - Homeowners insurance
   - Personal umbrella liability insurance
   - Earthquake insurance
   - Flood insurance
2. Commercial lines
   - Fire and allied lines insurance
   - Commercial multiple-peril insurance
   - General liability insurance
   - Products liability insurance
   - Workers compensation insurance
   - Commercial auto insurance
   - Accident and health insurance
   - Inland marine and ocean marine insurance
   - Professional liability insurance
   - Directors and officers liability insurance
   - Boiler and machinery insurance (also known as mechanical breakdown, equipment breakdown, or systems breakdown coverage)
   - Fidelity bonds and surety bonds
   - Crime insurance
   - Other coverages

Figure 1.6. Diagram of property and casualty insurance coverages (Source: George E. Rejda, Creative Commons License).

1.7.2. Government Insurance

There are currently numerous government insurance plans in place. Social insurance programs and other government insurance programs are the two categories of government insurance.

1.7.2.1. Social Insurance

Social insurance programs are government insurance programs with certain characteristics that distinguish them from other government insurance plans. These programs are financed entirely or in large part by mandatory contributions from employers, employees, or both, and not primarily by the general revenues of the government (Power, 1985) (Figure 1.7).

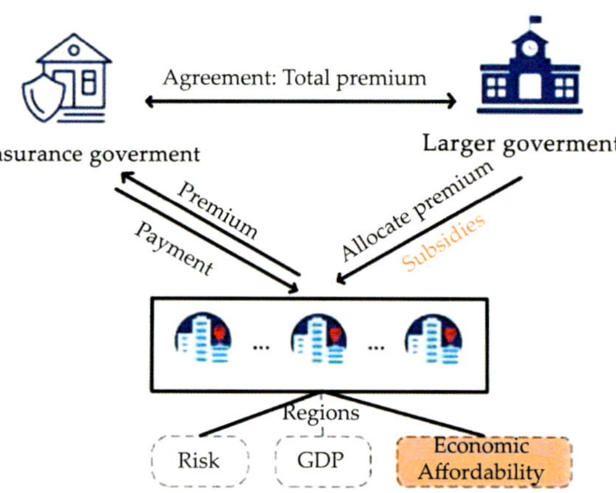

Figure 1.7. Illustration of mechanism for multi-region catastrophe insurance with government subsidies. (Source: Xihui et al., Creative Commons License)

The United States has several significant social insurance programs, which include the following:

a) Medicare
b) Compulsory temporary disability insurance
c) Unemployment insurance
d) Workers' compensation

e) Survivors, Old-Age, and Disability Insurance (Social Security)
f) Railroad Retirement Act
g) Railroad Unemployment Insurance Act

1.7.2.2. Other Government Insurance Programs

Other government insurance programs exist at both the federal and state levels. These programs lack the distinctive features of social insurance plans. Among the significant federal insurance initiatives are the following:

a) Federal employees employed after 1983 are eligible for survivor and disability benefits through the Federal Employees Retirement System (FERS).
b) Federal employees hired prior to 1984 are eligible to receive retirement, survivor, and disability benefits under the Civil Service Retirement System.
c) Insurance for checking and savings accounts is offered by the Federal Deposit Insurance Corporation (FDIC) to commercial banks, credit unions, and savings and loan associations.
d) In the event of the termination of a private defined-benefit pension plan, the Pension Benefit Guaranty organization (PBGC), a federal entity, provides a guarantee for workers' pension benefits, up to a specified limit.
e) Homeowners and commercial enterprises residing in flood zones have the option to acquire property insurance through the National Flood Insurance Program (NFIP), with certain limitations.
f) Other federal programs encompass federal crop insurance, war risk insurance, and various other initiatives. Veterans also have the opportunity to enroll in different life insurance schemes (Head & Porat, 1990).

1.7.3. Emerging Trends in Risk Management and Insurance

In the ever-evolving realm of risk management and insurance, it is crucial for industry professionals to stay informed about emerging trends. This section delves into significant developments and transformative shifts that are shaping the present and future of risk management and insurance.

1.7.4. Technological Innovations in Risk Assessment

In recent years, technology has become a game-changer in the risk management and insurance sector. Advancements in data analytics, artificial intelligence (AI), and machine learning have revolutionized the way risks are assessed and managed. Insurers now have access to vast amounts of data, enabling them to enhance underwriting accuracy, assess risks in real-time, and personalize insurance offerings. Telematics, for example, allows insurance companies to gather data from connected devices, such as vehicles, providing insights into policyholders' behavior and facilitating usage-based insurance.

1.7.5. Insurtech Disruption

The rise of Insurtech, a portmanteau of insurance and technology, has disrupted traditional insurance models. Startups are leveraging technology to streamline processes, enhance customer experiences, and introduce innovative insurance products. Blockchain technology, in particular, is being explored to improve transparency and efficiency in claims processing and reduce fraud. The intersection of finance and technology is fostering a new era of collaboration and competition within the insurance industry.

1.7.6. Cybersecurity Risks and Insurance

As businesses become increasingly reliant on digital infrastructure, the importance of cybersecurity has surged. The frequency and sophistication of cyber threats necessitate a specialized approach to risk management. Insurance products tailored to address cyber risks have gained prominence. These policies cover financial losses resulting from cyberattacks, data breaches, and other digital threats. The evolving nature of cyber risks requires constant adaptation in risk management strategies and insurance coverage.

1.7.7. Climate Change and Environmental Risks

With the growing recognition of climate change as a significant global challenge, insurers are increasingly focusing on environmental risks. Extreme weather events, rising sea levels, and other climate-related factors pose substantial threats. Insurers are reevaluating risk models and developing new products to address the evolving landscape of climate-related risks. Additionally, there is a rising trend in promoting sustainable and eco-friendly insurance practices, aligning risk management with broader environmental concerns.

1.7.8. Regulatory Developments

The regulatory landscape plays a pivotal role in shaping the risk management and insurance industry. Ongoing changes in regulations, both at national and international levels, impact how insurers operate and manage risks. Compliance with new standards and requirements introduces challenges and opportunities. This subheading delves into the latest regulatory developments, their implications for the industry, and how insurers are adapting to ensure compliance while maintaining effective risk management practices.

1.7.9. Changing Consumer Expectations and Demands

The digital age has transformed consumer expectations across all industries, and insurance is no exception. Consumers now demand seamless digital experiences, personalized services, and more transparent communication. Insurers are responding by embracing digital platforms, implementing user-friendly interfaces, and tailoring insurance products to meet the evolving needs of customers. Understanding and adapting to changing consumer preferences is a crucial aspect of modern risk management and insurance practices.

1.7.10. Globalization and Cross-Border Risks

In an interconnected world, businesses and individuals face risks that transcend national borders. Globalization introduces new challenges and opportunities for risk management and insurance. Insurers must navigate the complexities of cross-border regulations, geopolitical uncertainties, and diverse cultural contexts. This subheading explores how the industry is addressing the unique challenges posed by globalization and the strategies employed to effectively manage risks on a global scale.

SUMMARY

- This chapter offers a comprehensive introduction to risk management and insurance, delving into its historical origins, development, and current relevance. The narrative traces the origins of risk management in trading activities from prehistoric times to the historical evolution of the insurance industry.
- Emphasizing the broad significance and scope of risk, the discussion explores its vital role in various contexts.
- The classification of risk enhances readers' foundational understanding. By examining the characteristics of insurance, its essential nature within the framework of risk management is elucidated.
- The chapter underscores the crucial role that insurance plays in mitigating risk, explaining its function as a mechanism for risk transfer and its effectiveness in handling diverse types of risk.
- An in-depth examination of several types of insurance reveals how each one is specifically used to manage a variety of hazards. The advantages of combining risk management and insurance techniques are explained, offering guidance on how businesses can use both instruments for comprehensive risk reduction.
- The chapter concludes with a focus on the goals and definition of risk management, laying the groundwork for a better understanding of the frameworks and tactics used by businesses to effectively handle uncertainty.
- All things considered, this chapter provides a strong framework for understanding the relationship between risk management and insurance within the broader context of organizational risk.

MULTIPLE CHOICE QUESTIONS

1. **What is the primary purpose of risk management?**
   a. Profit maximization
   b. Loss minimization
   c. Asset accumulation
   d. Market expansion
2. **Which ancient civilization is credited with introducing risk-sharing agreements similar to insurance practices?**
   a. Ancient Greece
   b. Ancient Greece
   c. Ancient China
   d. Ancient Egypt
3. **What is the role of insurance in risk mitigation?**
   a. Risk amplification

b. Risk avoidance

c. Risk transfer

d. Risk acceptance

4. In the classification of risks, which category encompasses challenges related to internal processes, systems, and human factors?

a. Financial risks

b. Operational risks

c. Strategic risks

d. Legal risks

5. What term is used to describe the function of insurance in addressing various types of risks faced by an organization?

a. Risk acceptance

b. Risk transfer tool

c. Risk avoidance strategy

d. Risk amplification technique

REVIEW QUESTIONS

1. Identify and discuss three types of risks addressed by insurance, providing examples for each.
2. Explore the benefits of integrating insurance and risk management strategies for organizations.
3. Discuss the historical origins of risk management, focusing on its development from ancient trade practices to formalized structures.
4. What is the primary objective of risk management, and how does it align with achieving organizational goals?
5. Differentiate between financial risks and operational risks, providing real-world scenarios for each category.

Answers to Multiple Questions

1. (b) 2. (c) 3. (c) 4. (b) 5. (b)

REFERENCES

1. Aaron, H., (1966). The social insurance paradox. Canadian Journal of Economics and Political Science/Revue Canadienne de Economiques et Science Politique, 32(3), 371–374.
2. Abraham, K. S., (2001). Peril and fortuity in property and liability insurance. Tort & Insurance Law Journal, 777–802.

3. Acharya, V. V., Pedersen, L. H., Philippon, T., & Richardson, M., (2017). Measuring systemic risk. The Review of Financial Studies, 30(1), 2–47.
4. Acharyya, M., & Johnson, J., (2006). Investigating the development of enterprise risk management in the insurance industry: An empirical study of four major European insurers. The Geneva Papers on Risk and Insurance, 1(1), 55–80.
5. Acharyya, M., & Mutenga, S., (2013). The benefits of implementing enterprise risk management: Evidence from the non-life insurance industry. Enterprise Risk Management, 6(1), 22–24.
6. Adair, A., & Hutchison, N., (2005). The reporting of risk in real estate appraisal property risk scoring. Journal of Property Investment & Finance, 23(3), 254–268.
7. Akter, S., Brouwer, R., Choudhury, S., & Aziz, S., (2009). Is there a commercially viable market for crop insurance in rural Bangladesh? Mitigation and Adaptation Strategies for Global Change, 14, 215–229.
8. Altuntas, M., Berry-Stölzle, T. R., & Cummins, J. D., (2021). Enterprise risk management and economies of scale and scope: Evidence from the German insurance industry. Annals of Operations Research, 299, 811–845.
9. Anyika, E., (2015). Non-diversifiable risk in investment portfolios—An aid to investment decision making. Journal of Risk Analysis and Crisis Response, 5(1), 1–20.
10. Barth, M. E., & So, E. C., (2014). Non-diversifiable volatility risk and risk premiums at earnings announcements. The Accounting Review, 89(5), 1579–1607.
11. Ben-Horim, M., & Levy, H., (1980). Total risk, diversifiable risk and nondiversifiable risk: A pedagogic note. Journal of Financial and Quantitative Analysis, 15(2), 289–297.
12. Briys, E., Schlesinger, H., & Schulenburg, J. M. G. V., (1991). Reliability of risk management: Market insurance, self-insurance and self-protection reconsidered. The Geneva Papers on Risk and Insurance Theory, 16, 45–58.
13. Bromiley, P., McShane, M., Nair, A., & Rustambekov, E., (2015). Enterprise risk management: Review, critique, and research directions. Long Range Planning, 48(4), 265–276.
14. Calkin, D. E., Cohen, J. D., Finney, M. A., & Thompson, M. P., (2014). How risk management can prevent future wildfire disasters in the wildland-urban interface. Proceedings of the National Academy of Sciences, 111(2), 746–751.
15. Campbell, R. A., (1980). The demand for life insurance: An application of the economics of uncertainty. The Journal of Finance, 35(5), 1155–1172.
16. Cevolini, A., (2016). Time construction in insurance society. Journal of Historical Sociology, 29(2), 160–181.
17. Chen, H., Miao, J., & Wang, N., (2010). Entrepreneurial finance and non-diversifiable risk. The Review of Financial Studies, 23(12), 4348–4388.
18. Covello, V. T., & Mumpower, J., (1985). Risk analysis and risk management: An historical perspective. Risk Analysis, 5(2), 103–120.
19. Crockford, G. N., (1982). The bibliography and history of risk management: Some preliminary observations. Geneva Papers on Risk and Insurance, 1(1), 169–179.

20. Cutler, D. M., & Zeckhauser, R. J., (2000). The anatomy of health insurance. In: Handbook of Health Economics (Vol. 1, pp. 563–643). Elsevier.
21. Dickinson, G., (2001). Enterprise risk management: Its origins and conceptual foundation. The Geneva Papers on Risk and Insurance – Issues and Practice, 26(3), 360–366.
22. Dionne, G., (2013). Risk management: History, definition, and critique. Risk Management and Insurance Review, 16(2), 147–166.
23. Eikenhout, L. C. A., (2015). Risk Management and Performance in Insurance Companies, 1(1), 1–20. Master's thesis, University of Twente.
24. Elvik, R., Erke, A., & Christensen, P., (2009). Elementary units of exposure. Transportation Research Record, 2103(1), 25–31.
25. Ewold, F., (1991). Insurance and risk. The Foucault Effect: Studies in Governmentality, 197210, 201–202.
26. Fadun, O. S., (2013). Insurance, a risk transfer mechanism: An examination of the Nigerian banking industry. IOSR Journal of Business and Management, 7(4), 93–101.
27. Feng, R., (2023). Economics of risk and insurance. In: Decentralized Insurance: Technical Foundation of Business Models (Vol. 1, No. 1, pp. 55–84). Cham: Springer International Publishing.
28. Ferrer, R. C., & Mallari, N. C., (2011). Speculative and pure risks: Their impact on firms' earnings per share. Journal of International Business Research, 10(1), 115.
29. Fischer, J. A., (1990). The exclusion from insurance coverage of losses caused by the intentional acts of the insured: A policy in search of a justification. Santa Clara L. Rev., 30, 95.
30. Fischer, S., (1973). A life cycle model of life insurance purchases. International Economic Review, 1(1), 132–152.
31. Grace, M. F., & Klein, R. W., (2009). Insurance regulation: The need for policy reform. The Future of Insurance Regulation, 1(1), 117–143.
32. Gruber, J., (2000). Health insurance and the labor market. Handbook of Health Economics, 1, 645–706.
33. Hardwick, P., & Guirguis, M., (2007). The UK insurance industry—Structure and performance. In: Handbook of International Insurance: Between Global Dynamics and Local Contingencies (Vol. 1, No. 1, pp. 205–239).
34. Head, G. L., & Porat, M. M., (1990). Tax treatment of pre–loss risk financing costs–a public policy perspective. Journal of Insurance Regulation, 8(4), 1–20.
35. Hellner, J., (1963). The scope of insurance regulation: What is insurance for purposes of regulation? The American Journal of Comparative Law, 1(1), 494–543.
36. Henderson, R. C., (1970). Insurance protection for products liability and completed operations-what every lawyer should know. Neb. L. Rev., 50, 415.
37. Hiles, A., (2012). Enterprise risk management. The Definitive Handbook of Business Continuity Management, 1(1), 1–21.

38. Hoffman, C., & Paradise, J., (2008). Health insurance and access to health care in the United States. Annals of the New York Academy of Sciences, 1136(1), 149–160.

39. Holzmann, R., & Jørgensen, S., (2001). Social risk management: A new conceptual framework for social protection, and beyond. International Tax and Public Finance, 8, 529–556.

40. Houston, D. B., (1964). Risk, insurance, and sampling. The Journal of Risk and Insurance, 31(4), 511–538.

41. Hoyt, R. E., & Liebenberg, A. P., (2008). The Value of Enterprise Risk Management: Evidence from the US Insurance Industry, 1(1), 200.

42. Hoyt, R. E., & Liebenberg, A. P., (2011). The value of enterprise risk management. Journal of Risk and Insurance, 78(4), 795–822.

43. Ibragimov, R., Jaffee, D., & Walden, J., (2009). Nondiversification traps in catastrophe insurance markets. The Review of Financial Studies, 22(3), 959–993.

44. Ingram, J. D., & Ostfeld, L. R., (1984). The distinction between accidental means and accidental results in accidental death insurance. Fla. St. UL Rev., 12, 1.

45. Jitschin, A., (2015). From economic to political reality: Forming a nationalized Indian life insurance market. In: The Development of International Insurance (Vol. 1, No. 1, pp. 133–144). Routledge.

46. Kahane, Y., & Kroll, Y., (1985). Optimal insurance coverage in situations of pure and speculative risk and the risk-free asset. Insurance: Mathematics and Economics, 4(3), 191–199.

47. Keeton, R. E., (1954). Liability insurance and responsibility for settlement. Harvard Law Review, 67(7), 1136–1186.

48. Kling, B., & Wolthuis, H., (1992). Ordering of risks in life insurance. Insurance: Mathematics and Economics, 11(2), 139–152.

49. Leonard, A. B., (2016). Introduction: The nature and study of marine insurance. In: Marine Insurance: Origins and Institutions, 1300–1850 (pp. 2–22). London: Palgrave Macmillan UK.

50. Lewis, F. D., (1989). Dependents and the demand for life insurance. The American Economic Review, 79(3), 452–467.

51. Liebenberg, A. P., Carson, J. M., & Dumm, R. E., (2012). A dynamic analysis of the demand for life insurance. Journal of Risk and Insurance, 79(3), 619–644.

52. Lin, Y., Wen, M. M., & Yu, J., (2012). Enterprise risk management: Strategic antecedents, risk integration and performance. North American Actuarial Journal, 16(1), 1–28.

53. Lindsay, S. M., (1918). Purpose and scope of war risk insurance. The Annals of the American Academy of Political and Social Science, 79(1), 52–68.

54. Liu, J., Li, B., Lin, B., & Nguyen, V., (2007). Key issues and challenges of risk management and insurance in China's construction industry: An empirical study. Industrial Management & Data Systems, 107(3), 382–396.

55. Longnaker, J. L., (1962). History of insurance law. Ins. LJ, 1(1), 642.

56. Manes, A., (1942). Outlines of a general economic history of insurance. The Journal of Business of the University of Chicago, 15(1), 30–48.
57. Mantis, G., & Farmer, R. N., (1968). Demand for life insurance. Journal of Risk and Insurance, 1(1), 247–256.
58. Martin, R. J., Reza, A., & Anderson, L. W., (2000). What is an explosion? A case history of an investigation for the insurance industry. Journal of Loss Prevention in the Process Industries, 13(6), 491–497.
59. Martinez, L. P., (2012). A unified theory of insurance risk. U. Pitt. L. Rev., 74, 713.
60. Masci, P., (2011). The history of insurance: Risk, uncertainty, and entrepreneurship. Business and Public Administration Studies, 6(1), 25–25.
61. Maurer, R., & Somova, B., (2007). The German insurance industry: Market overview and trends. In: Handbook of International Insurance: Between Global Dynamics and Local Contingencies (Vol. 1, No. 1, pp. 305–345). Boston, MA: Springer US.
62. McNeely, M. C., (1941). Illegality as a factor in liability insurance. Colum. L. Rev., 41, 26.
63. McShane, M., (2018). Enterprise risk management: History and a design science proposal. The Journal of Risk Finance, 19(2), 137–153.
64. Meins, E., Wallbaum, H., Hardziewski, R., & Feige, A., (2010). Sustainability and property valuation: A risk-based approach. Building Research & Information, 38(3), 280–300.
65. Michel-Kerjan, E. O., (2010). Catastrophe economics: The national flood insurance program. Journal of Economic Perspectives, 24(4), 165–186.
66. Møller, T., (2002). On valuation and risk management at the interface of insurance and finance. British Actuarial Journal, 8(4), 787–827.
67. Nguyen, K. A. T., & Jolly, C. M., (2019). Steps toward the establishment of a commercial aquaculture insurance program: Lessons from an assessment of the Vietnamese pilot insurance program. Reviews in Fisheries Science & Aquaculture, 27(1), 72–87.
68. Nieuwoudt, W. L., (2000). An economic evaluation of a crop insurance program for small-scale commercial farmers in South Africa. Agrekon, 39(3), 269–291.
69. Njegomir, V., & Marovi⊠, B., (2012). Contemporary trends in the global insurance industry. Procedia-Social and Behavioral Sciences, 44, 134–142.
70. Nocco, B. W., & Stulz, R. M., (2006). Enterprise risk management: Theory and practice. Journal of Applied Corporate Finance, 18(4), 8–20.
71. Nyman, J. A., (1999). The value of health insurance: The access motive. Journal of Health Economics, 18(2), 141–152.
72. Odeyinka, H., (2000). An evaluation of the use of insurance in managing construction risks. Construction Management and Economics, 18(5), 519–524.
73. Paté-Cornell, M. E., (1994). Quantitative safety goals for risk management of industrial facilities. Structural Safety, 13(3), 145–157.

74. Patterson, E. W., (1919). The delivery of a life-insurance policy. Harvard Law Review, 33(2), 198–222.

75. Pauly, M. V., Zweifel, P., Scheffler, R. M., Preker, A. S., & Bassett, M., (2006). Private health insurance in developing countries. Health Affairs, 25(2), 369–379.

76. Pearson, R., (1997). Towards an historical model of services innovation: The case of the insurance industry, 1700–1914. The Economic History Review, 50(2), 235–256.

77. Pearson, R., (2002). Growth, crisis and change in the insurance industry: A retrospect. Accounting, Business & Financial History, 12(3), 487–504.

78. Pearson, R., (2015). Introduction: Towards an international history of insurance. In: The Development of International Insurance (Vol. 1, No. 1, pp. 1–24). Routledge.

79. Peters, J. F. M., (1993). Patterns of internationalization in insurance. Geneva Papers on Risk and Insurance: Issues and Practice, 1(1), 107–114.

80. Plomaritou, E., & Nikolaides, E., (2016). Commercial risks arising from chartering vessels. Journal of Shipping and Ocean Engineering, 6, 261–268.

81. Poolsappasit, N., Dewri, R., & Ray, I., (2011). Dynamic security risk management using Bayesian attack graphs. IEEE Transactions on Dependable and Secure Computing, 9(1), 61–74.

82. Power, M. L., (1985). Corporate risk management objective: A discounted cash flow approach. The Journal of Insurance Issues and Practices, 8(1), 98–104.

83. Powers, M. R., (2006). Pure vs speculative risk: False choice; sham marriage. The Journal of Risk Finance, 7(4), 345–347.

84. Prabhakar, S. V., Abu-Bakar, A., Becker, S., Pereira, J. J., & Solomon, D. S., (2015). Insurance for disaster risk reduction and climate change adaptation–an overview. Effectiveness of Insurance, 4, 1–20.

85. Radu, N., & Naghi, L. E., (2020). Catastrophic risk modeling—Residential and nonresidential exposure. J. Financ. Stud., 8, 96–112.

86. Re, III. V. L., Gowda, C., Urick, P. N., Halladay, J. T., Binkley, A., Carbonari, D. M., & Kostman, J. R., (2016). Disparities in absolute denial of modern hepatitis C therapy by type of insurance. Clinical Gastroenterology and Hepatology, 14(7), 1035–1043.

87. Reschovsky, J. D., Kemper, P., & Tu, H., (2000). Does type of health insurance affect health care use and assessments of care among the privately insured? Health Services Research, 35(1 Pt 2), 219.

88. Roll, K., Stargardt, T., & Schreyögg, J., (2012). Effect of type of insurance and income on waiting time for outpatient care. The Geneva Papers on Risk and Insurance-Issues and Practice, 37, 609–632.

89. Schwarcz, S. L., (2008). Systemic risk. Geo. LJ, 97, 193.

90. Schwartz, G. T., (1989). Ethics and the economics of tort liability insurance. Cornell L. Rev., 75, 312.

91. Schwartz, J., Bellinger, D., & Glass, T., (2011). Exploring potential sources of differential vulnerability and susceptibility in risk from environmental hazards to expand the scope of risk assessment. American Journal of Public Health, 101(S1), S94–S101.

92. Scordis, N., & Katrishen, F., (1997). The changing international insurance industry. Changing Roles of State Intervention in Services in an Era of Open International Markets, 1(1), 128–152.

93. Shaik, S., Barnett, B. J., Coble, K. H., Miller, J. C., & Hanson, T., (2006). Insurability conditions and livestock disease insurance. In: The Economics of Livestock Disease Insurance: Concepts, Issues and International Case Studies (Vol. 1, No. 1, pp. 53–67). Wallingford UK: CABI Publishing.

94. Smaga, P., (2014). The concept of systemic risk. Systemic Risk Centre Special Paper, (5), 1–20.

95. Smith, V. H., & Watts, M., (2019). Index based agricultural insurance in developing countries: Feasibility, scalability, and sustainability. Gates Open Res., 3(65), 65.

96. Snider, H. W., (1990). The importance of objectives in risk management. Risk Management, 37(1), 38–40.

97. Sommers, B. D., Gawande, A. A., & Baicker, K., (2017). Health insurance coverage and health—What the recent evidence tells us. N Engl. J. Med., 377(6), 586–593.

98. Stone, D. A., (1993). The struggle for the soul of health insurance. Journal of Health Politics, Policy, and Law, 18(2), 287–317.

99. Streit, E. F., (1952). The carrying of liability insurance as creating tort liability. Ins. LJ, 1(1), 602.

100. Syverud, K. D., (1993). On the demand for liability insurance. Tex. L. Rev., 72, 1629.

101. Wagstaff, A., & Lindelow, M., (2008). Can insurance increase financial risk?: The curious case of health insurance in China. Journal of Health Economics, 27(4), 990–1005.

102. Weimer, M., (2017). The origins of "risk" as an idea and the future of risk regulation. European Journal of Risk Regulation, 8(1), 10–17.

103. Williams, C. A., (1966). Attitudes toward speculative risks as an indicator of attitudes toward pure risks. The Journal of Risk and Insurance, 33(4), 577–586.

104. Woodard, J. D., Pavlista, A. D., Schnitkey, G. D., Burgener, P. A., & Ward, K. A., (2012). Government insurance program design, incentive effects, and technology adoption: The case of skip-row crop insurance. American Journal of Agricultural Economics, 94(4), 823–837.

105. Wu, M. T., Lin, P. C., Pan, C. H., & Peng, C. Y., (2019). Risk assessment of personal exposure to polycyclic aromatic hydrocarbons and aldehydes in three commercial cooking workplaces. Scientific Reports, 9(1), 1661.

CHAPTER 2

Principles and Aims of Risk Management and Insurance

LEARNING OBJECTIVES

After studying this chapter, you will be able to:

1. To understand principles for effective risk management and their application in the insurance domain.
2. To understand the practical importance of risk management in sustaining growth.
3. To learn risk management activities, exploring how these translate into operational strategies within the insurance landscape.
4. To understand efficiency principles for strategic risk management, applying optimization concepts to enhance decision-making, especially in insurance-related scenarios.
5. To understand fundamental insurance principles and their impact on relationships between insurers and policyholders.

INTRODUCTORY EXAMPLE

Let's examine risk management and insurance using a real-world example. Consider Sarah, a small company owner who owns and operates a bakery. Sarah enjoys baking and has invested a significant amount of capital and effort into her venture. However, she is aware that unforeseen events could potentially jeopardize the success of her bakery.

To safeguard her company, Sarah resolves to implement risk management strategies. She begins by identifying potential risks to her bakery's operations, such as fire, theft, or equipment failure. She then assesses the likelihood of these risks and their potential impact on her business. Based on this evaluation, she develops a risk management strategy that includes measures such as implementing security measures, installing fire extinguishers, and scheduling regular equipment maintenance.

Now, let's delve into the fundamentals of insurance. Recognizing that she cannot control every risk, Sarah decides to insure her bakery. This includes business interruption insurance, which would provide compensation for lost revenue in the event of a temporary closure due to unexpected circumstances. Additionally, she opts for property insurance to protect her tangible assets.

This example demonstrates how insurance concepts can be applied to create a financial safety net, while also integrating risk management principles by identifying and mitigating potential risks.

UNIT INTRODUCTION

Risk management and insurance are essential components of the modern-day business environment. They play a crucial role in protecting individuals and companies from unpredictability. This chapter explores the underlying ideas that support risk management and insurance practices, offering insight into the conceptual framework that governs decision-making in this crucial domain (Aven, 2016).

At its core, risk management entails identifying, evaluating, and mitigating potential risks that may affect the objectives of a business. It is now necessary for businesses to have a solid grasp of risks and successfully manage them to maintain their operations in an environment that is always changing and dynamic. This chapter will also shed light on the processes involved in identifying and reacting to the many different risks (Baker, 2011).

Insurance is examined in detail regarding risk management because it is an essential component. Insurance aims to act as a financial instrument enabling the transfer of risk between an individual or organization and an insurance provider. The fundamental concepts that regulate insurance mechanisms, such as compensation, substitution, and absolute honesty, are analyzed to clarify their importance in risk management. A thorough comprehension of these principles is essential for insurers and policyholders, as it influences the dynamics of risk distribution and financial safeguarding (Kozlova et al., 2019).

Furthermore, this chapter highlights the interdependent connection between risk management and insurance, emphasizing how both fields together strengthen the ability of both enterprises and individuals to recover from adversity. A thorough understanding of risk assessment, quantification, and treatment is essential for practitioners and scholars to make well-informed risk management and insurance judgments. Essentially, this chapter functions as a guide, providing directions to readers regarding the theoretical foundations that govern this dynamic and crucial topic (Priest, 2016).

2.1. PRINCIPLES OF RISK MANAGEMENT

Learning Objectives

- Understand the principles of risk management:
- Understand the concept of risk management
- Understand the importance of ongoing monitoring of identified risks

Risk management functions are based on a set of principles, and numerous endeavors have been made to define these principles. The British Standard BS 31100 outlines 11 principles for risk management, while the International Organization for Standardization ISO 31000 provides a comprehensive list of recommended risk management principles. The following list is a simplified representation of these documents. It is recommended that a risk management initiative will be successful when it is:

i. Proportionate to the degree of risk present in the organization;
ii. Aligned with other business operations;
iii. Comprehensive, methodical, and organized;
iv. Embedded into business procedures;
v. Dynamic, repetitive, and adaptable to changes;

The acronym PACED is presented and offers a highly effective collection of ideas that serve as the basis for a successful approach to risk management in any organization. Table 2.1 provides a comprehensive explanation of the PACED principles of risk management. The risk management strategy is founded on the belief that risk may be identified and controlled (Dickson, 1995).

The previously mentioned statement of principles relates to the fundamental characteristics of risk management. These principles explain the practical implementation of risk management. Some compilations of principles may also encompass guidelines regarding the objectives and outcomes that risk management should strive to achieve (Luko, 2013).

It is beneficial to categorize the principles of risk management into two distinct lists: the desired characteristics of risk management, as mentioned earlier; and the expected outcomes of risk management, as mentioned below:

i. Compliance to laws and regulations;
ii. Assurance in the handling of key risks;
iii. Decisions that fully evaluate risk factors;
iv. Efficiency, effectiveness, and efficacy in operations, projects, and strategy.

This document introduces the acronym CADE3 and affirms that risk management outcomes will result in reduced disturbance to regular operations, decreased confusion over change, and enhanced decision-making in evaluating and selecting alternative solutions (Pennock & Haimes, 2002).

Enhanced organizational decision making is a crucial component of risk management. Given the limited resources for risk management, the goal is to achieve the most effective response to risk by prioritizing based on a thorough examination of the risks. Uncertainty is an inevitable aspect, and it is imperative for any organization to proactively address it by implementing measures to control it to a degree that is deemed acceptable. The suitable spectrum of reactions to risk will be contingent upon the risk's inherent characteristics, magnitude, and intricacy (Just et al., 2003).

Did you know?

Lloyd's of London, founded in the late 17th century, is acknowledged as one of the oldest insurance exchanges worldwide. Initially, it functioned as a café where ship owners, merchants, and underwriters gathered to conduct maritime insurance operations.

Table 2.1. Principles of Risk Management

Principle	**Description**
Proportionate	The organization must ensure that its risk management operations are proportionate to the degree of risk it faces.
Aligned	It is essential to ensure that risk management efforts are synchronized with the other activities inside the firm.
Comprehensive	To achieve maximum effectiveness, the risk management strategy must be all-encompassing.
Embedded	The organization must integrate risk management initiatives.
Dynamic	Efforts to manage risks should be adaptable and promptly address emerging and evolving risks.

Source: Paul Hopkins, Creative Commons License.

2.2. IMPORTANCE OF RISK MANAGEMENT

Learning Objectives

- To learn the importance of risk management.
- To understand how effective risk management contributes to the achievement of organizational objectives.

The performance and sustainability of businesses depend heavily on effective risk management. This process ensures the protection of assets, maintains reputation, and facilitates strategic decision-making by methodically finding, evaluating, and responding to potential risks. It offers a systematic framework for aligning company goals with possible risks and opportunities, promoting innovation, and ensuring adherence to industry rules. The financial advantages are apparent, as efficient risk management reduces unexpected losses and optimizes the allocation of resources (Carvalho & Rabechini, 2015).

In addition to financial reasons, it cultivates a culture of ongoing improvement, promotes proactive planning, and strengthens an organization's ability to adapt to uncertainty. The protection of stakeholder interests, encompassing customers, employees, and investors, displays a dedication to appropriate corporate governance. Risk management is not solely a defensive measure but a strategic necessity that empowers firms to navigate dynamic terrain, pursue chances for growth, and prosper in an ever-evolving corporate climate (Duff, 2003). Table 2.2 provides some examples that demonstrate the significance of risk management. Risk management has gained significant importance in recent years due to the global financial crisis and the high-profile corporate failures worldwide. Furthermore, the significance of risk management has escalated due to the raising demands of stakeholders and the growing accessibility of communication channels (Ahmed et al., 2007).

Risk management not only helps with making better decisions and increasing efficiency, but it also provides more assurance to stakeholders. This assurance consists of two crucial elements.

i. The directors of any firm need to have confidence that risks have been identified.
ii. Adequate measures have been implemented to effectively manage risk to an acceptable level (Dionne & Triki, 2005).

Furthermore, firms are placing a stronger emphasis on the precise and reliable reporting of information, particularly when it comes to risk-related data. Stakeholders necessitate comprehensive data regarding corporate performance, encompassing a keen grasp of potential risks. The primary obligation of the Sarbanes–Oxley Act of 2002 (SOX) in the United States is to ensure the accuracy of financial reporting. The act emphasizes the need for precise reporting of results to a higher priority and mandates the complete and correct disclosure of all information about the organization (Power, 2004).

While Sarbanes–Oxley is a specific legal framework applicable only in certain situations, its underlying ideas hold great significance for all professionals involved in risk management (Doloi, 2009).

Table 2.2. Importance of Risk Management

Managing the Organization
Fluctuating costs or limited supply of raw materials.
Costs associated with retirement, pension, and social benefits.
Aspiration to enhance value for shareholders.
The organization must prioritize and enhance transparency.
The rate of change in the business world is always accelerating.
The influence of e-commerce on every facet of corporate life.
Greater dependence on information technology (IT) systems.
Raising significance of intellectual property (IP).
Increased intricacy and reliance within the supply chain.
The significance of reputation is increasing steadily.
Reputation harms, particularly to global brands.
High-profile losses and failures ruin reputations.
The intensity of regulatory pressures continues to escalate.
Fluctuations in national legislative mandates.
The prevalence of joint partnerships is increasing.

Changes in the Marketplace
Evolution of the business and market landscape.
Globalization of vendors, consumers, and goods.
Greater competition in the industry.
Higher client standards, frequently set by rivals.
Need to respond to stakeholder expectations more quickly.
Volatile markets with lower levels of client loyalty.
Diversification results in employment in new fields.
Continuous need to make risky strategic choices.
Must achieve short-term success without causing long-term harm.
Innovation in products and ongoing enhancements.
Technology for consumer products is changing quickly.
Dangers to the global or national economy.
Danger of pandemics or influenza.
Possibility of transnational organized crime.
Increasing instances of political risks and social unrest.
Extreme weather conditions that result in population displacement.

Source: Paul Hopkins, Creative Commons License.

Remember

The history of insurance begins in antiquity when Chinese traders dispersed their cargo across several ships to reduce the possibility of losing everything in a single catastrophe. The earliest method of risk distribution established the groundwork for modern insurance concepts.

Risk management is an essential process that provides an organization with the tools to identify and counter potential risks. Once a risk has been identified, it becomes easier to mitigate. Additionally, risk management serves as a basis for making informed decisions in a business context (Jorion, 2009).

The most effective way for a company to prepare for potential risks and facilitate growth and development is by recognizing and controlling those risks. By determining how potential risks will be managed and implementing necessary safeguards, an organization can enhance its chances of success. Furthermore, proactive risk management ensures that the most critical issues receive the highest level of attention possible. This approach also equips management with the necessary information to ensure continuous profitability and make well-informed decisions (Tchankova, 2002).

2.3. RISK MANAGEMENT ACTIVITIES

Learning Objectives

- To understand the risk management activities
- To understand how to integrate risk considerations into decision-making processes at various organizational levels

The process of managing risks can be broken down into multiple phases (Figure 2.1). The Institute of Risk Management Standard illustrates the steps in the risk management process. The International Organization for Standardization ISO 31000, the British Standard BS 31100, and other publications provide additional examples of the risk management process (Islam & Houmb, 2010).

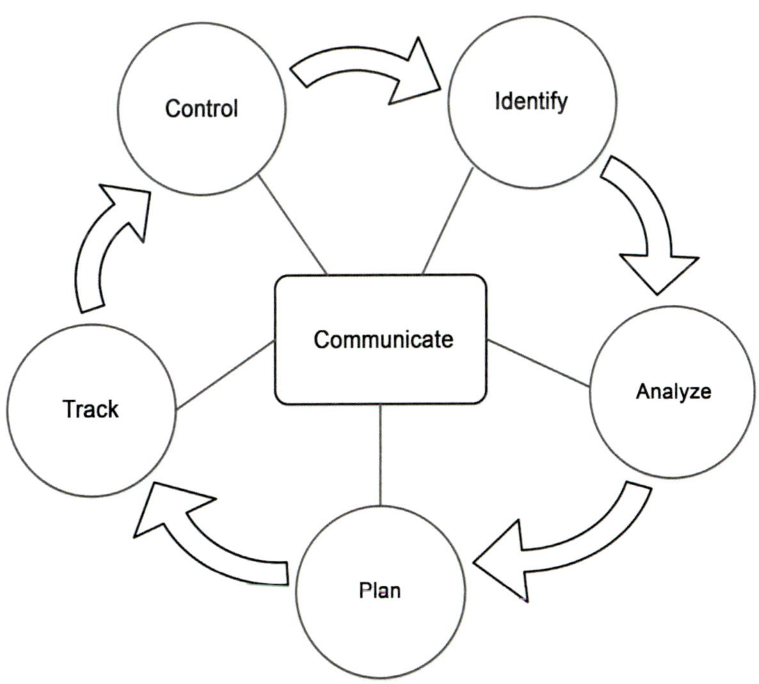

Figure 2.1. Illustration of risk management activities. (Source: M. Rizwan, Creative Commons License)

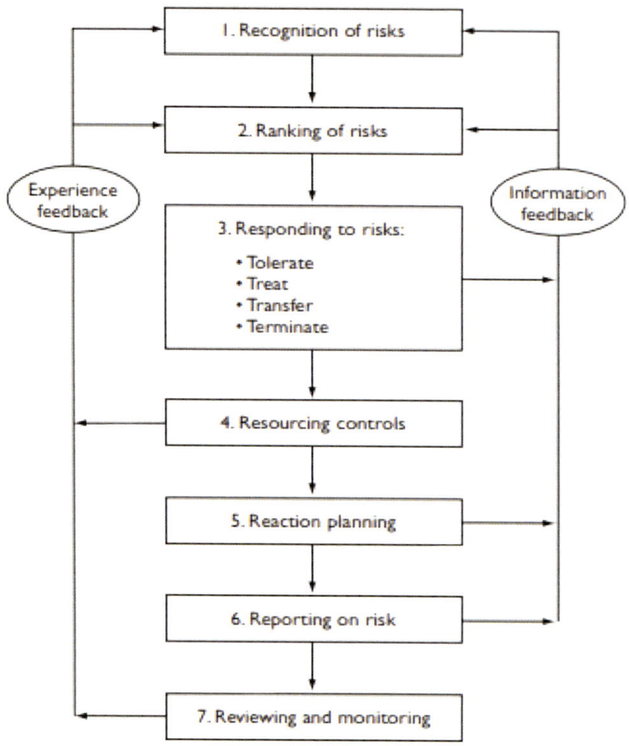

Figure 2.2. Representation of 7Rs and 4Ts of risk management. (Source: Paul Hopkin, Creative Commons License)

The steps in the risk management process are shown in Figure 2.2. To portray the process as the 7Rs and 4Ts of risk management, the language used to characterize the steps in the risk management process has been carefully chosen. For further details on each stage shown in Figure 2.2, refer to Table 2.3 (Bajek et al., 2008).

Table 2.3. 7Rs and 4Ts of (Hazard) Risk Management

1.	Identifying or recognizing risks, their nature, and the potential circumstances in which they could materialize.
2.	Risks are ranked or evaluated according to likelihood and magnitude to create a "risk profile" on file in a risk register.
3.	Reacting to significant risks, such as selecting the best course of action from the available possibilities: i. Tolerate ii. Treat iii. Transfer iv. Terminate

4.	Controls over resources are implemented to ensure adequate preparations for initiating and continuing the necessary control actions.
5.	Reaction planning and event management. Plans for disaster recovery or business continuity for risks will be included in this.
6.	Communicating about risk issues and reporting on and monitoring risk performance, actions, and occurrences using the organization's risk architecture.
7.	Analyzing the risk management system while considering internal auditing protocols, risk architecture, strategy, updates, and internal audit guidelines.

Source: Paul Hopkins, Creative Commons License.

The systematic application of management policies, procedures, and practices to communicate, consult, set the context, identify, analyze, evaluate, treat, monitor, and review risk is what ISO Guide 73 and British Standard BS 31100 refer to as the risk management process. Nonetheless, one could argue that the risk management framework, as opposed to the risk management process itself, consists of Communicating, advising, and developing that context along with developing rules, procedures, and practices (Takeuchi et al., 2014).

2.4. EFFICIENT, EFFECTIVE, AND EFFICACIOUS

Learning Objectives

- To discuss the examples of types of risk classifications
- To highlight the several distinct classes of risk

Risks that are insurable or hazardous may have an immediate impact on operations. Consequently, the original objective of implementing risk management principles was to ensure the continuity of productive and regular operations. As risk management has evolved, project management and the delivery of programs to enhance company processes have gained significance. It is essential for procedures to be efficient in order to achieve the desired outcomes. For example, an efficient software program is of little value if it cannot perform the necessary range of functions (Zidane & Olsson, 2017).

Strategic decisions are the most critical choices that an organization must make. Risk management provides valuable insights that enable more confident strategic decision-making. Any strategy adopted by an organization must yield the required results. Such a strategy can be deemed effective. There are numerous instances of businesses that either selected the wrong approach or failed to execute it successfully. Many of these businesses experienced corporate failure (Gould & Borer, 1996).

PRACTICE PROBLEM

Identify two possible hazards that a tech startup facing intense competition might encounter.

SOLUTION TO PRACTICE PROBLEM

Risk of Market Saturation: Evaluate the market to determine if it is already oversaturated with similar goods and services.

Technology Obsolescence Risk: Assess the potential for the startup's product to become outdated due to rapid technological advancements.

A strategy ought to be created with opportunities in mind. For example, a sports club might discover that it can sell more goods to its current clients. Certain clubs will set up a travel agency and offer connected travel insurance to the fans of the club who are going abroad. There is also a chance that a new finance division will oversee the creation of a club credit card. After identifying these options, the club must consider the risks involved in making these possible investments and create an appropriate project schedule to implement the chosen methods (Burches & Burches, 2020).

It will be easier to choose the most effective strategy, create the most effective processes, and, in the end, guarantee profitable and efficient operations if sufficient consideration of risk is given to each of these tasks. Businesses with good procedures and operations management will not succeed if their overarching plan is flawed. This will remain true no matter how effective the operational and project-level risk management procedures are. More company failures have been caused by incorrect strategy than inefficient operations or inadequate processes (Van et al., 2008).

2.5. FUNDAMENTALS PRINCIPLES OF INSURANCE

Learning Objectives

- To understand principles of insurance:
- To understand key insurance principles, such as indemnity and insurable interest.
- To apply these principles in insurance contracts for clarity and fairness.

The insurance principles constitute the fundamental structure that directs the interactions and operations of the insurance business. The core ideas of absolute good faith, insurable interest, indemnity, subrogation, contribution, and loss mitigation are at the center of these principles. Good faith requires complete sincerity and open communication between the insured and the insurer, guaranteeing that all pertinent data is submitted throughout the underwriting process (Jibril et al., 2018).

According to the definition of insurable interest, the policyholder must have a rightful financial interest in the insured person or property. According to the principle of indemnity, insurance is intended to avoid unfair enrichment by putting the insured back in the same financial situation as before the loss (Blackburn et al., 2005).

Through subrogation, an insurer can assume the policyholder's rights and pursue unidentified parties responsible for the loss after settling a claim (Figure 2.3). Loss mitigation emphasizes the policyholder's duty to prevent damages and losses, while contribution allows multiple insurance policies covering the same risk to share the loss proportionally. These principles collectively uphold the integrity and fairness of insurance agreements, fostering a stable and equitable system of risk transfer (Gephart, 1917).

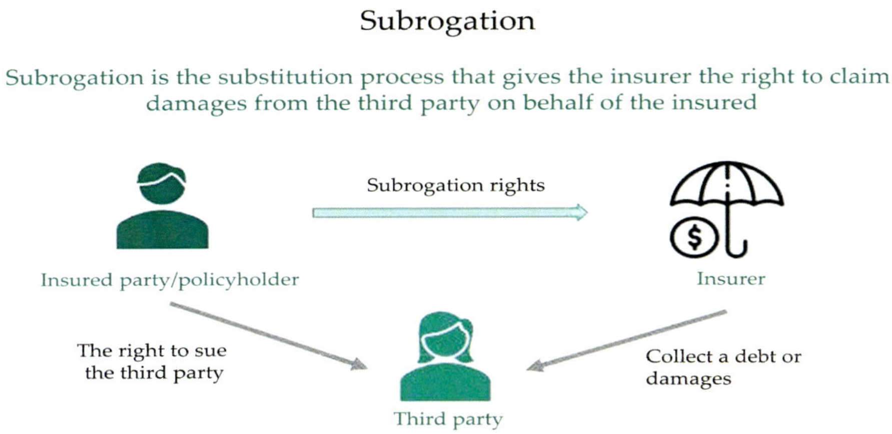

Figure 2.3. Diagram representing the process of subrogation. (Source: Gayatri, Creative Commons License)

Keyword

Indemnity: The concept and procedure of paying an insured party for the monetary loss or damage they have sustained as a result of a covered incident is known as "indemnity" in the context of insurance. In insurance, indemnification serves the function of returning the policyholder to their pre-loss financial situation without preventing financial gain.

2.5.1. Principle of Indemnity

The indemnity principle is one of the most important concepts in insurance. It states that the insurer commits to paying no more than the actual amount of the loss, ensuring that the insured does not profit from a loss. Many casualty and property insurance contracts operate on the basis of indemnity. In the event of a covered loss, the insurer should not be obligated to pay more than the actual loss amount. However, it is important to note that an indemnification contract does not guarantee full compensation for all covered damages. Factors such as deductibles, financial limitations, and other contractual requirements often result in the payment amount being less than the actual loss (Marandi & Moradmahi, 2016).

The indemnity principle serves two primary objectives. The first objective is to prevent the insured from gaining financially from a loss. For instance, if Kristin were to receive $200,000 for a partial loss of $50,000 covered by her home insurance, it would violate the concept of indemnity and be financially advantageous for her (Rosiak, 2014).

The second objective is to mitigate moral hazards. If dishonest policyholders could profit from a loss, they might intentionally cause losses to obtain insurance benefits. However, when the loss payment is less than the actual loss amount, there is less incentive for policyholders to engage in dishonest behavior (Williams, 1960).

2.5.2. Principle of Insurable Interest

Another crucial legal principle is that of insurable interest (Figure 2.4). According to the insurable interest principle, the insured must be able to suffer monetary loss in the event of a covered loss. For example, an individual possesses an insurable interest in their car, since they risk financial loss if the vehicle is stolen or damaged. Because one could suffer financial loss if their personal property—such as a computer, books, and clothes—is destroyed or damaged, they have an insurance interest (Patterson, 1918).

Consider a scenario when a person buys their spouse's health insurance. In this case, the person has an insurable interest in their spouse's well-being. The person acquiring the insurance would be immediately impacted emotionally, financially, and possibly regarding caring responsibilities if the spouse developed a medical condition or needed healthcare services. This financial and emotional connection creates a legitimate insurable interest since the individual will lose out if their partner has health issues. In this case, the health insurance coverage upholds the principle of insurable interest, which helps minimize potential financial obligations and provide required medical care (Campbell, 1949).

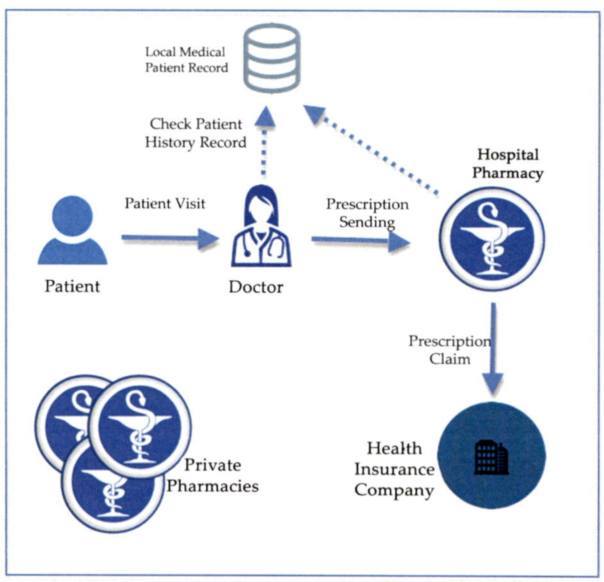

Figure 2.4. Illustration of insurance claim process. (Source: Kholoud Alqattan, Creative Commons License)

2.5.3. Principle of Subrogation

Subrogation is a principle that provides significant support to the indemnity principle (Figure 2.5). When an insurance policy covers a loss, subrogation means substituting the insurer for the insured to seek claiming indemnity from a third party. Put another way, the insurer can recoup any loss payments paid to the insured from a careless third party.

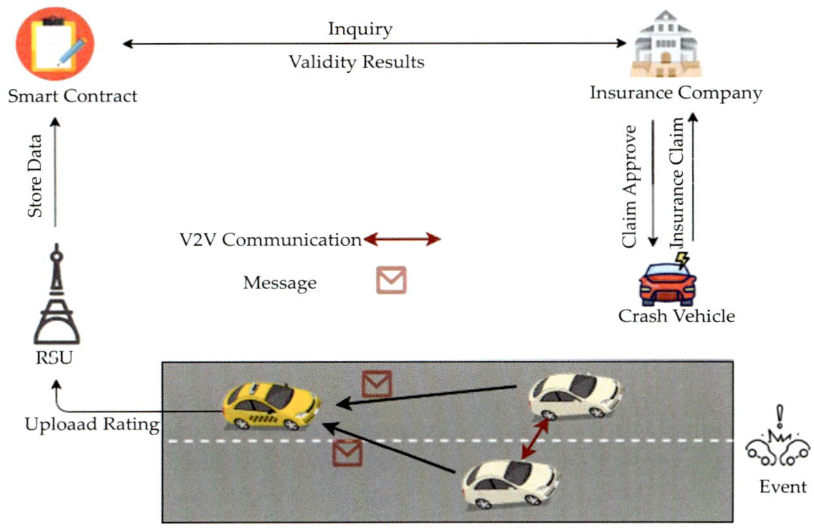

Figure 2.5. Representation of insurance claim model for vehicles. (Source: Tabinda Kokab, Creative Commons License)

For instance, if a negligent driver runs a red light, collides with Megan's car, and causes $5,000 worth of damage, assuming she has collision insurance on her vehicle, her insurer will cover the damage to the vehicle (minus any deductible) and pursue the irresponsible driver who caused the accident. Alternatively, Megan can attempt to obtain compensation for the damage to her vehicle directly from the negligent driver. Subrogation does not apply if the insurer does not pay for the loss. However, once a loss payment is made, the insured relinquishes any legal claims for reimbursement from the negligent third party to the insurer (Galt, 1891) (Figure 2.6).

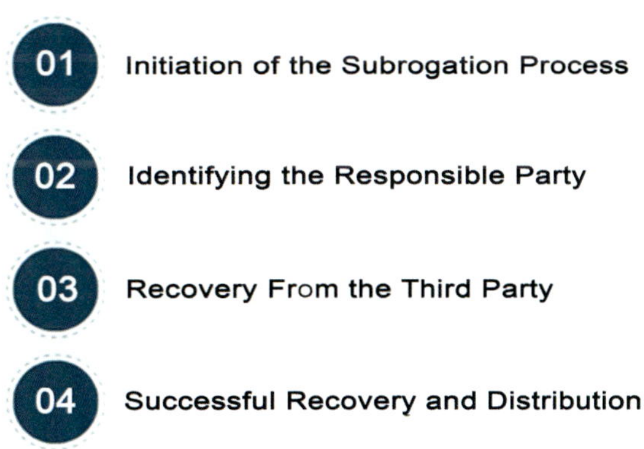

Figure 2.6. Depiction of Phases in subrogation process. (Source: True Tamplin, Creative Commons License)

Subrogation serves three main functions. Initially, subrogation prevents the insured from receiving payment for the same loss more than once. If subrogation were not allowed, the insured could receive payment from both the party responsible for the damage and their insurance company. This would violate the principle of indemnity (King, 1951).

2.5.4. Principle of Utmost Good Faith

The principle of ultimate good faith, which holds that both parties to an insurance contract must be more honest than they are in other contracts, is the basis of an insurance contract. This principle has its historical roots in ocean marine insurance. An ocean marine underwriter had to have great faith in statements made concerning the cargo that would be shipped in an insurance application. It is likely that the contract was formed away from the ship and its cargo, and the insured item was not visually inspected. As a result, the insurance applicant had to be extremely honest to comply with the concept of the highest good faith. Representations, secrecy, and warranty are three significant legal theories that uphold the highest good faith (Farrugia & Grima, 2021).

2.5.5. Principle of Contribution

The principle of contribution is one of the most fundamental concepts in insurance. It is closely related to the principle of indemnity. According to this principle, the insured is entitled to claim for the actual damage from any one insurer or all the other insurers (Ellis & McGuire, 1988).

For instance, let's consider the case of Mr. Bill Gates, who owns property worth 79 billion dollars. He has insurance coverage from three companies: Liberty Mutual Insurance Co. (20 billion dollars), State Farm Group (40 billion dollars), and All-State Insurance Group (30 billion dollars). If the actual property loss is valued at 40 billion dollars, Mr. Gates can only recover that amount from State Farm Group, and not from any other insurers (Maunah et al., 2023).

2.5.6. Principle of Mitigation of Loss

Another principle in insurance concepts is the principle of loss mitigation. According to this principle, the insured cannot simply stand by and allow their property to be destroyed; instead, they must make every effort to save it. Even though the property is covered by insurance, the insured should still try to minimize the losses (Goetz & Scott, 1983).

2.5.7. Principle of Causa Proxima

Another principle in insurance concepts is the principle of proximate cause. This principle states that in order to determine the insurer's liability, one or more causes must be identified, and the closest cause must be considered (Sahu, 2014).

For instance, let's consider a scenario where a trawler ship has insurance coverage for damages caused by collisions. Coincidentally, the trawler vessel collides with another vessel, resulting in additional delays of a few days. As a result of this delay, the bananas on the trawler ship become rotten and unfit for consumption. Therefore, there are two causes of the losses: the collision and the delay. The delay was the closest factor contributing to the spoilage of the bananas. Since the insurance coverage for the trawler vessel only includes collisions and not delays, the insured party will not receive compensation from the insurance company for the rotten bananas. However, the trawler ship will be compensated for the collision (Fujimoto, 1959).

2.6. LAW AND THE INSURANCE AGENT

Learning Objectives

- To understand the concept of law and insurance agent
- To discuss the types of risks addressed by insurance

Typically, an agent representing the principal (the insurer) sells an insurance contract. A person with the power to act on behalf of another is called an agent. The party on whose behalf action is to be taken is the principal, or insurer. Therefore, Patrick would be the agent and Apex Insurance Company would be the principal if he had the power to seek, initiate, or terminate an insurance contract on the company's behalf (McNeil, 1958) (Figure 2.7).

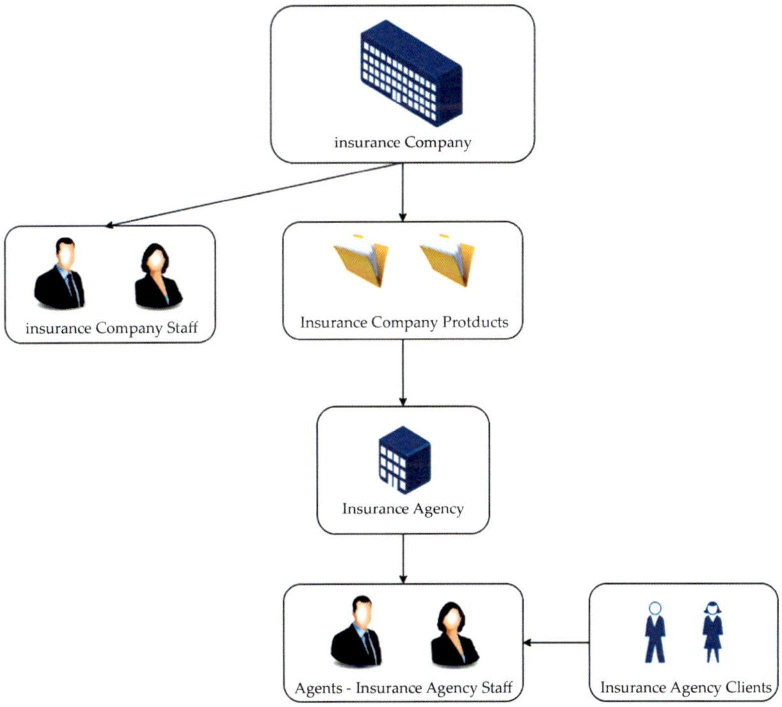

Figure 2.7. Illustration of the relationship between insurance companies and agencies. (Source: Stoyan Cheresharov et al., Creative Commons License)

2.6.1. Law of Agency

Significant legal requirements govern the acts of agents and their interactions with insureds. Among them are the following:

i. No agency relationship is presumed to exist.
ii. To represent the principle, an agent needs to be authorized.
iii. When an agent acts within the bounds of their authority, the principle is accountable for their actions.
iv. Agent authority may be subject to restrictions (Richmond, 2004).

2.6.1.1. No Presumptions of an Agency Relationship

The assumption that someone can lawfully represent another person as an agent is not always true. There must be some overt indication of an agency relationship. For instance, someone posing as a car insurance company agent might collect premiums and then steal the money. If the vehicle insurance has not taken any action to give the idea that an agency connection exists, it is not legally liable for the person's behavior. Nonetheless, it can be assumed that a legitimate agent is representing the insurer if the individual has the business card, rate information, and application blanks provided by the insurer (Huda et al., 2016).

2.6.1.2. Authority to Represent the Principle

An agent needs authorization to represent the principal. Three things can provide authority:

a) Express authority;
b) Implied authority;
c) Apparent authority.

The term "express authority" describes the specific powers of the agent. Typically, these rights are outlined in the agency agreement between the principal and agent. Moreover, the agency agreement may limit certain authorities. For example, a life insurance agent may have the authority to contact potential candidates and schedule in-person interviews. However, other rights, such as modifying contractual clauses or extending premium payment deadlines, may be restricted. Agents also possess implied authority. This refers to their ability to perform any necessary actions to fulfill the objectives of the agency agreement. For instance, an agent who is authorized to provide life insurance coverage to a customer is implicitly authorized to collect the initial premium (Krueger, 1952).

Furthermore, the principal may be bound by the agent's apparent authority. If the agent creates the impression that they are acting within reasonable and appropriate authority, and a third party is misled as a result, the principal may be held responsible for the agent's actions. Third parties only need to demonstrate that they exercised reasonable care in determining the agent's authority based on the agent's actual authority or the principal's conduct (Abraham, 2012).

2.6.1.3. Limitations on the Power of Agents Insurers

It can restrict the authority of agents. They are usually effective when limitations are appropriately disclosed to the policyholder and do not violate laws. This is accomplished by a nonwaiver clause in the application or policy, which usually specifies that only specific firm officials, like executive officers, can modify the policy terms or prolong the time to pay premiums (Feinman, 2012).

2.6.2. Principle Responsible for Acts of Agents

The principle is accountable for all actions taken by agents when acting within the bounds of their authority, according to another rule of agency law. This covers dishonesty in the form of deception, omissions, and acts. Furthermore, concerning topics falling under the purview of the agency relationship, knowledge of the agent is deemed to constitute knowledge of the principal. For example, even when the life insurance agent purposefully omits this information from the application, the insurer is assumed to be aware of the applicant's alcohol addiction. As a result, once the insurer issues the insurance, it cannot, after that, contest its validity on the grounds of alcoholism and significant misrepresentation (Stovall, 1962).

SUMMARY

- This chapter offers a thorough analysis of insurance and risk management, starting with a close look at the ideas behind sensible risk management tactics. These guidelines establish the foundation for comprehending the significance of risk management and highlighting its function in safeguarding resources, improving judgment, and cultivating organizational resilience.
- According to the concept of indemnity, the insurer should not pay more than the real amount of the damage; in other words, the insured should not profit from a covered loss. The indemnity principle has multiple exceptions. These exclusions include life insurance, replacement cost insurance, valued policy legislation, and valued policies.
- According to the principle of insurable interest, the insured must be financially disadvantaged in the event of a loss. For any insurance contract to be legally binding, it must be backed by an insurable interest.
- Property ownership, prospective legal obligation, secured creditors, and contractual rights may support the insurable interest requirement in property and casualty insurance.
- In the event of a loss, the insurable interest condition in property insurance must be satisfied. The insurable interest criterion for life insurance must only be satisfied when the policy is issued.
- Four general rules of agency govern agents' activities and interactions with insureds: The existence of an agency connection is not assumed. To represent the principle, an agent needs to be authorized. When agents behave within the bounds of their power, a principle is accountable for their acts. Agent authority may be subject to restrictions.

MULTIPLE CHOICE QUESTIONS

1. Which of the following is a key principle of risk management?

a. Avoidance

b. Ignorance

c. Procrastination

d. Acceptance

2. What is the purpose of diversification in risk management?

a. To concentrate risk in one area

b. To eliminate all risks

c. To spread risk across different assets or activities

d. To increase risk exposure

3. Which type of insurance provides coverage for damage to your own vehicle in an accident?

a. Liability insurance

b. Collision insurance

c. Comprehensive insurance

d. Underinsured motorist insurance

4. What is a deductible in an insurance policy?

a. The amount the insured receives after a claim

b. The maximum amount the insurer is liable to pay

c. The initial amount the insured must pay before the insurer covers the remaining loss

d. The premium paid monthly

REVIEW QUESTIONS

1. What are the fundamental principles of risk management, and how do they inform decision-making in organizations?
2. Discuss the significance of risk management in various industries, providing examples of situations where inadequate risk management could lead to negative consequences.
3. Explore the Principle of Insurable Interest in insurance contracts and explain its importance.
4. Outline the legal considerations that insurance agents need to be aware of in their profession and discuss potential ethical challenges they might face within the legal framework.
5. Provide an example of a real-world phenomenon or scenario that illustrates the application of the Principle of Utmost Good Faith in insurance transactions.

Answers to Multiple Questions

1. (a) 2. (c) 3. (b) 4. (c)

REFERENCES

1. Abraham, K. S., (2012). Four conceptions of insurance. *U. Pa. L. Rev.*, *161*, 653.
2. Ahmed, A., Kayis, B., & Amornsawadwatana, S., (2007). A review of techniques for risk management in projects. *Benchmarking: An International Journal*, *14*(1), 22–36.
3. Aven, T., (2016). Risk assessment and risk management: Review of recent advances on their foundation. *European Journal of Operational Research*, *253*(1), 1–13.
4. Bajek, R., Matsuda, Y., & Okada, N., (2008). Japan's Jishu-Bosai-Soshiki community activities: Analysis of its role in participatory community disaster risk management.

Natural Hazards, *44*, 281–292.

5. Baker, N., (2011). Managing the complexity of risk: The ISO 31000 framework aims to provide a foundation for effective risk management within the organization. *Internal Auditor*, *68*(2), 35–39.
6. Blackburn, W. E., Jones, D. A., Schwartzman, J., & Siegman, D., (2005). The application of fundamental valuation principles to property/casualty insurance companies. *Proceedings of the Casualty Actuarial Society-Arlington, Virginia 2005: XCII*, *1*(1), 257–491.
7. Burches, E., & Burches, M., (2020). Efficacy, effectiveness, and efficiency in the health care: The need for an agreement to clarify its meaning. *Int Arch Public Health Community Med*, *4*(1), 1–3.
8. Campbell, A. J., (1949). Some aspects of insurable interest. *Can. B. Rev.*, *27*, 1.
9. Carvalho, M. M. D., & Rabechini, Jr. R., (2015). Impact of risk management on project performance: The importance of soft skills. *International Journal of Production Research*, *53*(2), 321–340.
10. Davoudi, S. M. M., Arani, S. N., & Shojaei, S. H., (2012). The relationship between change management factors and efficacy, based on bitici change model: A survey in Alborz insurance. *Asian Journal of Research in Business Economics and Management*, *2*(8), 106–124.
11. Denenberg, H. S., (1963). The legal definition of insurance: Insurance principles in practice. *The Journal of Insurance*, *30*(3), 319–343.
12. Dickson, G., (1995). Principles of risk management. *Quality in Health Care*, *4*(2), 75.
13. Dionne, G., & Triki, T., (2005). *Risk Management and Corporate Governance: The Importance of Independence and Financial Knowledge for the Board and the Audit Committee, 1*(1), 1–20.
14. Doloi, H., (2009). Relational partnerships: The importance of communication, trust and confidence and joint risk management in achieving project success. *Construction Management and Economics*, *27*(11), 1099–1109.
15. Duff, C., (2003). The importance of culture and context: Rethinking risk and risk management in young drug using populations. *Health, Risk & Society*, *5*(3), 285–299.
16. Ellis, J., Feinstein, S., & Stearns, D., (2000). Scenario learning: A powerful tool for the 21st century planner. *Journal of Financial Planning*, *13*(4), 1–20.
17. Ellis, R. P., & McGuire, T. G., (1988). Insurance principles and the design of prospective payment systems. *Journal of Health Economics*, *7*(3), 215–237.
18. Farrugia, A., & Grima, S., (2021). A model to determine the need to modernize the regulation of the principle of utmost good faith. *Journal of Financial Regulation and Compliance*, *29*(4), 454–473.
19. Feinman, J. M., (2012). The law of insurance claim practices: Beyond bad faith. *Tort Trial & Insurance Practice Law Journal*, *1*(1), 693–740.
20. Feinman, J. M., (2018). Contract and claim in insurance law. *Conn. Ins. LJ*, *25*, 153.
21. Fujimoto, K., (1959). A tendency of arguments on the principle of: "Causa Proxima."

The Annals of the Hitotsubashi Academy, *10*(2), 158–170.

22. Galt, A. C., (1891). The principle of subrogation: A reply. *Can. L. Times*, *11*, 89.
23. Garg, M. C., & Garg, S., (2020). Operating efficiency and investment efficiency: General insurance companies. *SCMS Journal of Indian Management*, *1*(1), 131.
24. Gephart, W. F., (1917). *Principles of Insurance, 1*, 1–20.
25. Goetz, C. J., & Scott, R. E., (1983). The mitigation principle: Toward a general theory of contractual obligation. *Virginia Law Review*, 967–1024.
26. Gould, D. L., & Borer, J., (1996). Applied stapling technique in radical retropubic prostatectomy: Efficient, effective, and efficacious. *The Journal of Urology*, *155*(3), 1008–1010.
27. Huda, M. K., Nugraheni, N., & Komar, K., (2016). The nature of the contract of life insurance agency after enactment of the act number 40 of 2014 on insurance. *Journal of Advanced Research in Law and Economics*, 7(5 (19)), 1037–1041.
28. Islam, S., & Houmb, S. H., (2010). Integrating risk management activities into requirements engineering. In: *2010 Fourth International Conference on Research Challenges in Information Science (RCIS)* (Vol. 1, No. 1, pp. 299–310). IEEE.
29. Jibril, S. U., Baba, I. A., & Maude, A. K., (2018). Critical analysis of fundamental principles of insurance under the Nigerian law. *International Journal of Advanced Academic Research*, *4*(7), 28–40.
30. Jorion, P., (2009). Risk management lessons from the credit crisis. *European Financial Management*, *15*(5), 923–933.
31. Just, D. R., Wolf, S., & Zilberman, D., (2003). Principles of risk management service relations in agriculture. *Agricultural Systems*, *75*(2, 3), 199–213.
32. King, C. G., (1951). Subrogation under contracts insuring property. *Tex. L. Rev.*, *30*, 62.
33. Kintanar, A. Y., (1917). Subrogation. *Phil. LJ*, *4*, 285.
34. Kozlova, O. N., Kalacheva, E. A., & Kalacheva, I. V., (2019). Aims and perspectives of insurance company investments. In: *International Science and Technology Conference "FarEastCon" (ISCFEC 2019)* (Vol. 1, pp. 76–79). Atlantis Press.
35. Krueger, R. B., (1952). Agency: Imputation of agent's knowledge to principal: Insurance contracts. *Michigan Law Review*, *50*(5), 761–763.
36. Lee, C. C., Cheng, H. K., & Cheng, H. H., (2007). An empirical study of mobile commerce in insurance industry: Task-technology fit and individual differences. *Decision Support Systems*, *43*(1), 95–110.
37. Libby, G. E., (1952). Some aspects of protection and indemnity insurance. *Ins. LJ*, *1*(1), 684.
38. Luko, S. N., (2013). Risk management principles and guidelines. *Quality Engineering*, *25*(4), 451–454.
39. Lutvinoff, S., (1989). Subrogation. *La. L. Rev.*, *50*, 1143.
40. Marandi, M. R., & Moradmahi, R., (2016). The principle of indemnity in insurance law. *Journal of Social Sciences and Humanities Research*, *4*(3), 61–64.

41. Marasinghe, M. L., (1975). An historical introduction to the doctrine of subrogation: The early history of the doctrine II. *Val. UL Rev.*, *10*, 275.
42. Maysami, R. C., & Williams, J. J., (2006). Evidence on the relationship between takaful insurance and fundamental perception of Islamic principles. *Applied Financial Economics Letters*, *2*(4), 229–232.
43. McNeil, J. D., (1958). Liability of an insurance agent or broker in procuring or maintaining insurance for an owner. *Vand. L. Rev.*, *12*, 839.
44. Olorogun, L. A., (2015). A proposed contribution model for general Islamic insurance industry. *International Journal of Islamic and Middle Eastern Finance and Management*, *8*(1), 114–131.
45. Patterson, E. W., (1918). Insurable interest in life. *Columbia Law Review*, *18*(5), 381–421.
46. Pennock, M. J., & Haimes, Y. Y., (2002). Principles and guidelines for project risk management. *Systems Engineering*, *5*(2), 89–108.
47. Power, M., (2004). The risk management of everything. *The Journal of Risk Finance*, *5*(3), 58–65.
48. Priest, G. L., (2016). A principled approach toward insurance law: The economics of insurance and the current restatement project. *Geo. Mason L. Rev.*, *24*, 635.
49. Richmond, D. R., (2004). Insurance agent and broker liability. *Tort Trial & Insurance Practice Law Journal*, *1*(1), 1–58.
50. Rosiak, P., (2014). The implementation of the principle of equity in the context of indemnity. *Bialstockie Studia Prawnicze*, *17*, 217.
51. Sahu, M. K., (2014). The rule of causa Proxima as a principle of insurance. *Kathmandu Sch. L. Rev.*, *4*, 154.
52. Sanyare, F. N., & Tuolong, J. G., (2017). Administrative efficiency and policy failure: The national health insurance scheme of Ghana in perspective. *Global Encyclopedia of Public Administration, Public Policy, and Governance*, *1*(1), 1–9.
53. Schwarcz, D., (2016). Coverage information in insurance law. *Minn. L. Rev.*, *101*, 1457.
54. Scordis, N. A., Suzawa, Y., Zwick, A., & Ruckner, L., (2014). Principles for sustainable insurance: Risk management and value. *Risk Management and Insurance Review*, *17*(2), 265–276.
55. Stovall, E. S., (1962). Authority of insurance agents to bind the company. *Baylor L. Rev.*, *14*, 413.
56. Stulz, R. M., (2008). Rethinking risk management. In: *Corporate Risk Management* (Vol. 1, No. 1, pp. 87–120). Columbia University Press.
57. Tchankova, L., (2002). Risk identification–basic stage in risk management. *Environmental Management and Health*, *13*(3), 290–297.
58. Van, N. J. P., (1996). Maintaining the principle of indemnity: Theory and practice. *JS Afr. L.*, *1*(1), 572.

59. Van, T. D., Wickes, S., Stevens, V., Roosen, P., & Witvrouw, E., (2008). Effective prevention of sports injuries: A model integrating efficacy, efficiency, compliance, and risk-taking behavior. *British Journal of Sports Medicine*, *42*(8), 648–652.

60. Wang, Q., Lau, R. Y. K., Si, Y. W., Xie, H., & Tao, X., (2023). Blockchain-enhanced smart contract for cost-effective insurance claims processing. *Journal of Global Information Management (JGIM)*, *31*(7), 1–21.

61. Williams, W., (1960). The principle of indemnity: A critical analysis. *Ins. LJ*, *1*(1), 471.

62. Zidane, Y. J. T., & Olsson, N. O., (2017). Defining project efficiency, effectiveness, and efficacy. *International Journal of Managing Projects in Business*, *10*(3), 621–641.

CHAPTER 3

Risk Assessment and Identification Strategies

LEARNING OBJECTIVES

After studying this chapter, you will be able to:

1. To recognize the pivotal role of risk assessment in organizational decision-making and strategic planning.
2. To differentiate approaches and techniques for both quantitative and qualitative risk assessment.
3. To acquire proficiency in quantitative risk assessment using models.
4. To understand qualitative risk assessment methods.
5. To explore the synergy between qualitative and quantitative approaches.

INTRODUCTORY EXAMPLE

Imagine an insurance company, Quantum Risk Insure, navigating the complex landscape of risks inherent in the ever-evolving digital age. In this scenario, the company faces a multitude of challenges, from emerging cyber threats to shifts in customer expectations influenced by technological advancements. To effectively manage these risks, the company employs a comprehensive risk assessment strategy that integrates both quantitative and qualitative approaches. Actuarial models and predictive analytics are utilized to quantify the financial impact of potential cyber threats, while qualitative methods such as scenario analysis and expert judgment are employed to understand the nuanced cultural factors affecting customer behavior. This example illustrates the need for a synergistic approach in risk management to ensure that the insurer is well-prepared to address the intricacies of modern risk landscapes.

UNIT INTRODUCTION

This chapter focuses on risk assessment and identification methodologies, emphasizing their critical role in influencing informed decision-making in many fields. In this chapter, readers will explore several methods of risk assessment, offering valuable insights into the techniques employed for comprehending and controlling risks with efficiency. Furthermore, examination of specific risk assessment methodologies provides a clear understanding of the various tools that businesses can use to thoroughly examine their risk landscape (Manuj & Mentzer, 2008).

3.1. IMPORTANCE OF RISK ASSESSMENT

Learning Objectives

- To evaluate risk factors for informing underwriting decisions and ensuring effective insurance coverage terms.
- To apply risk assessment in premium determination by integrating loss history and emerging risks for accurate pricing.

Risk assessment is a crucial procedure in the insurance sector that serves as the basis for underwriting, pricing, and overall risk management methods (Figure 3.1). The insurance industry depends on meticulous risk assessment to identify and measure potential risks linked to insuring individuals, corporations, and assets (Naghavi et al., 2003).

Figure 3.1. Diagram of risk assessment process. (Source: Ozygein, Creative Commons License)

3.1.1. Underwriting Decision Making

Did you know?

The largest life insurance policy ever issued was valued at $201 million. It was for a Silicon Valley billionaire and set a Guinness World Record in 2014.

Insurers evaluate multiple characteristics, including the applicant's health, age, occupation, and lifestyle, to determine the probability of claims (Figure 3.2). This comprehensive assessment enables insurers to make well-informed judgments about the issuing of policies, determination of coverage limits, and pricing of premiums (Fan & Wang, 2017).

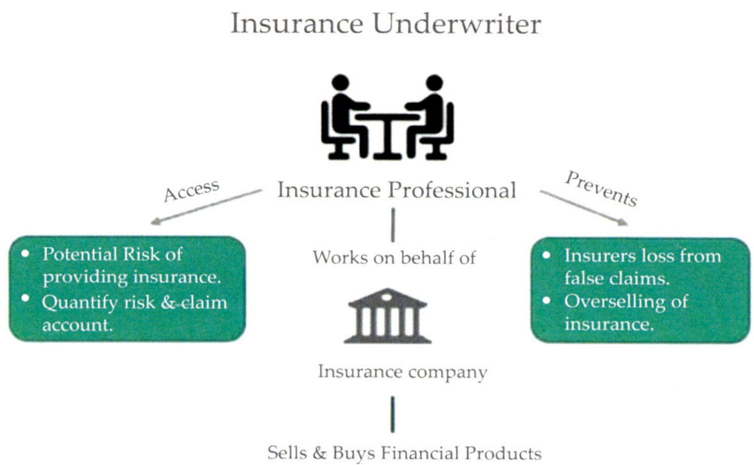

Figure 3.2. Illustration of insurance underwriter. (Source: Khalid, Creative Commons License)

3.1.2. Premium Determination

Risk assessment has a direct impact on the determination of insurance premiums. Insurers strive to establish premiums at a level that sufficiently covers projected claims and related administrative expenses, while also maintaining competitiveness in the market. Insurers can better match premiums to the risk level of the insured party or property by conducting a more precise and thorough risk assessment (Palliam, 2005).

3.1.3. Loss Prevention and Mitigation

Efficient risk assessment empowers insurers to recognize possible sources of loss and execute measures to prevent or mitigate these risks. For example, in property insurance, evaluating the risk of fire may result in suggestions to construct fire suppression systems, therefore diminishing the probability and intensity of potential losses. Insurers frequently engage in cooperation with policyholders to adopt risk management strategies that are mutually advantageous (Yang et al., 2018).

3.1.4. Data Analytics and Technology Integration

The insurance sector has seen a revolutionary transformation in risk assessment due to advancements in data analytics and technology. Insurers already utilize extensive information, artificial intelligence, and predictive modeling to improve the precision of risk assessment (Figure 3.3). By using technology, insurers can evaluate risks in real-time, adjust underwriting techniques in a flexible manner, and swiftly react to shifting market conditions (Nayak et al., 2019).

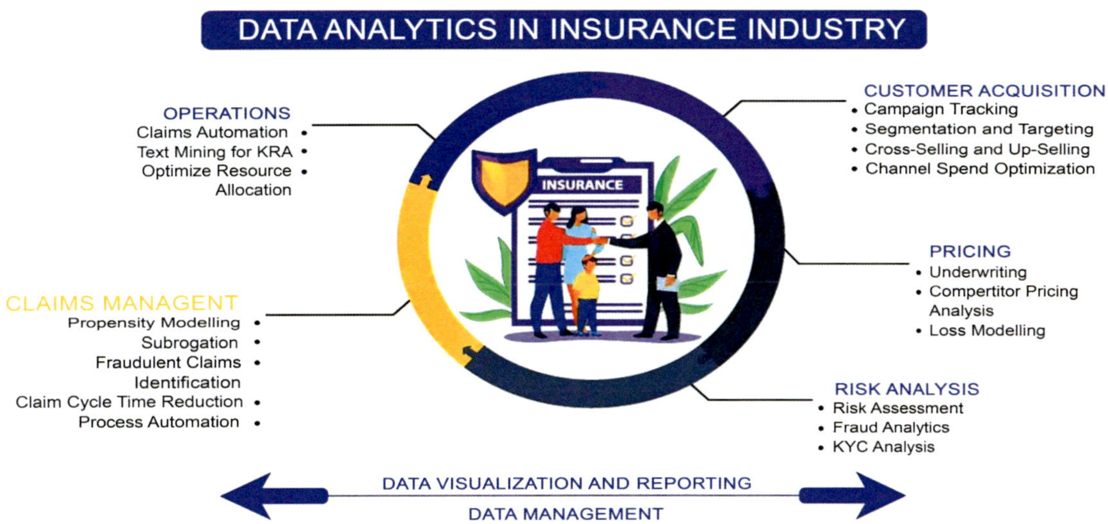

Figure 3.3. Representation of data analytics in insurance industry. (Source: Daniel, Creative Commons License)

3.1.5. Reinsurance Considerations

Reinsurance, a risk-sharing mechanism employed by insurance firms, is impacted by the results of risk evaluations. Insurers have the option to transfer a part of their risks to reinsurers, depending on the results of these evaluations. Reinsurers depend on their own risk assessment procedures to establish the specific terms and circumstances for accepting these risks, resulting in an intricate network of risk management in the insurance sector (Eden & Kahane, 1988).

Essentially, risk assessment in the insurance sector is a complex process that affects several aspects of the industry. A comprehensive risk assessment framework is crucial for insurers to effectively manage uncertainties and ensure financial stability in a constantly changing landscape. This framework encompasses underwriting decisions, premium determination, loss prevention, technological integration, regulatory compliance, and reinsurance considerations (Garven & Lamm, 2003).

3.2. APPROACHES TO RISK ASSESSMENT

Learning Objectives

- To understand the foundational principles and methodologies of qualitative and quantitative risk assessment approaches.
- To understand how to apply diverse risk assessment techniques and critically evaluate their efficacy in practical scenarios.

Within the insurance sector, the evaluative framework of risk involves a wide range of methodological approaches that strive to thoroughly examine and control potential uncertainties related to policyholders and insured assets. Underwriting guidelines serve as prescriptive frameworks that establish specific criteria, such as age and health, to guide the evaluation and decision-making process for policy acceptance. Actuarial analysis, based on statistical models, plays a crucial role in predicting future events and allowing for detailed estimates of the likelihood and severity of claims. By carefully examining past loss data and claims records, insurers can identify patterns, which in turn allows them to make adaptive changes to their underwriting procedures (Jobst, 2014).

Simultaneously, risk surveys and on-site inspections provide a tangible aspect to risk assessment. The incorporation of credit scoring, predictive modeling, and data analytics, which together form a technical toolkit, enhances the accuracy of risk assessment. Scenario analysis and stress testing are utilized as evaluative procedures to expose insurance portfolios to simulated extreme situations. Regulatory compliance requires maintaining sufficient capital, while reinsurance plans provide ways to transfer risk and support the risk mitigation framework. These methodological foundations enable insurers to effectively handle uncertainties, carefully adjust premiums, and maintain financial stability in the ever-changing insurance industry (Boyko & Roienko, 2014).

Remember

The first automobile insurance policy was issued in 1897 in the United Kingdom. It was intended to cover liability for accidents involving the vehicle.

3.3. QUALITATIVE VS. QUANTITATIVE RISK ASSESSMENT IN INSURANCE

Learning Objectives

- To understand the qualitative and quantitative risk assessment,
- To highlight the advantages of qualitative and quantitative risk assessment

There are two main ways for risk assessment: qualitative and quantitative approaches. Both strategies are essential for assessing and reducing risks in the insurance industry.

PRACTICE PROBLEM

Explain a real-world scenario where the lack of effective risk assessment impacted an insurance company. Discuss the practical repercussions on the company's financial stability and propose strategies that could have been employed through comprehensive risk assessment.

SOLUTIONS TO PRACTICE PROBLEM

Consider an insurance company that did not adequately assess the potential impact of climate-related events in a region prone to natural disasters. The lack of risk assessment might lead to substantial losses from unexpected claims, affecting the company's financial stability. Through comprehensive risk assessment involving climate data analysis and scenario planning, the company could have implemented strategies like revising coverage policies, setting aside sufficient reserves, and collaborating with reinsurers to mitigate such risks proactively.

3.3.1. Qualitative Risk Assessment

Qualitative risk assessment includes a subjective evaluation of risks using non-numeric data. This approach depends on the expertise, experience, and industry knowledge of professionals to assess the probability and consequences of risks. Qualitative assessment frequently employs descriptive scales, such as high, medium, and low, to categorize risks (Guo, 2009).

3.3.2. Advantages of Qualitative Risk Assessment in Insurance

Qualitative risk assessment in insurance involves subjective evaluations, focusing on non-numeric factors (Figure 3.4). This approach provides valuable insights into contextual risks that may not be easily quantifiable, enhancing the overall risk management process.

a) Subjective Insight: Qualitative assessments enable a sophisticated comprehension of risks by integrating expert perspectives and industry insights that may not be readily measurable.

b) Flexibility: Qualitative approaches are versatile and effective for evaluating emerging or unique risks in settings where there may be minimal historical data available.

c) Ease of Implementation: This approach is frequently more convenient and expeditious to execute, rendering it appropriate for early risk identification and rapid assessments (Tesliuc & Lindert, 2002).

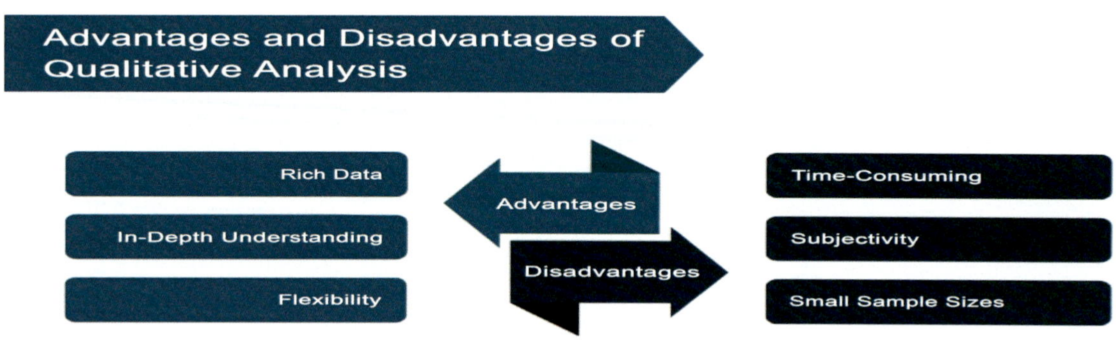

Figure 3.4. Diagram of advantages and disadvantages of qualitative analysis. (Source: True Tamplin, Creative Commons License)

3.3.3. Quantitative Risk Assessment

Quantitative risk assessment involves the use of numerical data and statistical models to analyze and quantify risks. This approach employs mathematical calculations to evaluate the probability and financial consequences of potential events, providing a more objective and measurable approach (Pap & Homolya, 2017).

3.3.4. Advantages of Quantitative Risk Assessment

a) Quantitative assessments provide a more precise understanding of risks by assigning numerical values, enabling insurers to accurately assess potential losses.

b) The use of historical data and statistical models enhances decision-making processes, enabling insurers to make well-informed choices based on empirical evidence.

c) Quantitative methods play a crucial role in effectively managing extensive risk portfolios, allowing insurers to optimize their risk exposure and allocate resources efficiently (Vnukova et al., 2020).

3.3.5. Comparative Analysis

a) Complementary Nature: Qualitative and quantitative methodologies are frequently employed together to offer a comprehensive risk assessment. Qualitative methods provide valuable insights and help identify new risks, while quantitative methods provide accurate estimates for more effective risk management (Drljaca, 2016).

b) Risk Complexity: Qualitative approaches are particularly suitable for analyzing complex and emerging risks, while quantitative methods are highly effective in assessing risks that have abundant historical data and a measurable impact.

c) Resource Requirements: Quantitative assessments may require additional resources in terms of data gathering, modeling, and analysis. On the other hand, qualitative approaches can be more cost-effective, especially for smaller insurance companies or when addressing fewer complex risks (Rose & Mackenzie, 1991).

3.4. MODELS OF QUANTITATIVE RISK ASSESSMENT

Learning Objectives

- To understand actuarial models for precise risk valuation in quantitative risk assessment.
- To understand and apply value-at-risk (VaR) metrics to assess and quantify portfolio impacts, enhancing proficiency in quantitative risk evaluation.

Quantitative risk assessment in insurance is a methodical and data-oriented process that uses mathematical models and statistical tools to measure the possible consequences of risks. Quantitative risk assessment, in contrast to qualitative methodologies, utilizes factual facts and computational studies to offer insurers a more objective comprehension of the likelihood and cost implications of different events (Deleris & Pate, 2012).

3.4.1. Actuarial Models and Predictive Analysis

Actuarial models are fundamental in quantitative risk assessment for insurance. They utilize mathematical and statistical techniques to analyze past data and forecast future events. Actuaries employ these models to assess risks associated with mortality, morbidity, and other essential elements in determining the prices of insurance products (Shaked, 1985).

3.4.1.1. Actuarial Models

Actuarial models assist insurers in forecasting future obligations, ascertaining suitable premium rates, and establishing reserve thresholds. These models integrate several elements, including policyholder behavior and demographic trends, to offer insurers a comprehensive framework for assessing risk (Kleffner & Lee, 2009).

3.4.1.2. Predictive Analysis

Predictive analytics use advanced statistical methodologies and machine learning algorithms to examine extensive datasets, unveil trends, and generate predictions.

Predictive analytics in the insurance industry aids in the identification of developing risks, enhancement of underwriting procedures, and improvement of fraud detection capabilities, ultimately leading to more precise risk assessment.

3.4.2. Financial Metrics in Risk Assessment

Financial metrics are crucial in quantitatively evaluating risks in the insurance sector. These measures offer a numerical foundation for assessing an insurer's financial well-being, resilience, and capacity to endure unfavorable events (Lee & Urrutia, 1996).

3.4.2.1. Solvency Ratios

Solvency ratios, such as the Solvency II ratio, assess the sufficiency of an insurer's capital in comparison to its liabilities. These ratios are crucial for evaluating an insurer's financial stability and ensuring that it has adequate funds to fulfill its responsibilities to policyholders.

3.4.2.2. Return on Equity

Return on Equity is a fundamental financial measure that assesses an insurer's profitability in relation to its equity. Insurers can evaluate their financial performance and detect potential risks that could affect their profitability and financial stability by examining the Return on Equity (ROE).

3.4.3. Probability and Severity

Quantitative risk assessment in insurance relies on quantifying the probability and severity of prospective risks, enabling insurers to assign numerical values to the probability of events occurring and their financial consequences (De Bandt & Overton, 2022).

3.4.3.1. Probability of a Loss

Insurers can evaluate the probability of certain events happening in order to determine the likelihood of claims and losses (Figure 3.5). Probability assessments utilize historical data, actuarial models, and predictive analytics to offer insurers a quantitative foundation for projecting risks.

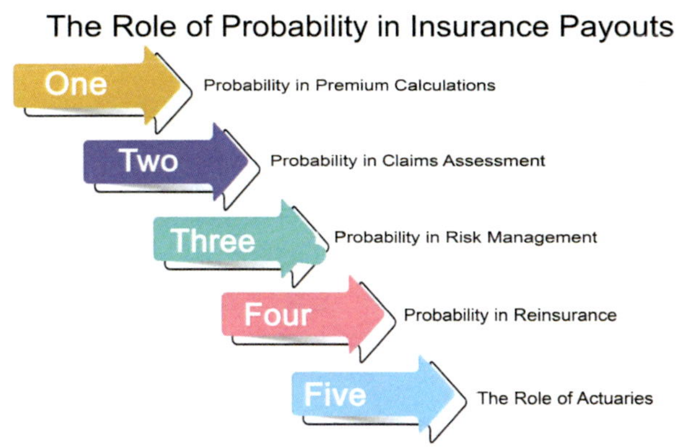

Figure 3.5. Illustration of role of probability in insurance. (Source: Hesham, Creative Commons License)

3.4.3.2. Severity of a Loss

Assessing the severity of potential losses involves analyzing the monetary consequences of unfavorable events. Insurers can utilize financial indicators, actuarial models, and scenario analysis to evaluate the potential seriousness of losses. This enables them to allocate reserves and implement effective risk reduction strategies.

Quantitative risk assessment in insurance employs actuarial models, predictive analytics, and financial metrics to provide insurers with a comprehensive framework for assessing and managing risks. The utilization of data in decision-making processes enhances financial stability and enables insurers to effectively mitigate risk in the insurance market (Wang & Van, 2021).

3.5. APPROACHES OF QUALITATIVE RISK ASSESSMENT IN INSURANCE

Learning Objectives

- To understand the key qualitative risk assessment methods employed in insurance.
- To comprehend how qualitative risk assessment informs decision-making processes within the insurance sector.

Qualitative risk assessment in the insurance sector is a systematic examination that depends on subjective judgment, expert opinions, and a comprehensive grasp of different risk factors. Qualitative assessment provides a deeper understanding of risks by examining complex characteristics that cannot be easily measured using numerical data, unlike quantitative methods. Qualitative approaches play a vital role in the insurance industry by facilitating the identification of developing risks, comprehension of intricate circumstances, and integration of expert viewpoints (Wrede et al., 2020).

3.5.1. Expert Judgment

Expert judgment adds important subjective viewpoints to risk assessment by utilizing the insights of seasoned underwriters, industry specialists, and risk management professionals. This human-centric approach improves the depth of risk understanding by considering subtle elements that may escape quantitative models.

3.5.1.1. Application in Insurance

Expert opinion is especially important in the insurance industry when evaluating new risks or those for which there is little historical evidence. To ensure a thorough awareness of risks that goes beyond statistical analysis, experts—such as seasoned underwriters and risk managers—play a crucial role in detecting and analyzing qualitative aspects of risks (Garayeta et al., 2022).

3.5.2. Delphi Method

The Delphi Method provides organized, collaborative expert perspectives (Figure 3.6). The Delphi Method enhances consensus on potential risks by fostering unbiased responses and maintaining participant anonymity through iterative questionnaires. The Delphi Method supports a collective intelligence approach in the insurance industry, where there are many developing risks and uncertainties. It provides a methodical means to extract expert views and tackle intricate, multiple problems.

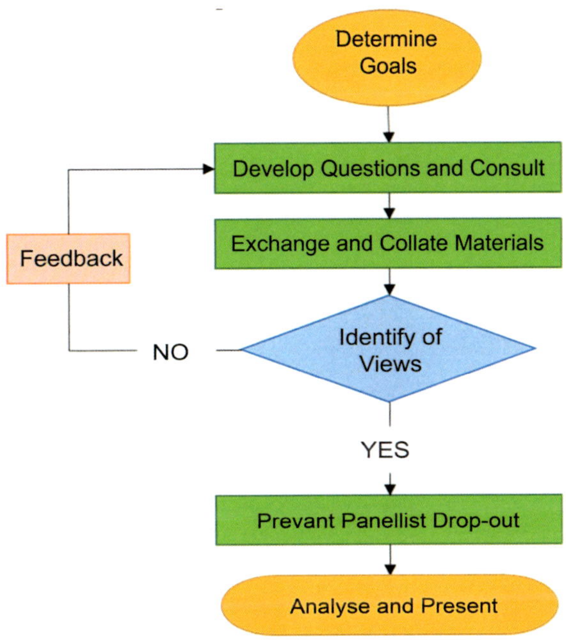

Figure 3.6. Flowchart of Delphi method. (Source: Jun Zhang, Creative Commons License)

3.5.2.1. Collaborative Expert Opinion

Through a series of repetitive surveys, a panel of experts' input is gathered and synthesized using the Delphi Method, a qualitative approach. This technique aids in the gathering of various expert perspectives in the insurance industry, promoting a cooperative evaluation process that might provide insights into possible risks and their effccts (Borch, 1963).

3.5.2.2. Enhancing Consensus

The Delphi Method seeks to improve expert consensus by requiring numerous rounds of input and anonymizing responses. This is especially helpful for the insurance sector, since a thorough risk assessment necessitates a variety of viewpoints on risks like geopolitical events, regulatory changes, and technological improvements (Ingram, 2005).

3.6. SWOT ANALYSIS AND CULTURAL FACTORS

Learning Objectives

- Investigate the emergence, characteristics, and propagation methods of viruses specifically targeting Macintosh systems.
- Assess the impact of Macintosh-specific viruses on system integrity and data security.

SWOT analysis provides a structured framework for assessing internal strengths and weaknesses, as well as external opportunities and threats, in qualitative risk assessment within the insurance sector (Figure 3.7). Insurance companies can ascertain their organizational capacities, knowledge, and assets internally, which facilitates a more comprehensive understanding of their innate advantages and possible disadvantages. To predict possibilities and challenges, external factors including market trends, regulatory changes, and new risks are closely examined. By using SWOT analysis, insurers may match their strategic goals with a thorough comprehension of the wider risk landscape through a qualitative lens (Dionne et al., 2009).

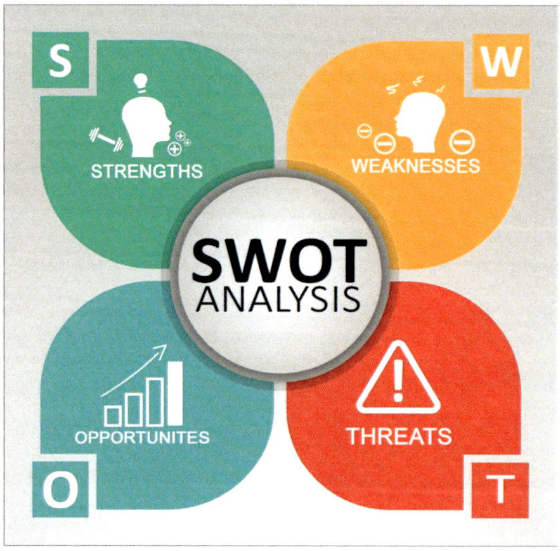

Figure 3.7. Diagram of SWOT analysis. (Source: Barry Pruit, Creative Commons License)

Cultural aspects play a crucial role in the qualitative evaluation of risk within the insurance industry. These variables encompass social, behavioral, and moral factors that can influence consumer choices, market dynamics, and legal frameworks. Insurers must delve into the cultural nuances that impact their business operations, client relationships, and overall risk environment (Campbell, 1980).

Understanding how cultural factors interact with the insurance industry can provide insights into qualitative risk aspects, such as reputational risks stemming from cultural misalignment or changes in customer preferences due to cultural shifts. Conducting a comprehensive review of cultural aspects through qualitative techniques like SWOT analysis enhances the overall risk assessment process, ensuring that insurers are cognizant of the intricacies of the contexts in which they operate.

To provide insurers with a comprehensive view of their internal and external risk landscapes, the integration of SWOT analysis with the study of cultural aspects in qualitative risk assessment is essential. This qualitative approach enhances strategic decision-making, enabling insurers to anticipate market dynamics, adapt to cultural changes, and navigate the complex interplay of elements unique to the insurance sector (Sankaramuthukumar & Alamelu, 2012).

SUMMARY

- This chapter delves into the critical aspects of risk assessment and identification within the insurance sector. It begins by highlighting the paramount importance of robust risk assessment practices, emphasizing their role in safeguarding an insurance company's financial stability and maintaining customer satisfaction.
- The chapter then explores various approaches to risk assessment, encompassing both qualitative and quantitative methods. Understanding the diverse methods is crucial for insurance professionals to effectively identify, evaluate, and mitigate risks inherent in their operations.
- The chapter emphasizes the need for a holistic and adaptive approach to risk management in the dynamic landscape of insurance. By integrating varied risk assessment strategies, insurance companies can proactively navigate uncertainties, ensuring resilience, and staying ahead in an ever-evolving industry. The chapter underscores the interconnectedness of risk assessment, effective decision-making, and organizational success within the intricate realm of insurance.

MULTIPLE CHOICE QUESTIONS

1. **What is the primary purpose of risk assessment in insurance?**
   a. To safeguard financial stability and customer satisfaction
   b. To ensure compliance with regulations
   c. To maximize profits
   d. To minimize competition
2. **Which of the following is a qualitative method commonly used in insurance for risk assessment?**
   a. Scenario analysis
   b. Actuarial modeling
   c. Regression analysis
   d. Monte Carlo stimulation
3. **What does a holistic risk management approach entail in the insurance sector?**
   a. Adapting risk management strategies based on evolving market trends
   b. Focusing solely on quantitative risk assessment
   c. Ignoring cultural factors in customer behavior analysis
   d. Relying exclusively on historical data for risk evaluation
4. **How can qualitative risk assessment benefit an insurance company entering a new market?**
   a. By minimizing the importance of cultural factors
   b. By tailoring strategies based on the local preferences

c. By solely relying on quantitative data
d. By avoiding customer surveys and focus groups

REVIEW QUESTIONS

1. Why is effective risk assessment crucial in insurance, and how does it impact financial stability and customer satisfaction?
2. Differentiate between qualitative and quantitative risk assessment in insurance and explain how combining these approaches enhances risk understanding.
3. Provide practical examples of how qualitative risk assessment methods, such as scenario analysis, are applied in the insurance sector.
4. Explain the significance of adopting a holistic and adaptive risk management approach in insurance, emphasizing the interconnected nature of risk assessment, decision-making, and organizational success.

Answers to Multiple Questions

1. (c) 2. (c) 3. (b) 4. (b)

REFERENCES

1. Borch, K., (1963). Recent developments in economic theory and their application to insurance. *ASTIN Bulletin: The Journal of the IAA*, *2*(3), 322–341.
2. Boyko, A., & Roienko, V., (2014). Risk assessment of using insurance companies in suspicious transactions. *Economic Journal*-XXI, (11, 12), 73–76.
3. Campbell, R. A., (1980). The demand for life insurance: An application of the economics of uncertainty. *The Journal of Finance*, *35*(5), 1155–1172.
4. De Bandt, O., & Overton, G., (2022). Why do insurers fail? A comparison of life and nonlife insurance companies from an international database. *Journal of Risk and Insurance*, *89*(4), 871–905.
5. Deleris, L. A., & Paté-Cornell, M. E., (2012). Insolvencies in the American property and casualty insurance industry: A systems' approach. *Risk and Decision Analysis*, *3*(1, 2), 3–18.
6. Dionne, G., Giuliano, F., & Picard, P., (2009). Optimal auditing with scoring: Theory and application to insurance fraud. *Management Science*, *55*(1), 58–70.
7. Drljača, D. S., (2016). Risk assessment through matrix model in insurance companies. *Poslovna Ekonomija*, *10*(2), 43–65.
8. Eden, Y., & Kahane, Y., (1988). Reinsurance contracts: A utility approach vs. insurance capacity considerations. *Journal of Banking & Finance*, *6*, 247–269.
9. Fan, C. K., & Wang, W. Y., (2017). A comparison of underwriting decision making between telematics-enabled UBI and traditional auto insurance. *Advances in Management and Applied Economics*, 7(1), 17.

10. Garayeta, A., De La Peña, J. I., & Trigo, E., (2022). Towards a global solvency model in the insurance market: A qualitative analysis. *Sustainability*, *14*(11), 6465.
11. Garven, J. R., & Lamm-Tennant, J., (2003). Economic and financial perspectives on the demand for reinsurance. *Rational Reinsurance Buying*, *1*(1), 163–186. London: Risk Publications.
12. Guo, L., (2009). A qualitative method for risk preference of insurance companies. In: *2009 International Conference on Intelligent Human-Machine Systems and Cybernetics* (Vol. 1, pp. 156–159). IEEE.
13. Htay, S. N. N., & Salman, S. A., (2013). Viability of Islamic insurance (Takaful) in India: SWOT analysis approach. *Rev. Eur. Stud.*, *5*, 145.
14. Ingram, J. D., (2005). Misrepresentations in applications for insurance. *U. Miami Bus. L. Rev.*, *14*, 103.
15. Jobst, A. A., (2014). Systemic risk in the insurance sector: A review of current assessment approaches. *The Geneva Papers on Risk and Insurance-Issues and Practice*, *39*, 440–470.
16. Kapasi, B. (n.d.). A study on the motion of IPO of life insurance corporation of India in the light of SWOT analysis. *Editorial Board*, *59*, 1–20.
17. Kleffner, A. E., & Lee, R. B., (2009). An examination of property and casualty insurer solvency in Canada. *Journal of Insurance Issues*, *1*(1), 52–77.
18. Lamond, J. E., (2014). The role of market-based flood insurance in maintaining communities at risk of flooding: A SWOT analysis. *Water Resources in the Built Environment: Management Issues and Solutions*, *1*(1), 258–270.
19. Lee, S. H., & Urrutia, J. L., (1996). Analysis and prediction of insolvency in the property-liability insurance industry: A comparison of logit and hazard models. *Journal of Risk and Insurance*, *1*(1), 121–130.
20. Manuj, I., & Mentzer, J. T., (2008). Global supply chain risk management strategies. *International Journal of Physical Distribution & Logistics Management*, *38*(3), 192–223.
21. Naghavi, M., Libby, P., Falk, E., Casscells, S. W., Litovsky, S., Rumberger, J., & Willerson, J. T., (2003). From vulnerable plaque to vulnerable patient: A call for new definitions and risk assessment strategies: Part I. *Circulation*, *108*(14), 1664–1672.
22. Nayak, B., Bhattacharyya, S. S., & Krishnamoorthy, B., (2019). Integrating wearable technology products and big data analytics in business strategy: A study of health insurance firms. *Journal of Systems and Information Technology*, *21*(2), 255–275.
23. Onwuegbuchunam, D. E., Igboanusi, C., & Ogwude, I. C., (2017). The performance of marine insurance firms in Nigeria: An augmented SWOT analysis. *International Journal of Transportation Engineering and Technology*, *3*(4), 83–90.
24. Palliam, R., (2005). Application of a multi-criteria model for determining risk premium. *The Journal of Risk Finance*, *6*(4), 341–348.
25. Paté-Cornell, E., & Deleris, L. A., (2009). Failure risks in the insurance industry: A quantitative systems analysis. *Risk Management and Insurance Review*, *12*(2), 199–212.

26. Rose, R., & Mackenzie, W. J. M., (1991). Comparing forms of comparative analysis. *Political Studies*, *39*(3), 446–462.

27. Sankaramuthukumar, S., & Alamelu, K., (2012). A SWOT analysis of Sri Lankan insurance sector. *IUP Journal of Risk & Insurance*, *9*(1), 27.

28. Shaked, I., (1985). Measuring prospective probabilities of insolvency: An application to the life insurance industry. *Journal of Risk and Insurance*, *1*(1), 59–80.

29. Tesliuc, E., & Lindert, K., (2002). Vulnerability: A quantitative and qualitative assessment. *Guatemala Poverty Assessment Program, 1*(1), 1–91.

30. Vnukova, N., Kavun, S., Kolodiziev, O., Achkasova, S., & Hontar, D., (2020). Indicators-markers for assessment of probability of insurance companies relatedness in implementation of risk-oriented approach. *Economic Studies*, *29*(1), 1–20.

31. Wang, W. L., & Van De, L. J. W., (2021). Quantitative modeling of residential building disaster recovery and effects of pre-and post-event policies. *International Journal of Disaster Risk Reduction*, *59*, 102259.

32. Yang, L., Cao, C., Wu, D., Qiu, H., Lu, M., & Liu, L., (2018). Study on typhoon disaster loss and risk prediction and benefit assessment of disaster prevention and mitigation. *Tropical Cyclone Research and Review*, 7(4), 237–246.

CHAPTER 4

Enterprise Risk Management

LEARNING OBJECTIVES

After studying this chapter, you will be able to:

1. Understand the principles of Enterprise Risk Management (ERM) and its strategic role in organizational resilience.
2. Explore the dynamics of the insurance market and its relevance in managing various risks.
3. Gain insights into the development of effective ERM frameworks aligned with organizational goals.
4. Recognize the global and dual nature of risks in the context of a multinational business environment.
5. Examine the interplay of insurance, reinsurance, and financial innovation in catastrophe risk management.
6. Explore innovations in risk management, including market enhancement and technical efficiency.

INTRODUCTORY EXAMPLE

Imagine a global company operating in the fast-paced business world of today, managing a complex web of risks. The company faces a wide range of risks that could affect its operations and financial health, from volatile market shifts and regulatory changes to the imminent threat of natural disasters. Recognizing the dual nature of risks, the organization must balance local and global risk considerations as it grows internationally. The management team is responsible for creating a strong framework for Enterprise Risk Management (ERM), coordinating risk management strategies with organizational goals, and maximizing exposure through the use of primary risk management techniques. This introductory scenario sets the stage for a comprehensive exploration of the principles and practices encompassed within the chapter on Enterprise Risk Management.

UNIT INTRODUCTION

The field of risk management has witnessed significant advancements in recent years. Firstly, specialized branches of risk management, such as project, energy, finance, operational, and clinical risk management, have emerged. Secondly, businesses are embracing the notion that risk management should be approached from a broader perspective.

This more comprehensive approach has been referred to by various names, including enterprise-wide, integrated, holistic, and strategic risk management. Currently, the most popular and widely accepted term for this comprehensive approach is enterprise or enterprise-wide risk management (ERM). The fundamental principle of the ERM method is to move away from the practice of managing individual risks separately (Bromiley et al., 2015).

ERM adopts a more cohesive, comprehensive, and integrated strategy. By employing the ERM technique, a company assesses all the risks associated with each of its operations. Enterprise risk management focuses on risk management that can impact the organization's goals, critical dependencies, or essential operations. It encompasses not only control and risk management but also opportunity management.

The fact that many risks are interconnected, and that typical risk management ignores these relationships, has also been taken into consideration. The identification of the relationship between two or more risks that may affect the same operation or goal is a key aspect of the ERM approach. The objective of the ERM approach is to assess all the risks that could have an impact on the item being assessed by closely examining the target, major dependencies, or core processes (D'arcy & Brogan, 2001).

To illustrate the ERM strategy, let's consider a sports club whose primary objective is to increase game attendance. In order to provide the best possible game experience, this process involves various operations such as marketing, advertising, ticket distribution and sales, as well as logistical planning. Ensuring sufficient parking and transportation options, along with appropriate catering and other amenities in the stadium, will all contribute to maximizing attendance during games.

The club can identify the risks that may influence these operations and the chosen core process by identifying the critical activities that contribute to the core process. The club's commercial director has been assigned the responsibility of overseeing the success of this crucial procedure, and targets for improved attendance at future games can be established. This more comprehensive approach may include an analysis of the potential for increasing game attendance (Hiles, 2012).

4.1. ENTERPRISE RISK MANAGEMENT

Learning Objectives

- Understand innovative approaches in ERM, covering market enhancement and technical efficiency.
- Understand the importance of considering both global and local factors in the ERM process.

Organizations independently develop strategies and plans to realize the potential benefits of enterprise risk management (Figure 4.1). The evaluation of all material risks that the organization faces is the primary characteristic of enterprise risk management. It is necessary to determine how risks are related to one another to assemble the organization's overall risk exposure. Once the organization's overall risk exposure has been determined, the board's appetite for risk and the organization's own risk capability can be contrasted (Nocco & Stulz, 2006) (Figure 4.2).

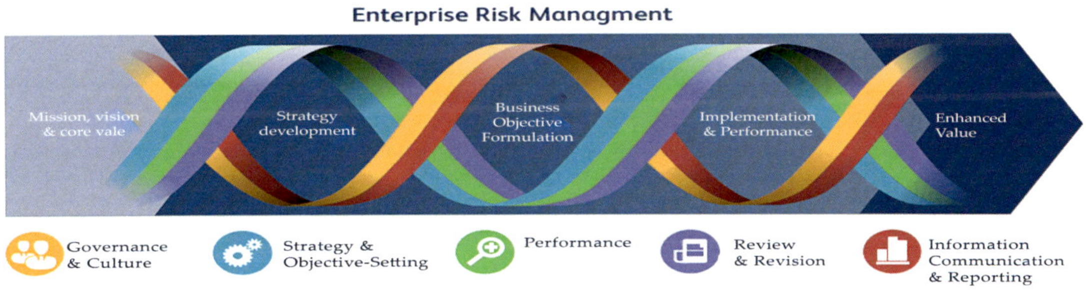

Figure 4.1. Diagram of Enterprise Risk Management. (Source: Yasuhide, Creative Commons License)

Did you know?

NASA employs rigorous enterprise risk management practices for space missions, emphasizing the identification and mitigation of potential risks.

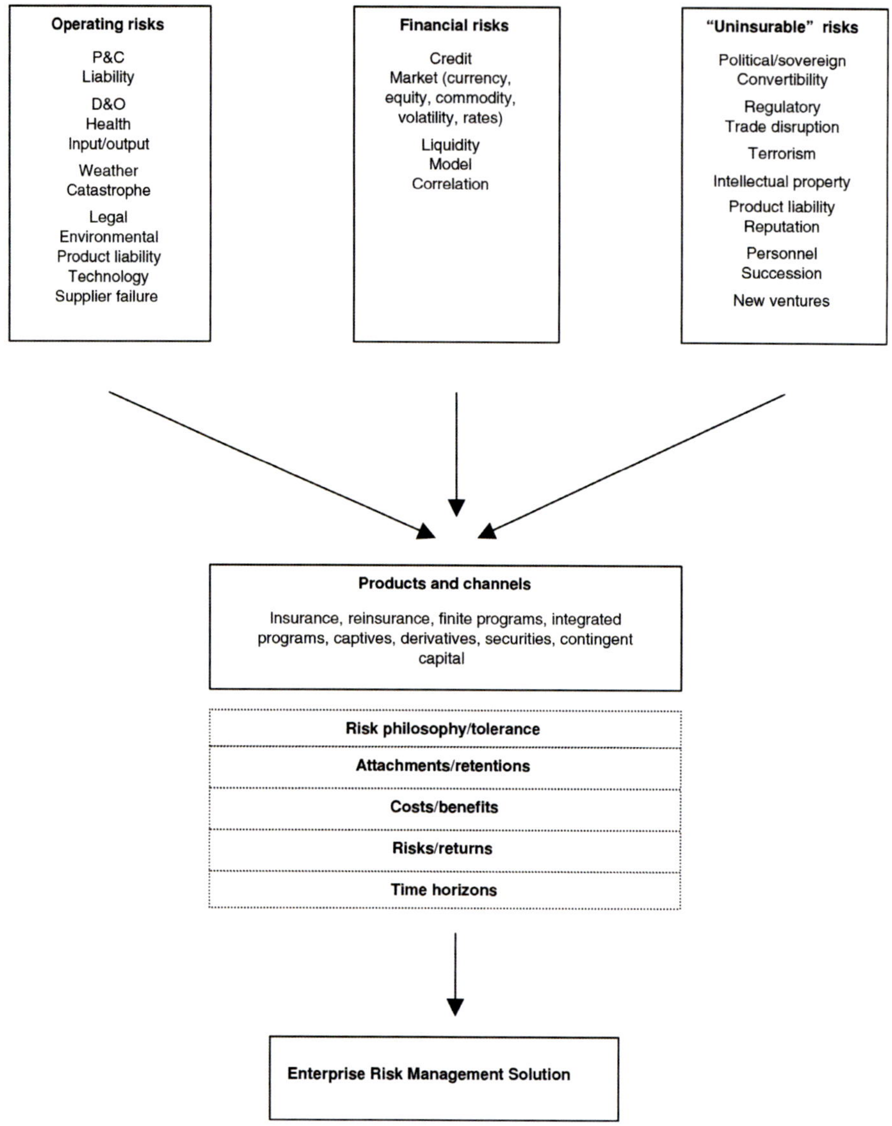

Figure 4.2. Diagram of ERM coverage. (Source: Erik Banks, Creative Commons License)

4.1.1. ERM and Business Continuity

Business continuity management (BCM) and enterprise risk management (ERM) are closely related. There is a direct relationship between the business impact analysis that forms the foundation of business continuity planning (BCP) and the risk assessment that is necessary as part of the risk management process.

The standard procedure for risk management involves assessing goals and determining each specific risk that has the potential to affect them. The identification of the essential tasks that must be completed for the firm to stay operational is the result of a business impact study (Suresh et al., 2020).

The ERM approach and the business impact analysis approach are very similar because they both focus on identifying the critical dependencies and functions that must be in place for the business to continue and succeed. This is evident from the definition of enterprise risk management provided above and the idea that it should be applied to the evaluation of core processes (Assibi, 2022).

Here's where ERM and BCP divide in the process: business continuity focuses on measures that should be performed to preserve the continuity of operations, whereas ERM focuses on risk management for processes. Therefore, the specific role of the business continuity strategy is to identify what steps should be taken to reduce the impact of the risk after it has been realized. As previously mentioned, business continuity planning is related to the cost-containment and damage-limitation aspects of loss management (Bertalan et al., 2016).

4.1.2. ERM in Energy and Finance

The energy and finance industries have developed their own well-established specialty area of risk management. The goal of an ERM initiative in the finance sector is to enhance shareholder value by:

i. Increasing capital and efficiency through objective resource allocation and leveraging portfolio effects and natural hedges;
ii. Supporting financial decision-making by capitalizing on risk-based advantages and considering regions with high potential for negative impact;
iii. Enhancing investor trust through proactive risk management, stabilizing outcomes, and safeguarding them from disruptions (Jonek, 2019).

In the energy industry, ERM often relies on the treasury department and specialized knowledge of oil price hedging. Many energy companies have established sizable divisions dedicated to this aspect of financial risk management. However, there is still a strong correlation between treasury risk management and the utilization of ERM in energy businesses.

The regulatory environment is one of the factors that motivates risk management in the finance industry. Basel II has been imposed on banks for several years now, and the Solvency II Directive will soon impose similar regulations on the European insurance industry. As a result, financial institutions have a duty to assess the extent of operational risk they are exposed to (Ittner & Oyon, 2020).

Financial institutions that engage in operational risk management (ORM) can determine the amount of capital that needs to be reserved to cover the consequences of identified risks materializing. Implementing ORM practices will improve risk identification and management, ultimately reducing the amount of capital required to cover the repercussions of materialized risks. In financial organizations, ORM can be seen as a specific application of the ERM methodology (Simkins, 2008).

The collapse of the entire banking system raised concerns about the effectiveness of risk management in banks, particularly in relation to operational risk management.

One of the effects of the global financial crisis is that risk is perceived as negative and risk management is seen as ineffective. However, taking risks is necessary for businesses to succeed (Rochette, 2009).

It is difficult to refute the claim that risk management in banks has failed. However, it is important to note that the banking crisis was not solely caused by the breakdown of risk management standards, but rather by the incorrect application of those standards. Many banks made two errors simultaneously:

i. Rather than adopting a more balanced perspective of the risks involved in pursuing higher rewards, banks made decisions based on the awards that were accessible since an accurate risk and reward analysis was not conducted.

ii Because of the banks' aggressive risk-taking approach, certain outcomes were deemed so rare that they could be disregarded, making it impossible to accurately quantify the level of risk involved.

A thorough examination of the 2008 banking crisis is outside the purview of this text. Nonetheless, it appears that the failure of two distinct sets of risk analysis models was the root cause of the crisis. Firstly, the banks' assumption that repackaged loans, such as sub-prime mortgages, would remain tradeable commodities was proven incorrect (Jermakyan, 2006).

Secondly, the banks believed that credit available for short-term borrowing would still be accessible in the wholesale money markets. Banks utilize this short-term capital to support their long-term lending activities at a higher profit margin. Most banks' credit models did not anticipate the collapse of the wholesale money markets (Otero et al., 2022).

4.2. INSURANCE MARKET DYNAMICS

Learning Objectives

- To understand the factors that contribute to the dynamic nature of the insurance landscape.
- To gain a comprehensive understanding of the dynamics influencing the insurance industry market.

When property and liability risks cannot be completely avoided, the resulting losses must be financed. The risk manager is faced with the decision of selecting between two approaches for financing losses: risk retention and risk transfer. Retained losses might be settled using current earnings, loss reserves, borrowing, or a captive insurance firm. Risk transfer involves the transfer of financial responsibility for losses to another entity, typically an insurance firm specializing in property and liability coverage. Decisions regarding the retention or transfer of risks are impacted by prevailing conditions in the insurance marketplace (Jurdi & AlGhnaimat, 2021). Three significant determinants impacting the insurance market are:

i. The underwriting cycle;
ii. Consolidation in the insurance industry;
iii. Capital market risk financing alternatives.

4.2.1. The Underwriting Cycle

Over the course of several years, a recurring trend has been noticed in various indicators of underwriting performance and financial success within the property and liability insurance sector. The underwriting cycle is the term used to describe the recurring pattern of changes in underwriting stringency, premium levels, and profitability. The property and liability insurance markets experience fluctuations characterized by periods of stringent underwriting standards and high premiums, known as a "hard" insurance market, as well as periods of relaxed underwriting standards and reduced premiums, referred to as a "soft" insurance market (Taylor, 2008). Various indicators can be employed to determine the current state of the underwriting cycle. The combined ratio represents the proportion of paid losses and loss adjustment charges, including underwriting expenses, in relation to premiums. If the combined ratio exceeds 1 (or 100%), it indicates that underwriting operations are not profitable (Fitzpatrick, 2003).

Remember

The modern ERM framework has evolved significantly over the years, influenced by financial disasters and global events such as the 2008 financial crisis.

For example, the combined ratio of 107 in 2002 signifies that insurers disbursed $1.07 in claims and expenses for every $1.00 they received in premiums. Insurance firms generate profits from underwriting operations when the combined ratio is below 1 (or 100%). In 2006, the combined ratio of 92.5 suggests that for every $1 of premium received, there was an underwriting profit of 7.5 cents (Feldblum, 2001).

When making judgments about retaining and transferring risks, risk managers need to consider the prevailing premium rates and underwriting standards. During a period of market softness, insurance can be obtained under favorable terms, such as lower premiums, expanded coverage, and the elimination of exclusions (Fitzpatrick, 2003).

In a "hard" market, higher retention rates are employed due to limited availability or unaffordability of certain insurance coverage. In response to the prolonged period of low demand in the insurance market during the late 1990s, several risk managers opted to acquire insurance contracts spanning numerous years to secure favorable terms (Simmons & Cross, 1986).

What are the factors that contribute to the volatility in property and liability insurance markets? (Feldblum, 2001). While several theories have been proposed, there are two clear aspects that impact the cost and underwriting decisions of property and liability insurance:

a) Insurance industry capacity;
b) Investment returns.

4.2.2. Consolidation in the Insurance Industry

As insurance product marketplaces evolve, organizations within this sector of the economy also undergo adjustments. The consolidation trend in the financial services business is continuing. Consolidation refers to the process of integrating business organizations by means of mergers and acquisitions (Berger, 1988). Several consolidation trends have significantly altered the insurance sector for risk managers:

a) Insurance company mergers and acquisitions;
b) Insurance brokerage mergers and acquisitions;
c) Cross-industry consolidations.

4.2.3. Capital Market Risk Financing Alternatives

Insurers and risk managers are increasingly seeking assistance from the capital markets to finance risk (Figure 4.3). Two methods of financing capital market risk include risk securitization and insurance options.

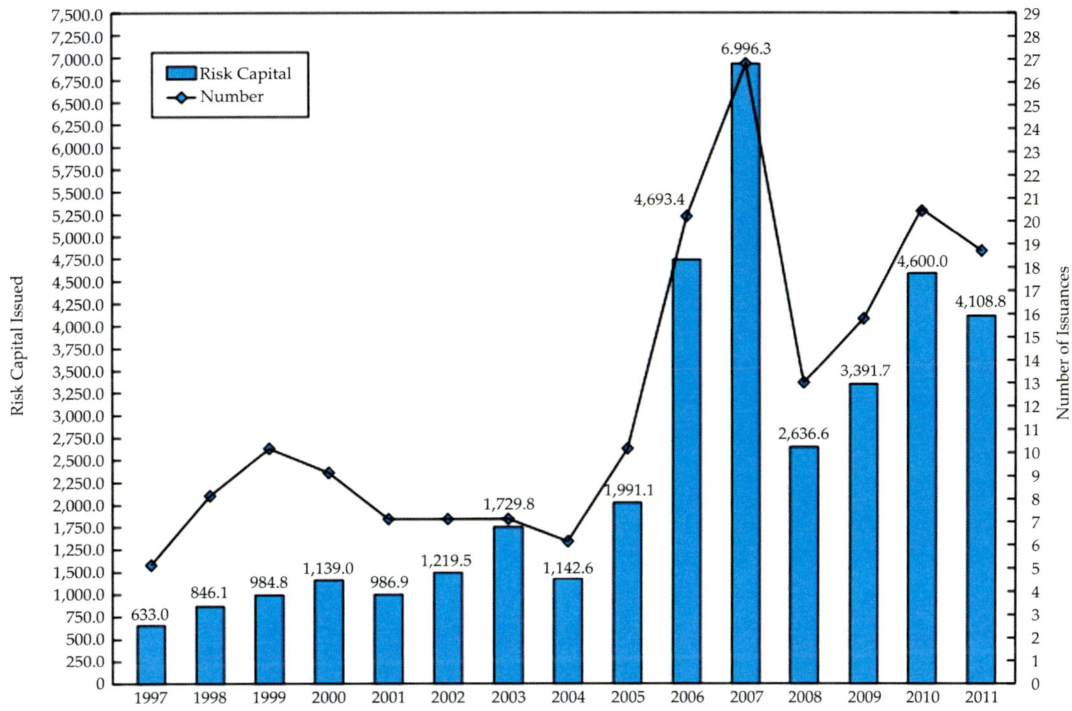

Figure 4.3. Catastrophe bonds: annual number of transactions and issue size. (Source: George E. Rejda, Creative Commons License)

4.2.3.1. Securitization of Risk

Risk securitization is a significant advancement in the field of insurance and risk management (Figure 4.4). Securitization of risk refers to the process of transferring insurable risk to the capital markets by creating a financial instrument, such as a catastrophe bond, futures contract, options contract, or other similar instrument. Risk securitization has an immediate effect on the insurance business by significantly increasing the capacity available to insurers and reinsurers. Securitization allows access to the money of other investors, instead of solely depending on insurance (Cummins et al., 1999).

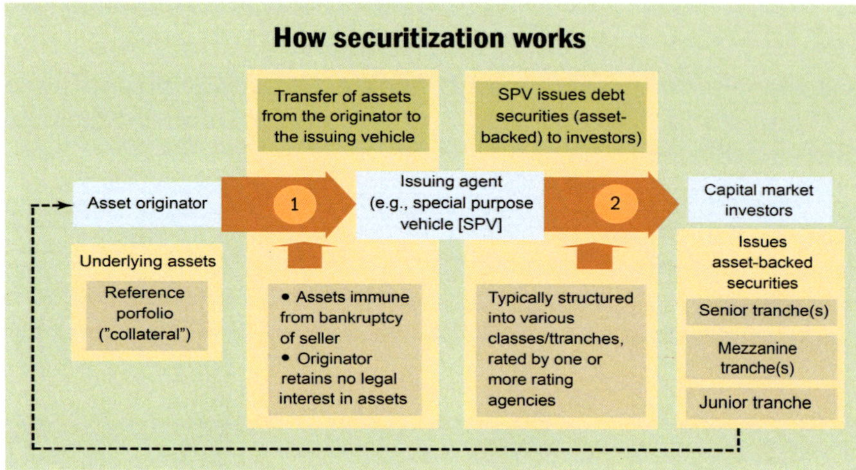

Figure 4.4. Flowchart of how securitization works. (Source: Daniel, Creative Commons License)

Insurers were early adopters of securitization. In 1997, USAA Insurance Company, using a subsidiary, issued a disaster bond to safeguard the company from significant financial losses caused by hurricanes (Thompson et al., 2018).

Catastrophe bonds are a type of corporate bond that grant the issuer the ability to forgo or delay making scheduled payments in the event of a catastrophic loss. Investors of the USAA bond received both the principal amount and interest, if the damages caused by hurricanes during a specific timeframe did not exceed a predetermined threshold. However, if hurricane claims surpass a specified threshold, both the principal and interest would be forfeited (Bouriaux & Scott, 2004).

4.2.3.2. Insurance Options

Insurance options can be utilized for the purpose of risk management. An insurance option is a financial instrument that gains value based on individual losses that can be insured or on the value of an index (Plowe et al., 2014).

Weather conditions have a significant impact on the profitability of numerous businesses. Utility firms, farmers, ski resorts, and other enterprises face weather-related risks and uncertainty. An increasing number of businesses are using weather derivatives to help manage this risk. A weather option provides compensation in the event of a predetermined weather condition, such as a temperature above a particular threshold or rainfall falling below a defined amount (Didier et al., 2021).

4.3. DEVELOPING AN ENTERPRISE RISK MANAGEMENT PROGRAM

Learning Objectives

- Understand the significance of a disaster recovery plan.
- Formulate a comprehensive disaster recovery plan.

It is becoming increasingly evident that contemporary corporations no longer have the choice of whether to safeguard their risk exposures. Instead, they must determine which exposures to safeguard against and in what precise manner. The significance of corporate risk management in safeguarding capital and improving shareholder value has been widely acknowledged and embraced. Consequently, the organization has successfully surpassed a substantial mindset "barrier," enabling them to consider implementing a more extensive enterprise initiative. However, it should be noted that not all organizations necessarily need or want an ERM program as a risk solution. The point is that there is a growing openness to evaluating the advantages and disadvantages of such programs when formulating a risk management plan (Murray, 2010).

A business must establish a risk strategy based on its risk tolerance and philosophy before launching an ERM program. Risk must be assessed in relation to its business objectives, which include financial targets (such as leverage, economic capital, and probability of insolvency), revenues, market share, presence in specific regions and industries, and financial risk tolerance. An organization cannot create an ERM strategy or a risk plan in a vacuum. Its actions need to be connected to the actualities of corporate business objectives (Abrams et al., 2007). Most businesses aim to maximize enterprise value as a general objective. Establishing a company risk strategy can help strengthen the connection between goals and implementation by identifying the barriers that stand in the way of this objective. Additionally, as resources are the financial assets that enable a business to function, it is evident that a focus on them is essential. Economic capital limits a firm's risk tolerance, or the maximum loss that can be incurred in each set of circumstances. It must be sufficient to support the financial and operating strategies of the company and lower the probability of ruin to the level defined by the company's executives and directors (Bello et al., 1997).

It is crucial to emphasize that taking risks is not a zero-loss endeavor, in contrast to other industrial production methods. A company must tolerate losses while limiting them because it is always vulnerable to them. Ultimately, economic capital should be allocated to different business units based on risk to serve as a guide for tolerance. This allows for continuous assessment of risk-adjusted performance and helps ascertain whether the company is indeed optimizing earnings for the risk it is assuming (Korac & Kakabadse, 2001) (Figure 4.5).

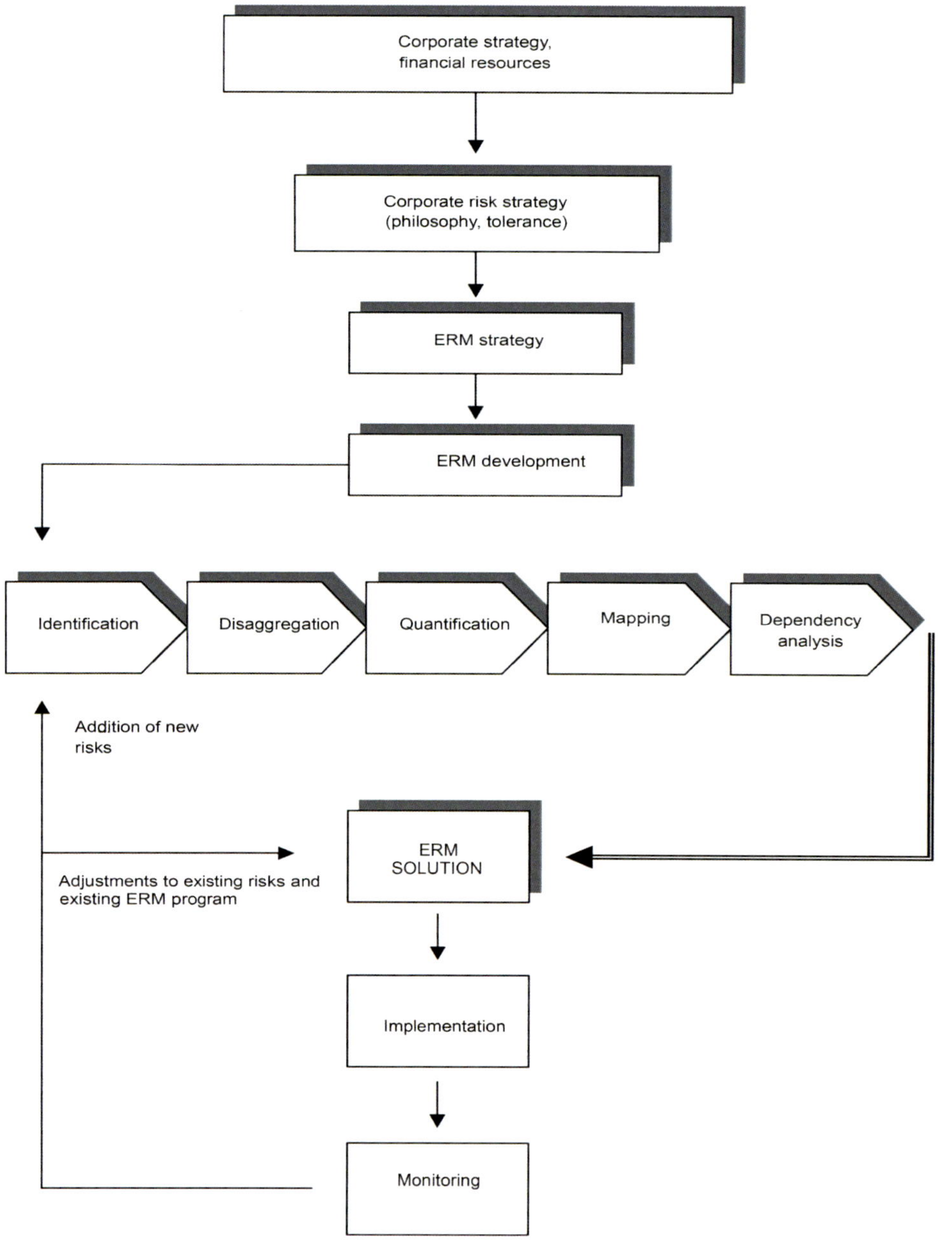

Figure 4.5. Illustration of ERM program development. (Source: Erik Banks, Creative Commons License)

4.4. GLOBALITY, DUALITY, AND FOUR PRINCIPLE STRATEGIES

Learning Objectives

- To develop an understanding of the concepts of globality and duality within the context of risk management.
- To understand the significance of balancing global and local factors in risk management decision-making.

The concept of evaluating the combined effect of all risks from all sources on the firm's value and developing a coordinated risk management plan is known as the "globality" issue. Duality is the outcome that comes in pairs when it comes to solutions for managing how risk affects business value. Regardless of the reason why risk is costly, value can be generated by hedging the risk or by changing the company's operations or organizational structure to allow for the cost-effective acceptance of risk. The second kind of strategy is "risk accommodation." Four basic general strategies that are at the core of contemporary financial innovation can be identified from these paired strategies of duality and globality (Crick et al., 2023).

PRACTICE PROBLEM

Identify and list two potential operational risks faced by a global logistics company expanding into new markets.

SOLUTIONS TO PRACTICE PROBLEM

Regulatory Compliance: Risks associated with adhering to diverse and evolving regulations in different countries.

Transportation Network Disruption: Potential disruptions in the transportation network due to geopolitical tensions or natural disasters.

4.4.1. Globality

The different justifications for the cost of risk to a company indicate that the point of impact occurs at a very broad level. For instance, the concept of tax non-linearity suggests that the firm incurs costs based on the risk associated with the revenues of the taxable organization in a certain jurisdiction. In the case of Federal US taxes, the relevant financial figure is the taxable income in the US. For a US firm, the source of income, whether it is generated from the Idaho facility or the Illinois distribution operation, is not relevant. These values are combined for tax purposes. The source of the risk, whether it is insurance exposure or an interest rate fluctuation affecting earnings, is irrelevant. The sole concern lies in the collective influence of every risk factor on taxable income (Luo, 2005).

When examining the reasons for financial distress, specifically the crowding out hypothesis, the level of aggregation is elevated. The crucial factor is the collective influence of all risk factors on the firm's probability of insolvency, its level of debt, the cost of its capital, stock price, and other related aspects. The level of risk associated with insurance exposure (or any other type of exposure such as interest or foreign exchange) is not significant when considered independently (Forss et al., 2000).

The crucial factor is the collective impact of all risks originating from various sources on the financial performance of the company. The aggregation of many insurance policies, assuming low correlation, will yield a diminished level of relative risk. Similarly, the combination of different categories of risk faced by enterprises, such as insurable, financial, interest rate, and marketing risks, will result in comparable advantages of diversification. This can be understood as the application of the law of large numbers, which serves as the fundamental principle of insurance. The agency costs between fixed income stakeholders and residual claimants of the firm emerge irrespective of the origin of risk. Furthermore, the crowding out of new investments is expected to be similarly significant if the depletion of internal funds occurred due to an uninsured liability loss or a sudden change in the price of the company's primary raw materials (Sparks, 2012).

4.4.2. Duality

The concept of duality is not complicated. If risk leads to the destruction of value, it is possible to restore value by either mitigating the risk or by reorganizing the firm and its activities in a way that reduces the cost associated with the risk. Table 4.1 presents a comprehensive overview of the five different types of risk costs. For each kind, a detailed description of two techniques that might be employed are: hedging and accommodation. Examine each of the mechanisms, beginning with tax convexity. If taxes exhibit convexity, then the anticipated tax amount will decrease as the level of risk decreases (Alfasi & Fenster, 2009).

Companies have an alternative approach to addressing this issue; they can choose to maintain the risk as it is, but strategically streamline their tax responsibilities. There exists a quasi-market where corporations can engage in the "trading" of tax shields. The primary characteristic of this market is the leasing arrangement, where the lessor maintains ownership of an asset and benefits from its tax advantages in comparison to the lessee, particularly in terms of asset depreciation. Likewise, there is some evidence indicating that the trading of reinsurance can be partially attributed to the practice of taking advantage of the differing marginal tax rates across insurers (Bednarek et al., 2021).

Table 4.1. Five Forms of Risk Cost

Type of risk cost	Hedge	Risk Accommodation
Tax non-linearities	Hedge	Tax arbitrage-reinsurance
Financial-distress-agency conflict	Hedge	Reduce leverage
Financial-distress-transaction costs	Hedge	Reduce leverage
Cost of capital-crowding out	Hedge	Alternative financing
Incentive-compatible compensation	Hedge	Re-write compensation contract

Source: Georges Dionne, Creative Commons License.

Risk diminishes value through a second process, which involves undermining organizations' capacity to design managerial compensation schemes that provide effective incentives. One risk management technique involves hedging the risk, allowing directors to design incentive-compatible compensation plans that tie compensation to stock price or performance, without the need to provide managers with a risk premium. The second approach involves connecting executive remuneration to alternative (accounting) performance metrics that have been adjusted to eliminate risk (Zeng et al., 2016).

This phenomenon is commonly referred to as a "phantom hedge" because there is no genuine need to hedge the risk in earnings, among other things. Instead, an accounting measure is calculated as if a hedge were in place, and pay is determined based on this accounting measure. It is desirable for these measurements to effectively indicate managerial success, while minimizing any irrelevant interference. In other words, they should have a low ratio of unnecessary noise to useful signal (Cheah & Doessel, 1994).

4.4.3. Four Principle Strategies

From the techniques listed in Table 4.1, we will focus on four fundamental types that are crucial to the debate.

4.4.3.1. Asset Hedge

An "asset hedge" refers to an asset that serves as a safeguard against the risk associated with another asset. A portfolio consisting of both the primary asset and the hedging asset carries minimal to no risk. The asset hedge can be expressed as a portfolio F, where a specific amount of money $ is invested in two assets. The initial fundamental asset yields a return of A_B for every dollar invested. The second asset, known as the hedging asset, yields a payment of A_H dollar. The capital $ is distributed between the two assets in the ratio {I : h}, and the correlation coefficient ρ_{BH} tends towards negative unity (Goffard & Lefevre, 2018).

$$ASSET\ HEDGE\ F = \$\left(A_B + hA_H\right) where 0 > \rho_{BH} \geq -1$$

If ρ_{BH} = -1, then some hedge ratio h* can be chosen such that the portfolio is riskless; i.e.,

$COV\left\{ü\left(A_B + h^* A_H\right)\right\} =$ A reinsurance contract serves as a conventional means for insurers to hedge their assets. A more recent financial instrument is the catastrophe option, which is an option based on the value of an index representing insurance company claims. It provides a payout when the index reaches a certain amount, known as the striking price.

4.4.3.2. Liability Hedge

A hedge can be established on the opposite side of the balance sheet. The portfolio incorporates a liability L_H instead of the hedging asset.

$$LIABILITY\ HEDGEF = \$\left(A_B + hL_H\right) where\ O < \rho_{BH} \leq 1$$

If $\rho_{BH} = 1$ then some hedge ratio h* can be chosen such that the portfolio is riskless, i.e., $COV\left\{\$\left(A_B + h^* L_H\right)\right\} = 0.$ Many of the newer risk management strategies are indeed liability hedges (Scordis et al., 2014).

4.4.3.3. Leverage Hedge

There are various risk accommodation solutions available, which rely on the specific type of risk and its associated costs. Utilizing tax arbitrage can be suitable for minimizing the impact of tax non-linearities, while modifying managerial remuneration contracts can alleviate the negative consequences of risk on managerial decision-making. However, one would argue that the most crucial approach to managing risk is the regulation of leverage. This approach can be employed to tackle the subsequent expenses incurred due to financial difficulties, the expenses associated with the delegation of authority resulting from leverage and prospective insolvency, and the crowding of new investments (Emms et al., 2007).

Leverage management may entail the straightforward act of decreasing the quantity of leverage. This minimizes the agency cost between creditors and residual claimants, hence decreasing the expected value of bankruptcy expenses. Additionally, in the event of an unexpected loss, the company will be better equipped to seek financing from capital markets for the purpose of either rebuilding damaged assets or supporting new investment initiatives. Alternatively, the issue of crowding out can be directly tackled by the implementation of a dividend policy. Reducing dividend payouts can improve the firm's capacity to finance future projects using internal funds and decrease the likelihood of losing projects due to limited access to affordable capital (Abraham, 2012).

4.4.3.4. Postloss Equity Re-Capitalization

Managing corporate risk is necessary to prevent bankruptcy expenses and safeguard the firm's capacity to cover unexpected losses and fund investment prospects. One strategy to tackle these concerns is to recapitalize the company following a financial loss. The advantage is that the company receives an infusion of capital at a crucial time without raising its level of debt. In addition, an insurer may be unable to cover losses from catastrophic events using their current liquid assets, even if they have significant illiquid assets, particularly the franchise value of future operations. Re-capitalization is a method used to free up illiquid assets and enable a company to keep functioning while safeguarding its franchise value (Verezubova, 2015).

4.5. CATASTROPHE RISK: RISK, INSURANCE, REINSURANCE, AND FINANCIAL INNOVATION

Learning Objectives

- To understand the nature and significance of catastrophe risk within the context of risk management.
- To explore the roles of insurance and reinsurance in managing and mitigating catastrophic risks.

Catastrophic events, including both natural calamities and large-scale accidents, pose significant risks to individuals and enterprises. Acquiring a comprehensive understanding and effectively managing catastrophic risk is crucial in mitigating the financial consequences of such incidents (Maroofi et al., 2017).

4.5.1. Insurance

a. **Insurance as a Risk Transfer Mechanism:** Insurance serves as the main method for transferring the financial responsibility of catastrophic risk. Policy premiums collected from individuals and businesses form a collective fund that insurers use to reimburse losses resulting from catastrophic events.

b. **Customizing Policies to Catastrophic Risk:** Customizing Policies to Catastrophic Risk: Insurers utilize advanced risk assessment algorithms to customize policies that effectively protect policyholders from the distinctive risks presented by catastrophic events. This requires a balance between comprehensive coverage and reasonable cost, guaranteeing that policyholders have efficient safeguarding (Doherty, 1997).

4.5.2. Reinsurance

Reinsurance is crucial in strengthening the insurance industry's ability to manage and absorb significant losses caused by catastrophic events. Reinsurers undertake a share of the risk transferred by primary insurers, thus distributing the financial consequences more widely. This cooperative approach strengthens the industry's ability to withstand and recover from major calamities.

Reinsurers enhance risk management strategies by providing supplementary layers of protection. Primary insurers frequently find themselves unable to handle large and complex risks, necessitating the inclusion of reinsurance as a crucial element in ensuring stability within the insurance ecosystem (Doherty, 2000).

4.5.3. Financial Innovation

Financial innovation has introduced instruments such as catastrophe bonds, which facilitate the transfer of catastrophic risk to capital markets. These bonds enable investors to share in the risk and serve as alternate funding sources for insurers following catastrophic events.

Insurance Linked Securities (ILS) is a financial innovation that enables insurers and reinsurers to shift risk to investors. The process of diversifying risk portfolios improves the industry's capacity to handle losses, promoting resilience when faced with unforeseen catastrophic events.

The future of managing catastrophic risks depends on technical breakthroughs, improved risk modeling approaches, and enhanced communication among stakeholders. Utilizing data analytics and artificial intelligence can improve the precision of risk assessment and facilitate the creation of inventive risk transfer solutions (Zhao et al., 2021).

4.6. INNOVATION (MARKET ENHANCEMENT AND TECHNICAL EFFICIENCY)

Learning Objectives

- To understand the concept of innovation in the context of risk management, specifically focusing on market enhancement and technical efficiency.
- To explore how innovations in market enhancement contribute to more effective risk mitigation strategies.

Innovation serves two overarching purposes. Firstly, it has the potential to enhance the market. Figure 4.6 displays the key characteristics of hedging instruments, with its notable feature being the ability to manage basis risk. Hedging instruments may encounter moral hazard and credit risk. Innovation expands the range of options within this multidimensional domain. The diagram illustrates the features of the primary instruments under consideration. However, it is important to acknowledge that product design requires ongoing compromises within this domain. The value of market enhancement is derived from the distinct nature of insurers (Tian & Zuo, 2007).

An analysis of the trade-off between moral hazard and basis risk helps simplify the matter. Figure 4.7 illustrates the various options for a hedge buyer, with line AB representing these possibilities. Positions closer to point A involve lower basis risk and higher moral hazard. The configuration and placement of line AB depend on technical considerations, which will be promptly addressed. An insurer with a portfolio spread across different geographical locations may choose to address the issue of moral hazard by trading CBOT options (near point A on line AB) instead of relying on reinsurance. This approach entails accepting a certain level of basis risk (Nasierowksi, 2010).

The insurer's basis risk will be relatively low since its portfolio closely aligns with the structure of the "market portfolio" of insurance risks. If another insurer has a more focused portfolio, they may consider the basis risk associated with an available index to be undesirable and instead choose reinsurance (around point B on line AB).

The primary purpose of market enhancement is to improve efficiency, while the secondary role is to alter technological efficiency. Examine the compromise between moral risk and basis risk illustrated in Figure 4.7 as line AB. Shifting this line closer to the origin will decrease the loss of efficiency caused by hedging. Reinsurance tackles this trade-off by employing one of two methods. A classic reinsurance contract eliminates basis risk and establishes a long-term connection between the parties involved, effectively managing moral hazard through monitoring of the primary party (Aldieri et al., 2021).

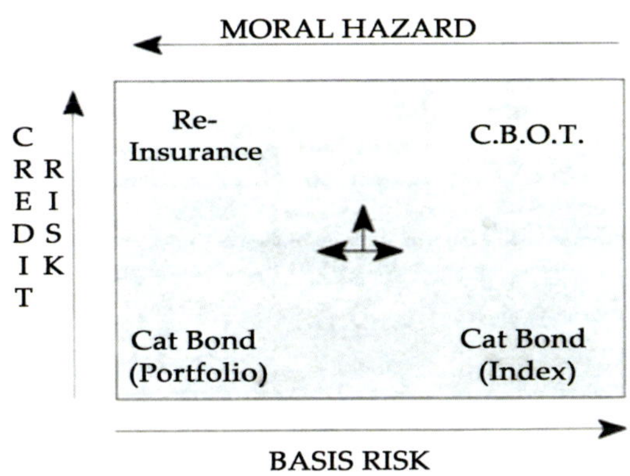

Figure 4.6. Representation of hedging instruments properties. (Source: Georges Dionne, Creative Commons License)

Through the selection of the attachment level for the reinsurance contract, the insurer can determine their position on the AB line. Opting for a higher retention level entails accepting greater risk and reducing the likelihood of moral hazard. An alternative approach involves restructuring the reinsurance contract as a debt-like instrument, similar to the practice of finite reinsurance. The reinsurance contract's hedging features are constrained by this, as it increases basis risk (Mekonnen et al., 2015).

However, it effectively reduces moral hazard. Currently, the primary has reduced incentive to allow claims to become excessive, resulting in a decreased need for reinsurer oversight. By altering the combination of debt and insurance in the finite risk plan, it is possible to attain various positions within the moral hazard-basis risk spectrum. The current inquiry pertains to determining whether this approach offers the most optimal balance between effectiveness and efficiency: modifying the reinsurance attachment point or altering the insurance debt composition. To enhance efficiency, it is necessary to reduce the trade-off line in Figure 4.7 from AB to CB (Dutta & Sengupta, 2010).

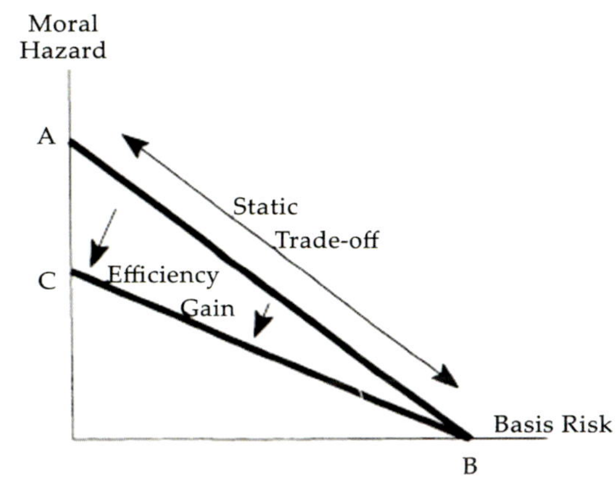

Figure 4.7. Representation of increase efficiency trade-off. (Source: Georges Dionne, Creative Commons License)

Additional alternatives for enhancing technical efficiency can be envisioned. John Major (1996) demonstrated in a recent study that insurers can achieve significant reductions in volatility by utilizing a state-wide index of industry loss experience for hedging purposes. State-wide indexes do entail a certain level of basis risk, which varies among firms based on their portfolio compositions. The availability of industry loss experience indexes by zip code would greatly mitigate basis risk. The reduction in basis risk is partly attributed to the insurer's increased concentration and higher market share in specific zip codes (Al Amri et al., 2012).

To mitigate basis risk, it is necessary to increase the hedging ratio in these zip codes with high concentration. However, this approach may amplify moral hazard as the losses incurred by the hedging insurer constitute a significant proportion of the overall industry losses in those zip codes. The current inquiry pertains to a technical matter. Which approach is more optimal: utilizing a state index and balancing moral hazard and basis risk by employing a relatively high hedge ratio, or employing a zip code index with a lower hedge ratio? Which strategy is represented by line AB, and which by line CB? (Ilyas & Rajasekaran, 2019).

There are more options to consider for altering technological efficiency. Reinsurer monitoring is a technique used to manage ex post moral hazard. Another option is for the primary insurer to establish direct agreements with policyholders, offering them incentives for mitigating losses after they occur. These incentives may include deductibles, coinsurance, and retrospective premium changes. The trade-off between moral hazard and basis risk might vary between insurers and even within the same insurer. The only reliable inference is that there is no universally applicable solution. The diversity present in the insurance industry allows for the creation of value through innovation, as insurers strive to identify combinations of basis risk, credit risk, and moral hazard that align with their financial and organizational framework (Lyu et al., 2022).

Keyword

Insurance Linked Securities: Insurance-Linked Securities (ILS) are financial instruments directly tied to insurance or reinsurance risks. These securities enable insurers to transfer risk to capital markets, typically through structures like catastrophe bonds or collateralized reinsurance. Investors receive returns based on the occurrence of predefined insurance events, providing a means for insurers to manage risk and investors to access uncorrelated returns.

4.7. LOSS FORECASTING

Loss forecasting within the context of Enterprise Risk Management (ERM) acts as a strategic necessity for firms endeavoring to navigate the complexities of potential financial setbacks. It involves the systematic estimation and prediction of future financial losses, offering a proactive approach to understanding the potential consequences of identified risks. Loss forecasting seamlessly integrates with risk assessments in ERM by employing quantitative methodologies, including statistical models, scenario studies, and stress testing (Cook & Cummins, 1994).

A comprehensive comprehension of risk dynamics is imperative due to the interconnected nature of risks and the challenges posed by data limitations and uncertainty. Despite these challenges, the insights gained from loss forecasting empower companies to make well-informed decisions regarding risk management techniques, such as risk mitigation, utilization of risk transfer mechanisms like insurance, or the acceptance of certain risks. Loss forecasting plays a pivotal role in enhancing organizational resilience by providing guidance for strategic decision-making and enhancing the ability to effectively navigate uncertainties and disruptions (Fildes & Makridakis, 1988).

4.8. FINANCIAL ANALYSIS IN RISK MANAGEMENT DECISION MAKING

Learning Objectives

- To understand financial statement interpretation and ratio analysis for effective risk assessment in decision-making.
- To understand financial analysis tools in evaluating and enhancing risk management strategies, ensuring informed decision-making within the organizational context.

Financial analysis is crucial in risk management decision-making, as it plays a vital role in evaluating, measuring, and reducing potential financial risks. Financial analysis plays a crucial role in risk management decision-making by conducting a thorough assessment of the potential effects that different risks can have on an organization's financial well-being.

This entails analyzing historical financial data, employing predictive modeling, and conducting scenario assessments to assess the potential financial impacts linked to identified risks. Through the incorporation of financial analysis into risk management frameworks, companies acquire a more comprehensive understanding of the potential expenses and advantages linked to risk mitigation techniques (Bastos, 2010).

An essential component of financial analysis in risk management is determining risk tolerance and appetite. Organizations utilize financial measures and benchmarks to establish thresholds for acceptable levels of risk exposure. Financial analysis enables decision-makers to synchronize risk management techniques with the organization's overarching financial goals, guaranteeing that risk-taking is in line with the desired equilibrium between risk and return (Santomero & Babbel, 1997).

Financial analysis is essential for choosing and maximizing the effectiveness of risk management methods. This entails assessing the cost-effectiveness of risk reduction strategies, such as insurance, hedging, and diversification. By conducting careful financial analysis, companies can evaluate the trade-offs between the expenses associated with risk reduction measures and the potential monetary consequences of unfavorable events. This process helps in selecting the most effective risk management solutions (Pirson & Turnbull, 2011).

Furthermore, financial analysis plays a crucial role in the creation of stress testing and scenario assessments, enabling businesses to predict the possible financial consequences of extraordinary events. These exercises provide valuable insights into the resilience of an organization's financial standing during challenging circumstances, facilitating the identification of weaknesses and the development of backup plans (Powell & Ansic, 1997).

Financial analysis is a fundamental aspect of making informed decisions in risk management. Organizations can enhance their ability to recognize, assess, and address risks that align with their financial objectives and strategic goals by utilizing financial data and analytical tools. Incorporating financial analysis within the framework of risk management decision-making ensures a comprehensive and well-informed approach to navigating the uncertainties inherent in today's ever-changing corporate environments (Alexander, 2005).

SUMMARY

- The chapter provides a comprehensive exploration of Enterprise Risk Management (ERM), offering insights into its principles and practices. Insurance market dynamics are examined, highlighting the complexities and challenges inherent in the insurance landscape and its role in risk management.
- The development of an ERM framework is emphasized, stressing the need for aligning risk management strategies with organizational objectives. Globality and duality in risk management are discussed, recognizing the importance of considering both global and local factors and understanding the dual nature of risks.
- Four principal strategies in ERM are outlined, demonstrating their crucial role in optimizing risk exposure and ensuring a resilient risk management approach. The chapter consistently emphasizes an integrated approach, recognizing the interconnected nature of various elements in creating a holistic and adaptive risk management strategy.

MULTIPLE CHOICE QUESTIONS

1. **Enterprise Risk Management (ERM):**
   a. This is only applicable to small businesses.
   b. Involves identifying and managing risks to achieve organizational objectives.
   c. Focuses solely on financial risks
   d. This is unrelated to strategic decision-making.
2. **Why are insurance market dynamics considered complex?**
   a. They are static and unchanging.
   b. They play a minimal role in risk management.
   c. They involve challenges and complexities.
   d. This is only relevant for large corporations.
3. **What does the concept of Globality and Duality in Risk Management emphasize?**
   a. Risks are only local in nature.
   b. Acknowledges the interconnectedness of risks on a global scale.
   c. Ignores the need to balance local and global factors.
   d. Propose a singular approach to risk management.
4. **Which objective do the Principal Strategies in ERM primarily aim to achieve?**
   a. This is irrelevant for organizations with a low-risk profile.
   b. Focus on increasing risk exposure.
   c. Optimization of risk exposure and enhancement of resilience.
   d. Exclude considerations for risk mitigation.

5. What does Catastrophe Risk Management encompass in addition to insurance solutions?

a. Excludes reinsurance as a risk management strategy.

b. Involves financial innovation but not insurance.

c. Only involves insurance solutions.

d. Encompasses the interplay of insurance, reinsurance, and financial innovation.

REVIEW QUESTIONS

1. Define and explain the significance of risk management in organizational resilience.
2. Explore the complexities and challenges associated with dynamics in the insurance market.
3. Discuss the interconnected nature of risks on a global scale and the concept of duality in risk management.
4. Identify and elaborate on key strategies employed in enterprise risk management for optimizing risk exposure.
5. Examine the interplay of insurance, reinsurance, and financial innovation in the context of catastrophe risk management.

Answers to Multiple Questions

1. (b) 2. (c) 3. (b) 4. (c) 5. (d)

REFERENCES

1. Abraham, K. S., (2012). Four conceptions of insurance. *U. Pa. L. Rev.*, *161*, 653.
2. Abrams, C., Von, K. J., Muller, S., Pfitzmann, B., & Ruschka-Taylor, S., (2007). Optimized enterprise risk management. *IBM Systems Journal*, *46*(2), 219–234.
3. Al-Amri, K., Gattoufi, S., & Al-Muharrami, S., (2012). Analyzing the technical efficiency of insurance companies in GCC. *The Journal of Risk Finance*, *13*(4), 362–380.
4. Aldieri, L., Brahmi, M., Chen, X., & Vinci, C. P., (2021). Knowledge spillovers and technical efficiency for cleaner production: An economic analysis from agriculture innovation. *Journal of Cleaner Production*, *320*, 128830.
5. Alexander, C., (2005). The present and future of financial risk management. *Journal of Financial Econometrics*, *3*(1), 3–25.
6. Alfasi, N., & Fenster, T., (2009). Between the "global" and the "local": On global locality and local globality. *Urban Geography*, *30*(5), 543–566.
7. Aronczyk, M., (2008). 'Living the brand': Nationality, globality, and the identity strategies of nation branding consultants. *International Journal of Communication*, *2*, 25.

8. Assibi, A. T., (2022). The role of enterprise risk management in business continuity and resiliency in the post-COVID-19 period. *Open Access Library Journal*, *9*(6), 1–19.
9. Baker, T., (2004). Medical malpractice and the insurance underwriting cycle. *DePaul L. Rev.*, *54*, 393.
10. Barrientos, S., Kabeer, N., & Hossain, N., (2004). The gender dimensions of globalization of production. *ILO Working Paper*, *17*, 1–20.
11. Bastos, J. A., (2010). Forecasting bank loans loss-given-default. *Journal of Banking & Finance*, *34*(10), 2510–2517.
12. Bednarek, R., Chalkias, K., & Jarzabkowski, P., (2021). Managing risk as a duality of harm and benefit: A study of organizational risk objects in the global insurance industry. *British Journal of Management*, *32*(1), 235–254.
13. Bello, D. C., Dant, S. P., & Lohtia, R., (1997). Hybrid governance: The role of transaction costs, production costs and strategic considerations. *Journal of Business & Industrial Marketing*, *12*(2), 118–133.
14. Berger, L. A., (1988). A model of the underwriting cycle in the property/liability insurance industry. *The Journal of Risk and Insurance*, *55*(2), 298–306.
15. Bertalan, Z., Nagy, K., Csedo, Z., & Tamus, A., (2016). Innovations in operational risk management and business continuity planning methodologies of transmission system operators: Implications of the operational security network code. *Innovations*, *6*(2), 1–20.
16. Błaszczyszyn, B., & Sigman, K., (1999). Risk and duality in multidimensions. *Stochastic Processes and Their Applications*, *83*(2), 331–356.
17. Bouriaux, S., & Scott, W. L., (2004). Capital market solutions to terrorism risk coverage: A feasibility study. *The Journal of Risk Finance*, *5*(4), 34–44.
18. Bromiley, P., McShane, M., Nair, A., & Rustambekov, E., (2015). Enterprise risk management: Review, critique, and research directions. *Long Range Planning*, *48*(4), 265–276.
19. Cheah, C. W., & Doessel, D. P., (1994). Welfare cost and health insurance: A disaggregated approach using duality theory and Australian data. *Applied Economics*, *26*(6), 567–574.
20. Cheung, K. C., He, W., & Wang, H., (2023). Multi-constrained optimal reinsurance model from the duality perspectives. *Insurance: Mathematics and Economics*, *113*, 199–214.
21. Cook, D. O., & Cummins, J. D., (1994). *Productivity and Efficiency in Insurance: An Overview of the Issues, 1*(1), 1–20.
22. Crick, J. M., Crick, D., & Chaudhry, S., (2023). Governance considerations and non-linear international scale-up behavior among INVs. *International Small Business Journal*, *41*(6), 647–681.
23. Cummins, J. D., Tennyson, S., & Weiss, M. A., (1999). Consolidation and efficiency in the US life insurance industry. *Journal of Banking & Finance*, *23*(2–4), 325–357.
24. D'arcy, S. P., & Brogan, J. C., (2001). Enterprise risk management. *Journal of Risk Management of Korea*, *12*(1), 207–228.

25. Didier, T., Levine, R., Montanes, R. L., & Schmukler, S. L., (2021). Capital market financing and firm growth. *Journal of International Money and Finance*, *118*, 102459.

26. Doherty, N. A., (1997). Innovations in managing catastrophe risk. *The Journal of Risk and Insurance*, *64*(4), 713–718.

27. Doherty, N. A., (2000). Innovation in corporate risk management: The case of catastrophe risk. *Handbook of Insurance, 1*, 503–539.

28. Emms, P., Haberman, S., & Savoulli, I., (2007). Optimal strategies for pricing general insurance. *Insurance: Mathematics and Economics*, *40*(1), 15–34.

29. Ezu, G., (2020). Effect of consolidation of the Nigerian insurance industry on the growth of the Nigerian economy (1996–2018). *IOSR Journal of Economics and Finance (IOSR-JEF)*, *11*(2), 22–32.

30. Feldblum, S., (2001). Underwriting cycles and business strategies. In: *Proceedings of the Casualty Actuarial Society* (Vol. 88, pp. 175–235).

31. Fildes, R., & Makridakis, S., (1988). Forecasting and loss functions. *International Journal of Forecasting*, *4*(4), 545–550.

32. Fitzpatrick, S. M., (2003). Fear is the key: A behavioral guide to underwriting cycles. *Conn. Ins. LJ*, *10*, 255.

33. Forss, M., Kalimo, E., & Purola, T., (2000). Globalization and the concept of insurance. *The Year*, *1*(1), 1–20.

34. Gabel, J. R., & Jensen, G. A., (1992). Can a universal coverage system temper the underwriting cycle? *Inquiry*, *1*(1), 249–262.

35. Gatzert, N., & Martin, M., (2015). Determinants and value of enterprise risk management: Empirical evidence from the literature. *Risk Management and Insurance Review*, *18*(1), 29–53.

36. Goffard, P. O., & Lefèvre, C., (2018). Duality in ruin problems for ordered risk models. *Insurance: Mathematics and Economics*, *78*, 44–52.

37. Hiles, A., (2012). Enterprise risk management. *The Definitive Handbook of Business Continuity Management*, *1*(1), 1–21.

38. Hoyt, R. E., & Liebenberg, A. P., (2011). The value of enterprise risk management. *Journal of Risk and Insurance*, *78*(4), 795–822.

39. Ilyas, A. M., & Rajasekaran, S., (2019). An empirical investigation of efficiency and productivity in the Indian non-life insurance market. *Benchmarking: An International Journal*, *26*(7), 2343–2371.

40. Ittner, C. D., & Oyon, D. F., (2020). Risk ownership, ERM practices, and the role of the finance function. *Journal of Management Accounting Research*, *32*(2), 159–182.

41. Jermakyan, M., (2006). Enterprise risk management in the energy and power industry. In: *Risk Management,* (Vol. 1, pp. 41–58). Academic Press.

42. Jonek-Kowalska, I., (2019). Efficiency of enterprise risk management (ERM) systems. Comparative analysis in the fuel sector and energy sector on the basis of Central-European companies listed on the Warsaw stock exchange. *Resources Policy*, *62*, 405–415.

43. Jones, K. D., & Oshinsky, R. C., (2009). The effect of industry consolidation and deposit insurance reform on the resiliency of the US bank insurance fund. *Journal of Financial Stability*, *5*(1), 57–88.

44. Jurdi, D. J., & AlGhnaimat, S. M., (2021). The effects of ERM adoption on European insurance firms performance and risks. *Journal of Risk and Financial Management*, *14*(11), 554.

45. Korac-Kakabadse, N., & Kakabadse, A., (2001). IS/IT governance: Need for an integrated model. *Corporate Governance: The International Journal of Business in Society*, *1*(4), 9–11.

46. Kunreuther, H., & Pauly, M. V., (2015). Behavioral economics and insurance: Principles and solutions. *Research Handbook on the Economics of Insurance Law*, *1*(1), 15–35.

47. Lemieux, V. L., Rowell, C., Seidel, M. D. L., & Woo, C. C., (2020). Caught in the middle? Strategic information governance disruptions in the era of blockchain and distributed trust. *Records Management Journal*, *30*(3), 301–324.

48. Leng, C. C., & Meier, U. B., (2006). Analysis of multinational underwriting cycles in property-liability insurance. *The Journal of Risk Finance*, 7(2), 146–159.

49. Levy, B., & Fukuyama, F., (2010). Development strategies: Integrating governance and growth. *World Bank Policy Research Working Paper*, *1*(1), (5196).

50. Luo, Y., (2005). How does globalization affect corporate governance and accountability? A perspective from MNEs. *Journal of International Management*, *11*(1), 19–41.

51. Lyu, C., Xie, Z., & Li, Z., (2022). Market supervision, innovation offsets and energy efficiency: Evidence from environmental pollution liability insurance in China. *Energy Policy*, *171*, 113267.

52. Maroofi, F., Ardalan, A. G., & Tabarzadi, J., (2017). The effect of sales strategies in the financial performance of insurance companies. *International Journal of Asian Social Science*, 7(2), 150–160.

53. Mekonnen, D. K., Spielman, D. J., Fonsah, E. G., & Dorfman, J. H., (2015). Innovation systems and technical efficiency in developing-country agriculture. *Agricultural Economics*, *46*(5), 689–702.

54. Murray, J. P., (2010). Capital markets financing alternatives for leasing companies. *The Journal of Equipment Lease Financing (Online)*, *28*(3), 1A.

55. Nasierowski, W., (2010). Technical efficiency of efforts to enhance innovativeness in the European Union. *International Journal of Innovation and Technology Management*, 7(04), 389–404.

56. Nocco, B. W., & Stulz, R. M., (2006). Enterprise risk management: Theory and practice. *Journal of Applied Corporate Finance*, *18*(4), 8–20.

57. O'Sullivan, N., & Diacon, S. R., (2003). Board composition and performance in life insurance companies. *British Journal of Management*, *14*(2), 115–129.

58. Otero-González, L., Durán-Santomil, P., & Marouf, D., (2022). Can ERM ratings explain the performance and risk of EMEA insurance companies? *Journal of Risk Research*, *25*(6), 738–763.

59. Peng, X., & Huang, H., (2020). Fuzzy decision-making method based on CoCoSo with critic for financial risk evaluation. *Technological and Economic Development of Economy*, *26*(4), 695–724.

60. Pirson, M., & Turnbull, S., (2011). Corporate governance, risk management, and the financial crisis: An information processing view. *Corporate Governance: An International Review*, *19*(5), 459–470.

61. Plowe, J., McMahon, D., Phillips, J., & Rosen, G., (2014). Alternative capital markets solutions in renewable energy finance. *Journal of Structured Finance*, *20*(3), 46.

62. Powell, M., & Ansic, D., (1997). Gender differences in risk behavior in financial decision-making: An experimental analysis. *Journal of Economic Psychology*, *18*(6), 605–628.

63. Robinson, J. C., (2004). Consolidation and the transformation of competition in health insurance. *Health Affairs*, *23*(6), 11–24.

64. Rochette, M., (2009). From risk management to ERM. *Journal of Risk Management in Financial Institutions*, *2*(4), 394–408.

65. Santomero, A. M., & Babbel, D. F., (1997). Financial risk management by insurers: An analysis of the process. *Journal of Risk and Insurance*, *1*(1), 231–270.

66. Scordis, N. A., Suzawa, Y., Zwick, A., & Ruckner, L., (2014). Principles for sustainable insurance: Risk management and value. *Risk Management and Insurance Review*, *17*(2), 265–276.

67. Simkins, B., (2008). Enterprise risk management: Current initiatives and issues journal of applied finance roundtable. *Journal of Applied Finance*, *18*(1), 115.

68. Simmons, L. F., & Cross, M. L., (1986). The underwriting cycle and the risk manager. *Journal of Risk and Insurance*, *1*(1), 155–163.

69. Sparks, R., (2012). 'Bringin' it all back home': populism, media coverage and the dynamics of locality and globality in the politics of crime control. In: *Crime, Risk and Justice* (Vol. 1, pp. 194–213). Willan.

70. Suresh, N. C., Sanders, G. L., & Braunscheidel, M. J., (2020). Business continuity management for supply chains facing catastrophic events. *IEEE Engineering Management Review*, *48*(3), 129–138.

71. Taylor, G., (2008). A simple model of insurance market dynamics. *North American Actuarial Journal*, *12*(3), 242–262.

72. Thompson, J., Boschmans, K., & Pissareva, L., (2018). *Alternative Financing Instruments for SMEs and Entrepreneurs: The Case of Capital Market Finance*, *1*(1), 1–20.

73. Tian, L., & Zuo, F., (2007). Catastrophe bond: As a financial innovation in management of catastrophe risk. In: *2007 International Conference on Wireless Communications, Networking and Mobile Computing* (Vol. 1, pp. 3899–3902). IEEE.

74. Verezubova, T., (2015). Financial strategy of insurance companies. *Polish Journal of Management Studies*, *11,* 1–20.

75. Wanyama, D. W., & Olweny, T., (2013). Effects of corporate governance on financial performance of listed insurance firms in Kenya. *Public Policy and Administration Research*, *3*(4), 96–120.

76. Young, V. R., & Zariphopoulou, T., (2002). Pricing dynamic insurance risks using the principle of equivalent utility. *Scandinavian Actuarial Journal*, *2002*(4), 246–279.

77. Zeng, X., Carson, J. M., Chen, Q., & Wang, Y., (2016). Optimal life insurance with no-borrowing constraints: Duality approach and example. *Scandinavian Actuarial Journal*, *2016*(9), 793–816.

78. Zhao, Y., Lee, J. P., & Yu, M. T., (2021). Catastrophe risk, reinsurance, and securitized risk-transfer solutions: A review. *China Finance Review International*, *11*(4), 449–473.

CHAPTER

5

Key Drivers of Risk Management

LEARNING OBJECTIVES

After studying this chapter, you will be able to:

1. To understand the concept of risk management drivers.
2. To explore replacement and abandonment decisions as integral components of risk management.
3. Analyze the costs and benefits associated with loss control, financing, and risk reduction strategies.
4. To evaluate strategies for accessing new risk capacity and diversifying credit risk.
5. To understand the impact of deregulation on organizational strategies and risk management.

INTRODUCTORY EXAMPLE

The manufacturing company, Advanced Manufacturing Solutions, is currently grappling with a pivotal decision – whether to replace its aging production facility or opt for ongoing maintenance and upgrades. This decision underscores the core principles of risk management drivers, requiring a careful evaluation of potential risks against anticipated benefits. The company is tasked with navigating considerations such as costs, potential business interruptions, and the dynamic nature of the market landscape. This scenario vividly illustrates how risk management drivers hold a central role in strategic decision-making. This introductory example lays the foundation for a comprehensive exploration of the intricate facets of risk management drivers and their profound impact on organizational outcomes.

UNIT INTRODUCTION

Risk management drivers are the essential factors and considerations that businesses use to determine how they detect, evaluate, and mitigate risks. These drivers play a crucial role in guiding decision-making in the field of risk management. The term pertains to the critical elements that influence how firms traverse uncertainty and make strategic decisions to maximize results while mitigating potential setbacks. The drivers encompass a range of factors, including judgments regarding replacement and abandonment, thorough assessment of costs and benefits related to loss management, available financing options, and measures for reducing risk. By comprehending these factors, firms acquire a comprehensive perspective of the intricate interaction among many aspects of risk management, enabling them to actively control possible difficulties and capitalize on opportunities for value enhancement (Luke & Heyns, 2014).

The chapter presents a comprehensive decision framework that covers replacement and abandonment decisions, as well as a detailed examination of the costs and benefits related to loss control, financing, and risk reduction (Cohen, 2015).

The exploration encompasses the understanding of market cycles, including insurance pricing dynamics and the differentiation between "hard" and "soft" market conditions. The chapter also discusses important factors such as acquiring additional risk capacity, diversifying credit risk, and implementing sophisticated enterprise risk management methods. Additionally, the chapter addresses obstacles such as tax reduction, overcoming regulatory restrictions, and capitalizing on opportunities arising from deregulation. Overall, the chapter provides a thorough and informative guide, offering readers a deep understanding of the key factors that influence strategic risk management decisions. It also assists organizations in building resilience and maximizing value in a constantly changing and challenging business environment (Hudin & Hamid, 2014).

5.1. MAXIMIZING ENTERPRISE VALUE

Learning Objectives

- To understand the concept of enterprise value and its significance in organizational success.
- To explore strategies for maximizing enterprise value through effective risk management.

A corporation is held accountable and responsible to a diverse range of stakeholders, with a particular focus on its stock investors (Figure 5.1). Equity risk capital providers expect a suitable return on their investment, and directors and management, acting as their representatives, must work towards maximizing the return within the firm's business objectives. The share price of a company is a measure of its value, representing the discounted value of the firm's future cash flows, taking into account the associated risks. The primary objective of many corporations is to maximize their enterprise value, which aims to increase the share price for investors. Various claimholders inherently possess distinct stakes and attitudes towards risk; the principle of value maximization takes into consideration the costs of risk placed on all corporate claimholders, rather than solely shareholders (Renault et al., 2016).

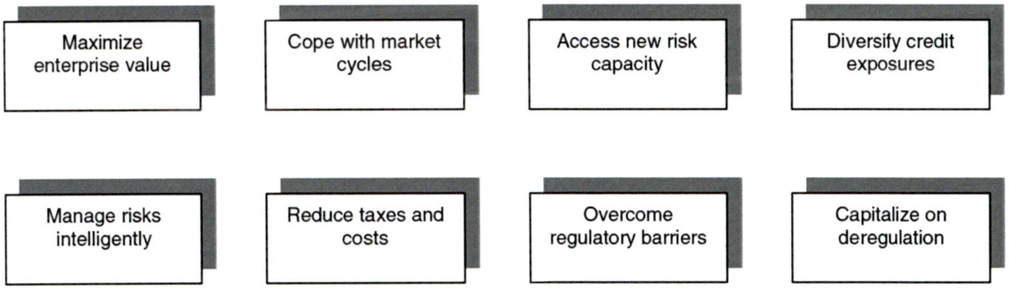

Figure 5.1. Illustration of art market growth and innovation drivers. (Source: Erik Banks, Creative Commons License)

A firm endeavors to enhance its enterprise value by undertaking projects that generate a rate of return surpassing the firm's cost of capital. In practical terms, management aims to maximize the firm's discounted future cash inflows. The primary objective of corporate risk management systems is to minimize projected losses, thereby maximizing net cash flows. Essentially, this process involves a corporation allocating present resources to create future value (Bohnert et al., 2019).

Numerous academic studies provide substantial support for the benefits of utilizing risk management products to enhance cash flows and reduce expected loss volatility. While the ultimate goal is to maximize value, a company aims, at the very least, to prevent financial difficulties and the expenses associated with a weakened financial state. The company must understand potential losses that could adversely affect its financial performance and creditworthiness. Within the confines of a logical cost/benefit analysis (for example, it may not be practical to spend more on risk protection than the expected loss value), the company must take necessary measures to mitigate the impact of such events (Lai et al., 2010).

Value creation focuses on the net returns generated by company assets after deducting the capital cost required to sustain those assets. Value is generated when the net return is favorable, and the emphasis is placed on the earnings of assets, the cost of funding them, and the level of leverage employed (Yow & Sherris, 2008). For example, an insurance business generates value when the net return from underwriting and investment operations (the main sources of income for a typical insurer) exceeds the capital expenses. Implementing measures to reduce the cost of capital can generate additional value. By setting up diversification and reinsurance strategies, an insurance company can reduce the volatility of its underwriting outcomes and the expenses associated with its capital. Additionally, these measures can enhance the company's value, if the costs incurred from diversification and reinsurance do not outweigh the benefits derived from the decreased volatility of underwriting results (Tahir & Razali, 2011).

A corporation may face several financial and operational risks. These risks can potentially influence a company's value by impacting the expected net cash flows in terms of their magnitude, timeliness, and unpredictability. The risk management process enables a company to employ various strategies, such as loss control, loss financing, risk reduction, and related approaches, to minimize the probability of unforeseen alterations in anticipated net cash flows. However, these achievements come with a price tag and consequently affect the overall worth of the business. Essentially, while developing a risk management strategy, a company must consider the cost of risk, which refers to the price, whether stated or implied, paid to handle potential risks. This is important because the cost of risk directly impacts the company's overall worth (Hoyt & Liebenberg, 2011).

The cost of risk encompasses multiple theoretical elements, such as:

i. Expected cost of direct and indirect losses arising from retained risks.
ii. Expected cost of loss control activities.
iii. Expected cost of loss financing activities.
iv. Expected cost of risk reduction activities.

The primary objective of any profit-maximizing company should be to reduce risk costs. This does not necessarily equate to risk minimization. Figure 5.2 provides a concise overview of this fundamental connection (Nocco & Stulz, 2006).

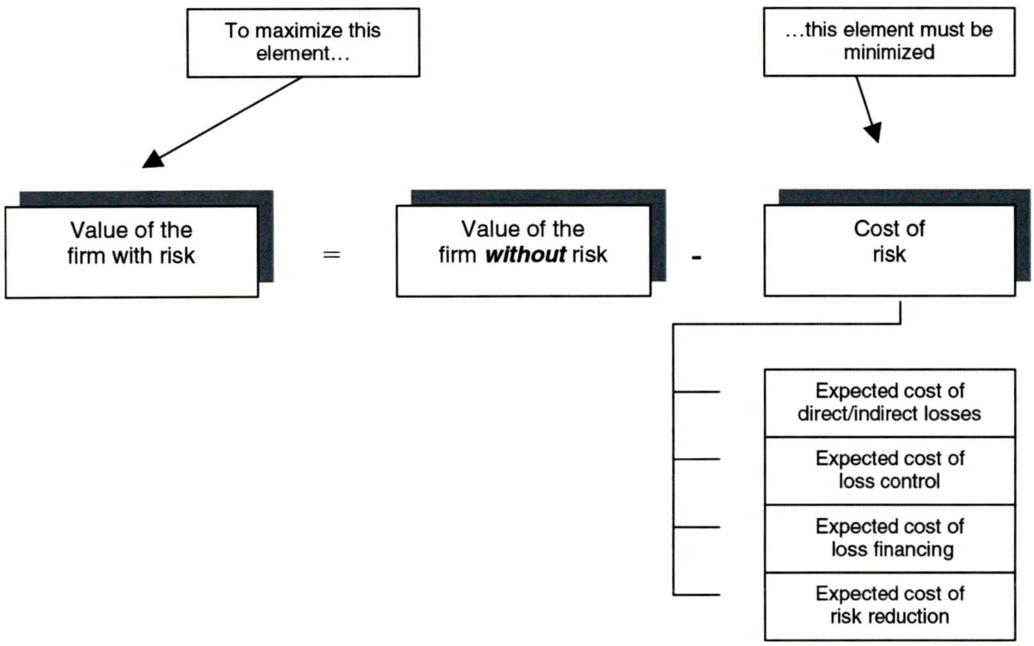

Figure 5.2. Illustration of value-maximizing relationship. (Source: Samantha Whittaker, Creative Commons License)

As a corporation increases its expenditure on risk costs, it concurrently decreases the level of uncertainty in its predicted net cash flows. However, this also leads to a reduction in its operational profitability. Assuming all other factors remain constant, a company with smaller anticipated net cash flows decreases its probability of insolvency (which incurs its own expenses). Nevertheless, there will come a time when the additional cost of implementing measures to prevent losses, financing losses, and reducing risks will outweigh the benefits of reducing expected losses. At this point, the strategies employed by the company to eliminate risks, diversify, and maintain control will no longer be effective in maximizing the overall value of the operation (Schiller & Prpich, 2014).

Let's examine a straightforward structure to highlight many important ideas. Initially, it might be assumed that the present value of predicted NCFs must be maximized to maximize enterprise value. Accordingly, the predicted NFC after a year is $97 if a firm has a 90% chance of earning NCFs of $100 (outcome 1) and a 10% probability of earning $70 (outcome 2). After applying a 5% discount rate, the present value (PV) of the predicted NCFs comes to $92.38. This represents the enterprise value as of right now, before the company implements any risk management measures. The firm's predicted worth in a year will be 5% more than it is now (e.g., $92.38), but the actual value will depend on whether outcomes 1 or 2 materialize. Either 8.25% (outcome 1) or –24.23% (outcome 2) will be the return; this is expected to equal 5%, or 90% × 8.25% + 10% × –24.23% (Li, 2019).

Now, let's examine certain parts of this example. In the first case, a discount rate of 5% was applied. This is essentially the rate required to raise capital to support operations or the firm's cost of capital, and it consists of two parts: a risk premium r(p) and a risk-free benchmark rate r(f). The rate r(f) compensates the investor for the time value of money, whereas the rate r(p) compensates for the investment's risk. Investors will demand a higher r(p) if predicted NCFs are more variable or risky. This will result in a higher total cost of capital, or r. Second, the company should consider taking that move if it finds a cost-effective risk management strategy to lower the probability of producing \$70 to 5% or even 0% (raising the \$100 scenario to 95% or 100% and raising predicted NCFs). If NCF variability (the \$70 scenario) has been reduced, then even though the cost of risk is increasing, the firm's value should also increase (Demidenko & McNutt, 2010).

A company that can reduce the variability of its expected NCFs indicates less risk and volatility and needs less return to draw in investors. Because of this, the r(p) component of r decreases, lowering its cost of capital. There is a trade-off: decreasing NCF variability can have a cost associated with it, and decreasing NCF variability can eventually result in reducing the r(p) element. Thus, a company has to decide which of the following risk management options to use: risk reduction (e.g., withdrawal or diversification), loss control (e.g., safety), or loss financing (e.g., insurance, self-insurance, or derivatives hedging) (Manab et al., 2010). The choice is always based on a cost/benefit analysis:

i. To the extent that hedging, diversifying, or providing other protection for predicted non-current liabilities (NCLs) is likely to result in higher costs than benefits from lower capital costs, enterprise value may not be enhanced by these risk management strategies.
ii. Hedging, diversifying, or in some other way safeguarding forecasted NCFs may raise enterprise value if the anticipated cost of risk management strategies is lower than the gain from a lower cost of capital.

To reduce NCF variability, a business may consider purchasing insurance. For instance, it could pay a premium to earn \$30 if the \$70 scenario occurs. Acquiring loss-financing insurance and eliminating uncertainty is reasonable if the expected cost of protection is lower than the projected future net cash flow. However, if the business deems insurance to be too costly, it can proceed without protection, allowing room for uncertainty (Rao, 2009).

In such a case, the business must decide whether to borrow against anticipated future cash flows and invest in an alternative project or utilize internal funds to cover the loss when it arises, provided it has sufficient cash on hand to offset any losses resulting from a future event. Once again, a cost/benefit analysis must be conducted. If the project's positive net present value (NPV) justifies borrowing money from a bank instead of issuing securities or paying fees, borrowing funds to cover the loss may be the optimal option from an enterprise value perspective. A business that lacks adequate cash on hand or loss-financing protection faces a slightly different situation. It can either file for bankruptcy or borrow against future cash flows to settle its losses (Lai, 2010).

A company may also consider implementing a diversification plan. Theoretically, investors should demand a lower r(p) if a corporation can diversify away risk. The question is whether a business can effectively diversify. There are two types of risk: non-diversifiable risk (also known as systematic risk) and diversifiable risk (sometimes referred to as idiosyncratic risk).

Maintaining a portfolio with multiple commitments and exposures can reduce company-specific diversifiable risk. All companies face non-diversifiable risks that cannot be completely eliminated. Although diversification seems to offer a corporation a lower r(p) (and therefore r), the actual savings may be insignificant because investors can often diversify more effectively than individual companies. However, this depends on the specific details of the company and its operations. Figure 5.3 illustrates these connections (Segal, 2006).

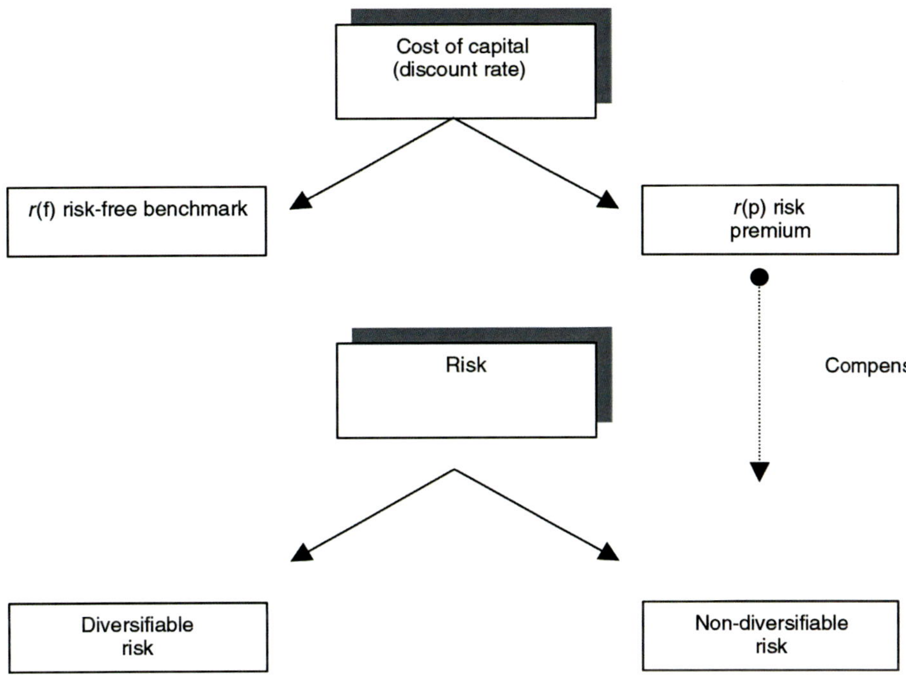

Figure 5.3. Representation of cost of capital and risk. (Source: Patricia Morrison, Creative Commons License)

The primary thing to emphasize is that a business needs to make decisions about risk management and how those decisions will affect enterprise value. These can be ascertained using a technique like cost/benefit analysis during the risk management process quantification stage; if a specific strategy is demonstrated to provide more value by reducing expected NCF variability, it might be the best option.

5.2. THE DECISION FRAMEWORK

Learning Objectives

- Understand the decision framework in risk management.
- Understand how to apply this framework by assessing real-world scenarios and their impact on organizational outcomes.

A company that practices active risk management must make several financial decisions to continue operating. These fall into the general categories of funding and investment decisions. For example, a company must determine how to finance a loss control program if it invests in such measures as part of its risk strategy. Financing is not required if the company chooses not to use any loss control. Similarly, no funding is needed if a company chooses to drop a project that has been physically harmed. If it chooses to reinvest (replace) after a loss, it must determine whether to arrange funding before or after the loss. There will be clear cost/benefit ratios for each of these that must be considered (Greenspan, 2006).

Pre-loss financing refers to anticipatory financing that is set up before a loss scenario arises; this can involve instruments like insurance, derivatives, or contingent capital. Ex-ante costs are connected to each type of pre-loss financing, such as a bid-offer spread, arrangement charge, or premium payment. Funding set up in reaction to a loss event is known as post-loss financing; it can originate from cash or reserves, short- or long-term debt, or equity, each having its own ex-post cost (such as interest or dividend expense or lost investment income). Term loans, bonds (long-term securities being a form of semi-permanent financing), balance sheet cash/liquid securities, lines of credit (often as a form of bridge rather than permanent financing), and stock (a permanent form of funding that results in dilution) are common strategies. Nevertheless, post-loss finance options will not be examined in more detail (Weaver et al., 2013).

Any of these scenarios can lead to the classic debt vs equity trade-off. While debt is less expensive for the company to issue and less risky for investors, it increases leverage and raises the probability of financial distress. Naturally, when the average cost of capital declines, so does the enterprise value and the discounted value of the company's earnings. Although equity is more costly than debt, it decreases leverage and can lessen the likelihood of experiencing financial issues (Gold et al., 2017). It is crucial to understand that post-loss financing does not indicate a lack of risk management strategy; rather, it indicates that a business has chosen not to incur ex-ante costs for an uncertain event after weighing the pros and cons and the possibility of suffering losses of a specific size. On the other hand, finance arrangements made following a loss event will likely be more costly. If the loss is particularly significant, the business may be vulnerable to financial instability and thus unable to get acceptable financing terms. Any financing will inevitably come under market examination, and the financing's size about the losses incurred will be reflected in the borrowing rates or issue price. Figure 5.4 summarizes the major kinds of finance and investment decisions (Bachrach & Baratz, 1963).

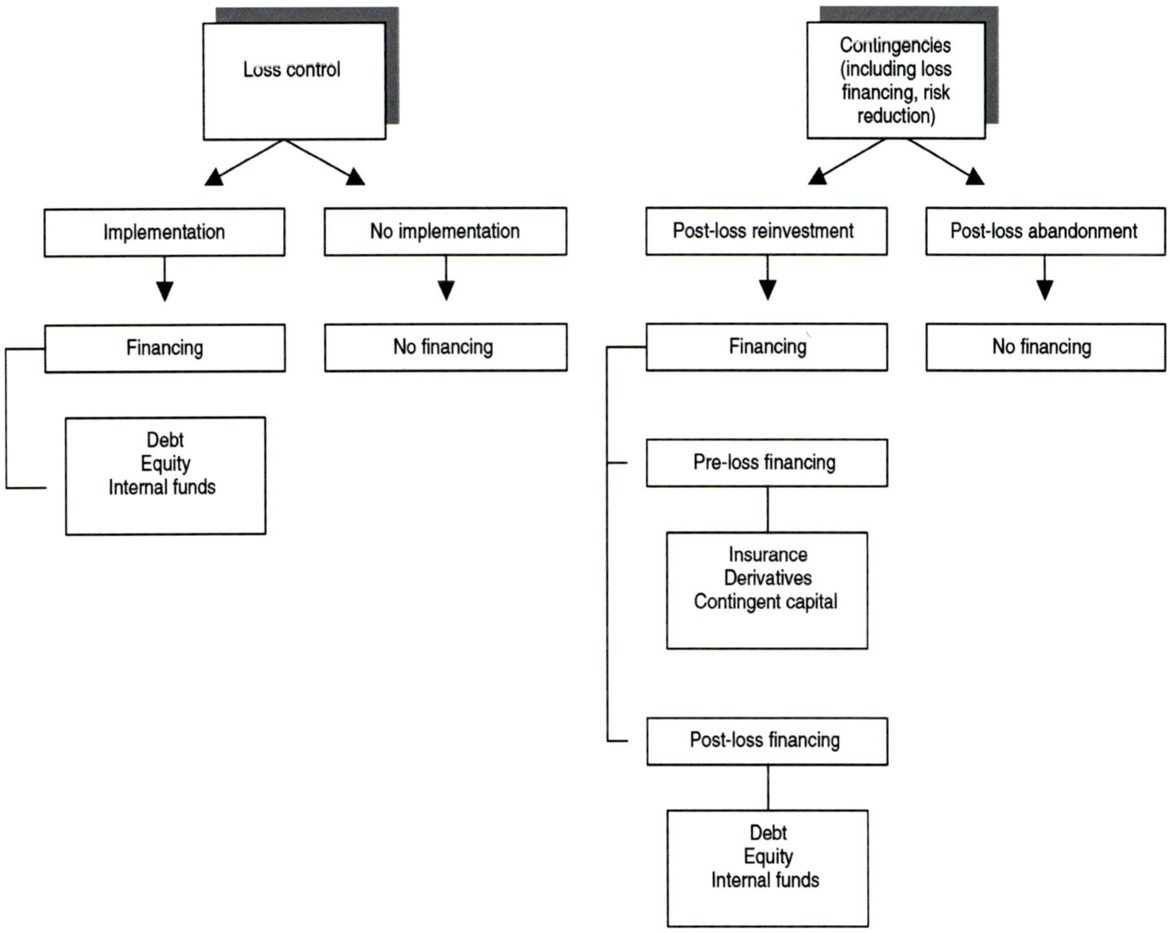

Figure 5.4. Diagram of investment and financing decisions. (Source: Carole Millet, Creative Commons License)

5.2.1. Replacement and Abandonment

A company manages its risks to protect the value of its revenue-generating assets. The company's enterprise value decreases, and its earnings power is temporarily or permanently lowered if the assets are destroyed or damaged. A company will replenish lost assets as soon as possible and resume output at its pre-loss level if it can do so without incurring any transaction expenses (Howe & McCabe, 1983). When the return exceeds the cost of capital, the sensible firm—assuming no transaction expenses—will always choose a replacement. Nevertheless, if the return on damaged or destroyed assets is lower than the cost of capital, it is not advisable to replace them. In fact, it is more advantageous to abandon these assets without incurring any transaction costs, as this will enhance the overall value of the enterprise. Pre-loss abandonment is recommended when the immediate sale value of an asset is more than its discounted future cash flows (Furneaux & Rieser, 2022).

Remember

Space agencies meticulously use risk management to navigate uncertainties in space exploration.

Conversely, if the sale value is lower than the discounted future cash flows, which are themselves lower than the cost of investment, it is not advisable to replace the assets after the loss. However, it is not advisable to completely disregard them either, as the insured company will benefit from an injection of funds that can be utilized for more efficient objectives. Under no circumstances should assets be abandoned, even in the event of a loss, if the investment value is less than the discounted future cash flows. The act of replacing or abandoning productive assets is a fundamental aspect of any risk management procedure (Parvin & Beruvides, 2021).

5.2.2. Costs and Benefit of Loss Control

Loss control, where the specific benefit can be regarded as a lesser quantity of losses, is the culmination of all physical actions and precautions used to lower the expected value of aggregate losses. The procedure usually requires an initial financial outlay for infrastructure and safety precautions that pay off later. As a result, an NPV framework may be used to evaluate costs and benefits. Safety precautions can be procedural or educational, such as through safety training, although they are typically physical (e.g., sprinklers, hazardous storage, and alarms). Either way, they need cash upfront before making direct or indirect profits. Gains must be calculated on a net basis since the loss control plan may need recurring maintenance expenses (Merisalu et al., 2021).

In typical NPV/capital budgeting scheme one can observe that:

$$NPV = \sum_{i=1}^{t} \frac{CF_i}{(1+r)^i} - I_0$$

where CF_i represents the net periodic benefit achieved through the implementation of loss control techniques, and I_0 represents the initial cost of investment. A reinvestment framework (e.g., reinvestment of CF_i) is utilized to evaluate the effectiveness of loss control strategies, as they safeguard funds that can be allocated to other wealth-enhancing endeavors. When considering loss control, it is crucial to take into account the complete time horizon, as it is a multi-year process, in contrast to the standard one-year insurance horizon (Brass et al., 2011).

5.2.3. Costs and Benefit of Loss Financing

Loss-financing approaches play a central role in the risk management process for many companies and require extensive study due to the involvement of numerous variables and options. Although loss control is undeniably crucial, it may be perceived as a relatively unchanging procedure directly influenced by the extent to which risks are retained (e.g., once the initial loss control procedures are implemented, they require periodic evaluation) (Raju et al., 2016).

Similarly, when a company chooses to mitigate risk by eliminating its risks, it no longer needs to be concerned about them (the process of diversification, of course, is more dynamic and demanding). When deciding how to handle losses, a corporation must consider the comparative costs and benefits of retaining, transferring, and hedging. Some companies may choose a strategy that focuses on retaining fundamental risks while transferring or hedging non-fundamental risks. While this approach may be convenient, it may not yield optimal results, and only a thorough evaluation can determine if enterprise value is truly being maximized through this process (Schanze, 2006).

5.2.4. Costs and Benefits of Risk Reduction

Removing an activity that creates unintended risks—those whose preservation cannot be commercially justified by a cost-benefit analysis or the company's business aims and strategies—is one way to reduce risk. Alternatively, it can happen via the methods of diversification (i.e., building portfolios of uncorrelated risks). An abandonment or sale scenario can be used to quantify the relative costs of exiting the market. The ensuing benefits include lower operational cash flow variability after an undesirable risk has affected the business and cost savings from not having to continue providing protection against that exposure (Hall & Solomatine, 2008).

When a portfolio diversification strategy lowers risks, the cost/benefit analysis concentrates on the additional expenses needed to reach a specific portfolio balance. This outcome will vary based on the specific risks at hand (such as speculative or pure risks), the chosen technique of diversification (such as purchasing uncorrelated risk assets, utilizing synthetic baskets, or employing portfolio mechanisms), and the extent to which the risk is reduced. The primary benefits include reduced volatility in cash flow (Cummins, 1991).

The costs and benefits framework, or a comparable objective metric capable of quantifying inflows and outflows, is a crucial component in decision-making and assessing the worth of a business, regardless of the risk management strategy adopted (Laeyen & Goovaerts, 2008).

5.3. COPING WITH MARKET CYCLES

Learning Objectives

- To understand strategies for navigating market cycles.
- To learn the concept of insurance pricing and the difference between "hard" and "soft" market conditions.

One of the most important aspects of risk management is managing market cycles, which entails strategically adjusting organizational strategies to navigate the dynamic fluctuations in the economy. A thorough grasp of market dynamics, including changes in insurance prices, is necessary for this procedure.

5.3.1. Insurance Pricing

Let's begin by providing a concise summary of insurance pricing. The primary objective of an insurer is to maximize return on investment, even if a corporate risk manager aims to minimize the cost of a risk transfer mechanism. Otherwise, the insurer will lack the necessary resources and financial incentives to compete effectively. In theory, insurance premiums must be set at a level that covers projected claims (expected value loss), operational and administrative costs, and provides fair remuneration to providers of risk capital (Emms et al., 2007). This estimation takes into account projected future claims (losses), expenses, and profit margins, and may be considered a fair premium, sometimes referred to as the gross rate. The cost imposed on the cedant is commonly known as the "rate on line," which is calculated by dividing the premium amount by the total coverage (or limit) granted. Therefore, a premium of $1 million for a line of coverage worth $10 million is equivalent to a rate of 10% on the line. The insurance cost is typically calculated by dividing the premium rate by the actuarial likelihood of loss minus 1. The insurance coverage is considered 'actuarially fair if the resulting price is zero' (Lindholm et al., 2022).

Premiums must be sufficient to accurately cover expected losses and expenses. Failure to do so may result in the insurer experiencing financial distress and potentially jeopardizing the status of all cedants. The pricing should adhere to principles of equity, reasonableness, and non-discrimination. An insurance policy's fair premium is divided into two components, as shown in Figure 5.5. The first part is the pure premium, which covers the total required for loss adjustment costs and losses. The second element is the premium loading, which covers extra costs and generates a suitable profit margin (Embrechts, 2000). This second element is crucial as insurers need to provide their shareholders with a reasonable return on capital. Within a conventional risk/return framework, the level of risk associated with an insurer's business directly correlates with the necessary level of profitability. This is because riskier ventures have increased variability of claims. A business with higher claim variability requires more capital support, resulting in a higher economic return for shareholders. Inaccurate determination of profit loading may lead to inadequate compensation for shareholders, causing their reluctance to provide capital (Young & Zariphopoulou, 2002).

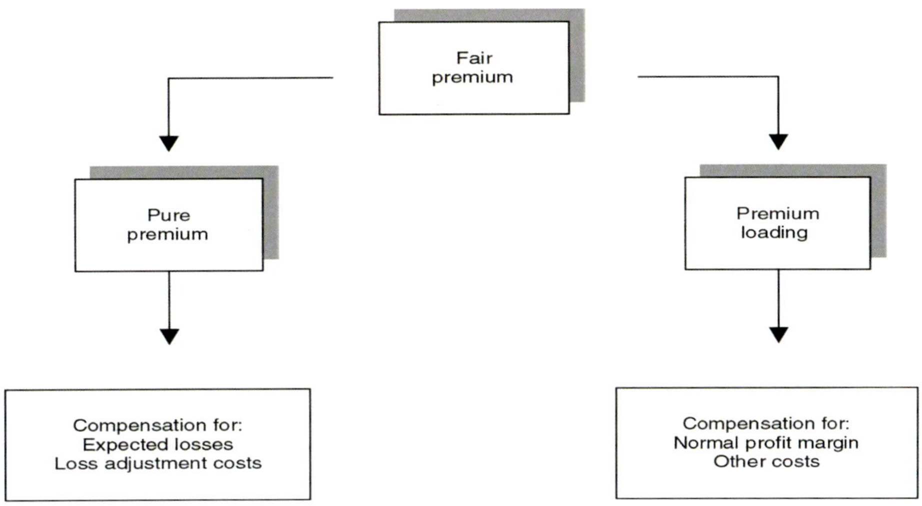

Figure 5.5. Illustration of insurance premium pricing components. (Source: Merrill Lynch, Creative Commons License)

When risks are independent and homogeneous, insurers can easily ascertain the appropriate premium. Exposures with comparable attributes are categorized and subjected to the same rate, namely one that reflects the average loss experience. This can be enhanced by additional merit adjustments, which can be increased or decreased based on specific merit criteria (Liberti & Petersen, 2019). These criteria include the schedule rating, which is a rate influenced by the coverage's physical qualities, or the experience rating, which is a rate modified by the previous loss experience. Nevertheless, determining prices becomes significantly more intricate when risks are diverse and cannot be easily categorized. Rate-setting may rely on subjective rather than objective criteria, resulting in less accurate outcomes. As previously mentioned, the absence of proper information classification can give rise to adverse selection (Harrington et al., 2008).

5.3.2. Hard Versus Soft Market

Like other segments of the international financial market, the insurance industry undergoes cycles of varying lengths. During a typical market cycle, the supply and demand of insurance are balanced, and insurers charge cedants a reasonable premium. By employing a traditional economic model based on supply and demand, as illustrated in Figure 5.6, one can observe the equilibrium point N where the supply and demand curves intersect. This point represents the quantity of insurance available in Q1, with a corresponding premium price of P1 (Harrington et al., 2008).

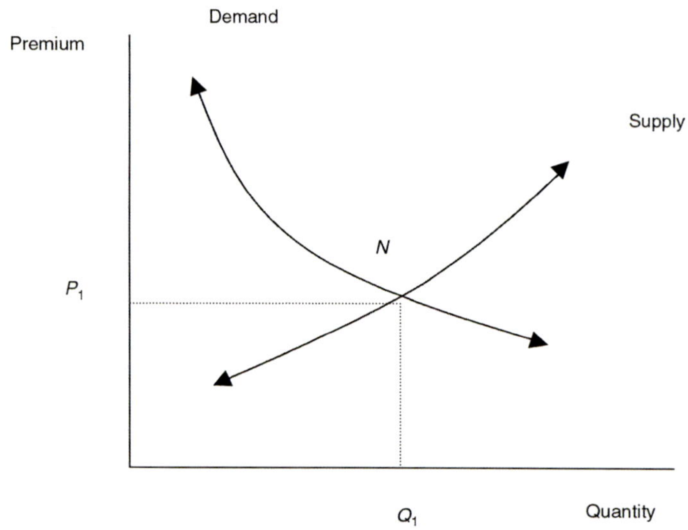

Figure 5.6. Representation of equilibrium market for insurance. (Source: Milena, Creative Commons License)

A soft market can arise when capital is abundant in the system and must be allocated efficiently. Insurers tend to relax their underwriting requirements in such circumstances to attract more business. Additionally, they may decrease their premiums when more rivals enter the market (Tesselaar et al., 2020).

The end result is a shift of the supply curve towards the right, indicating that insurance companies are more inclined to offer larger coverage amounts at reduced prices. In Figure 5.7, the new equilibrium price of insurance coverage is shown by point N.' This is accompanied by a decrease in premiums from P1 to P2 and an increase in supply from Q1 to Q2. During a period of low demand, conventional insurance policies are priced highly competitively and emerge as an appealing option within the cost-benefit analysis of risk management (Alff, 2022).

An excessive amount of risk capacity is not a sustainable long-term condition for the market. Insurers have implemented more lenient underwriting criteria in order to gain a larger market share, resulting in underwriting losses that surpass the reserves allocated for covering actual loss experience. As a result, the market enters a challenging phase known as a hard market. Insurers limit the extent of coverage they are willing to offer, causing a leftward shift in the supply curve. This shift establishes a new equilibrium position, referred to as N',' as shown in Figure 5.8 (Winter, 1988).

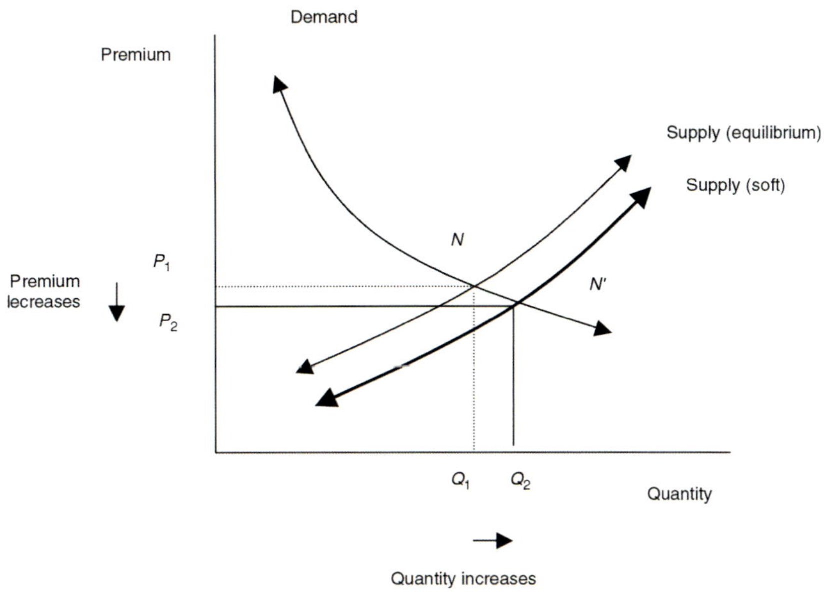

Figure 5.7. Diagram of soft market for insurance. (Source: Erik Banks, Creative Commons License)

This leads to a decrease in insurance coverage and an increase in insurance premiums, with the actual premium received (P3) exceeding the fair equilibrium premium (P1). A catastrophic event has the potential to accelerate the challenging market cycle, leading to a surplus of insurance claims. These events can include infrequent but highly impactful occurrences such as hurricanes, earthquakes, terrorism, or situations where multiple insurance lines are affected simultaneously, such as business interruption, property and casualty, life, and health insurance. In the midst of a challenging insurance market, new risk transfer methods emerge as compelling alternatives (Denenberg, 1967).

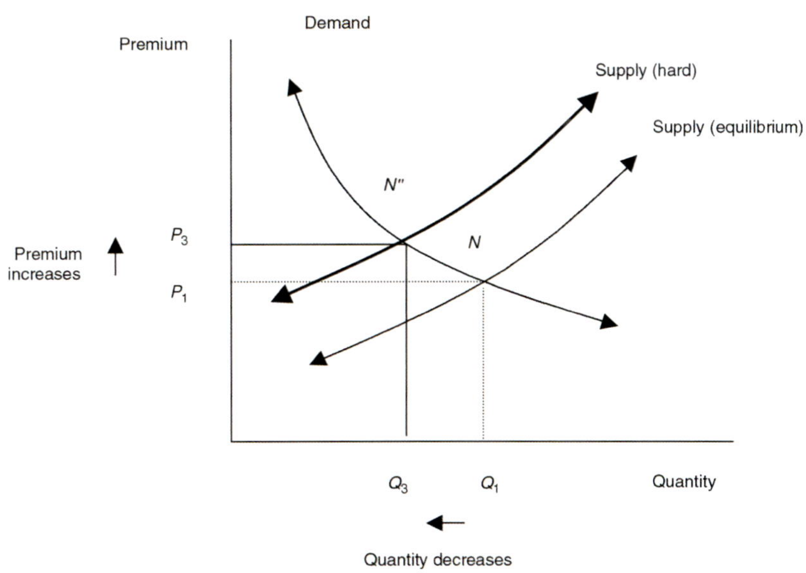

Figure 5.8. Illustration of hard market for insurance. (Source: Erik Banks, Creative Commons License)

5.4. ACCESSING NEW RISK CAPACITY

Learning Objectives

- To understand the concept and significance of accessing new risk capacity.
- Develop proficiency in analyzing emerging risks through comprehensive assessments and quantitative analysis.

To make reasonable risk management decisions within a cost/benefit framework, a company must be able to thoroughly evaluate a wide range of options. If it is unable to do so, it will assume a passive role in the market, accepting prices as they are, and is unlikely to achieve the highest possible value for its business. Due to the cyclical nature of risk management markets, new channels and procedures emerge to address their deficiencies (Stanford et al., 2016). In the event of a challenging insurance market and excessively high premiums for coverage, a company can explore alternative avenues to manage its risk. These alternatives include establishing a captive insurance company, joining a risk retention group, utilizing derivative contracts, issuing capital markets instruments, and employing other similar strategies (Vincent et al., 2018).

While undoubtedly significant, the precise mechanism is of lesser importance than the fact that a corporation can choose an economically logical alternative technique. When a firm gains access to additional risk capacity, which refers to the ability to shift exposures through risk coverage, it eliminates the uncertainties associated with coverage and safeguards its enterprise value (Tadesse et al., 2015).

By utilizing ART (Alternative Risk Transfer) products and methods, firms endeavor to establish a risk management plan, reducing their reliance on conventional sources of capacity and decreasing the likelihood of encountering unpredictable or costly coverage. They have transitioned from being passive price takers to actively seeking the most cost-effective options. Accessing additional risk capacity is feasible due to the varying specializations, resources, and objectives of different intermediaries and capacity suppliers. Furthermore, these entities are bound by distinct rules, regulations, and legal/accounting practices, which can result in disparities in pricing (Peterson, 2012).

The presence of alternative mechanisms ensures the continuous availability of adequately priced risk capacity. Traditional insurance companies primarily offer renewable coverage for specific lines of exposure, while banks specialize in providing packaged risks with a longer duration. These factors can exhibit distinct variations in supply, demand, and pricing patterns at any given moment. By utilizing either one or a combination of the two options as necessary, a company can mitigate or completely eliminate the uncertainty associated with obtaining the most suitable coverage at a certain cost (Winton, 1997).

PRACTICE PROBLEM

A manufacturing company is considering the feasibility of replacing a deteriorating production facility. The new facility is expected to reduce the risk of operational disruptions, albeit at a higher initial cost. Please determine the cost-benefit ratio for the decision to replace.

SOLUTIONS TO PRACTICE PROBLEM

Cost-Benefit Ratio = (Present Value of Benefits) / (Present Value of Costs)

In this scenario, the company needs to assess the present value of benefits (e.g., reduced operational risks) against the present value of costs (e.g., upfront investment in the new facility).

5.5. DIVERSIFYING THE CREDIT RISK OF INTERMEDIARIES

Learning Objectives

- To understand the concept of diversifying credit risk of intermediaries and its importance in mitigating financial vulnerabilities within an organization's risk management strategy.
- Understand methods for diversifying credit risk among intermediaries in order to enhance overall risk management effectiveness.

Corporate end-users who engage in risk transfer, risk-financing, or hedging arrangements with intermediaries may face credit risk. If the broker, acting as a counterparty, breaches its contractual obligations, there could be a potential for financial damage. For example, if a business and a bank enter into a derivative hedging agreement and the hedge grows in value (offsetting a loss in the business's core operations), the company will suffer a loss should the bank default (Ibragimov et al., 2011). In the same way, the business loses money if it buys an insurance policy from an insurer who breaches their obligations at a critical moment (such as when an insured loss happens or a claim is made). The credit risk dimension is a critical element of the financial markets in general and the risk management markets in particular. It is assumed that any business participating in risk management operations would have credit exposure to intermediaries; this exposure must be considered (Infante et al., 2020).

Suppose a firm's credit risks are primarily associated with high-rating intermediaries (such as A, AA, or AAA), and the exposures are not significant, concentrated, or long-term. In that case, the firm may find the credit risk acceptable. Nevertheless, in cases where this is inaccurate, it becomes necessary to carefully regulate exposure. A firm with significant or intricate financial and operational risks can engage with many insurers, reinsurers, or financial institutions. This makes it possible to diversify the credit exposures in the company's portfolio. In order to establish a more equal distribution of exposures, risks might be assigned to different institutions using a variety of mechanisms, including those provided by the financial market and the ART market (Delis et al., 2014). A company can utilize specialized mechanisms within the ART market to eliminate the credit risk associated with the insurer or reinsurer. For instance, issuing a capital market security or employing a pure captive effectively eliminates the company's vulnerability to the insurer or reinsurer. Consequently, the ability to modify, reduce, or eliminate the potential for financial loss due to the failure of intermediaries is an additional factor that drives participation in the ART market (Kimbrough & Componation, 2009).

5.6. MANAGING ENTERPRISE RISKS INTELLIGENTLY

Learning Objectives

- Understand the principles of intelligently managing enterprise risks through data-driven insights and technology integration.
- Understand how to implement intelligent risk management strategies for enterprises, focusing on proactive identification and mitigation using advanced analytics.

Corporate and end-use clients seeking innovative solutions to manage both traditional and non-traditional risks have a significant impact on the demand for the ART market. While it may be relatively simple for companies to acquire conventional insurance/reinsurance or basic derivative hedges, larger corporations that prioritize prudent risk management require more sophisticated and comprehensive solutions (Bromiley et al., 2015). This necessitates an increased need for:

a) Programs that span three to five years or longer, providing coverage for a range of risks associated with different exposures (such as business interruption, workers' compensation, hurricane and earthquake coverage, etc.);

b) Non-traditional insurance plans that cover emerging risks resulting from trade and financial deregulation, terrorist activity, reputation management, technology, intellectual property, geopolitics, fraud, professional negligence, non-hazardous weather phenomena, environmental concerns, and similar issues;

c) Various flexible coverage methods, including the option to choose between derivatives, insurance/reinsurance, capital market instruments, captives, and other alternatives;

d) Integrated risk programs that utilize platforms to combine various exposures in a customized manner, generating the most cost-effective and resource-efficient coverage available.

The ART market effectively allocates risk to the institution, product, or solution with the appropriate expertise and advantage, which may differ from those involved in absorbing or managing the risk (Gruber, 2002).

5.7. REDUCING TAXES

Learning Objectives

- Understand effective tax reduction strategies through legal and strategic financial planning.
- Understand the implementation of tax-efficient practices.

Tax considerations can play a significant role in any economic choice. A tool, means of transportation, or financial deal that reduces taxes (assuming all other factors remain constant) will ultimately enhance operating/net income and, thus, the business's overall value. Consequently, it is crucial to comprehend the tax consequences associated with different risk management strategies.

Let's examine the tax implications of insurance contracts as one example. A company's insurance premiums are often considered an essential and regular business expense in many tax jurisdictions. As a result, these premiums can be deducted from the firm's income as they are incurred, increasing net income. Insurance earnings received after a loss and claim are often not subject to taxation unless the amount exceeds the tax base of the destroyed property or represents lost business profits. This has the potential to enhance a company's net profits (Parry, 2005).

If a firm is not covered by insurance and experiences a loss, it can subtract the portion of the loss not covered by insurance from its income. For example, the company may deduct the adjusted book value of the property or the difference between the asset's fair market value before and after the loss, whichever is smaller, in the event of property and casualty losses. The insurance's place of origin may also impact how taxes are computed (Pritchard & DeBoer, 1995).

Derivatives have highly complex tax effects that need to be carefully considered. Many jurisdictions still have subjective rules that depend on the specifics of the reference index and underlying transaction. The main tax benefit, however, usually varies based on whether a derivative is considered a speculative position or a hedge for risk management. If the company can be legally categorized as a hedge, it can deduct derivative earnings and losses from its regular revenue. A tax hedge refers to a swap or option that minimizes the impact associated with interest rate, item, or currency risks on a company's financial statement. It may also include "anticipatory" hedging. On the other hand, a derivative that guards against price and volatility risks for revenue streams or net income could not always be seen as a tax hedge. Derivative losses, in turn, become capital losses if a derivative is not a hedge and are normally only deductible against capital gains before being abandoned (Boyer, 2000).

Derivative contracts, insurance, and reinsurance are not the only areas with tax deductibility difficulties. Loss control strategies that reduce a company's risk exposures by taking preventative action could qualify for a deduction. For example, under certain accounting regimes, loss control costs, like education and training about safety, dangers, inspection, and other topics, might be automatically subtracted from income. Irrigation systems, safety fencing, security, and other capital assets utilized for loss control are depreciated throughout the asset's useful life and removed in each appropriate period (Bodenheimer & Grumbach, 1992).

5.8. OVERCOMING REGULATORY BARRIERS

Learning Objectives

- Understand key approaches for overcoming regulatory barriers by navigating legal frameworks and compliance requirements effectively.
- Understand and implement strategies to successfully navigate and overcome regulatory barriers, fostering a compliant yet adaptive approach to regulatory challenges.

Financial institutions and insurance/reinsurance firms are subject to distinct regulations and are overseen by several regulatory bodies. Therefore, efforts to remove regulatory obstacles that might otherwise restrict or forbid business impact the activity in the ART market (this is different from profiting from deregulation). To overcome regulatory obstacles, great consideration must be given to the type of risk management solution being developed or utilized.

Finding out if the national regulator categorizes a product as a derivative or insurance is vital. If a contract is labeled as a derivative, it's critical to determine whether it meets the requirements for being a hedge and whether the intermediary has the legal capacity to make the contract. This affects how taxes and regulations are applied and the costs and advantages for intermediaries and final consumers (Churchill, 2007).

A cedant and insurer acting under English law may agree to the payment of a certain amount through a risk transfer product, even in the event that a loss does not materialize. Under these circumstances, the product will be regarded as an "unenforceable wager" and will not be handled similarly to an insurance contract in terms of accounting, taxes, and loss mitigation. Before trading, one needs to understand these differences.

Regulations governing insurers are typically stricter than those governing reinsurers because regulators are under more pressure to shield individual policyholders from the risk of insurer failure. Insurance firms are subject to stringent underwriting, investment, and capital prudency criteria regulations in numerous nations where state or federal regulatory organizations govern them. Conversely, reinsurers conduct business internationally and across borders (Schwarcz, 2013).

Their primary target market is the professional market. They can underwrite a wider range of risks than primary insurers because they are not as bound by strict regulatory regulations and oversight. As a result, the legislative environment facilitates the transfer of some ART-related business from the insurance market to the reinsurance market. Some significant insurers have set up reinsurance subsidiaries to deal in specific goods and risks offshore to "circumvent" regulations that may otherwise obstruct commerce. Additionally, several have created capital market companies to provide their professional client with derivatives and other financial instruments (Zaring, 2018).

5.9. CAPITALIZING ON DEREGULATION

Learning Objectives

- Understand how to leverage deregulation for business advantage.
- Implement strategies to capitalize on deregulation effectively.

Although regulatory hurdles within and between market segments limit the kind and amount of risk management activities that certain institutions can undertake, deregulation forces are contributing to increased activity across sectors. This deregulation has allowed insurance and financial organizations to engage in cross-sector fusion of economic activity, or each other's markets. This is accomplished by putting in place procedures that allow financial and insurance risks to be assumed and transferred. Owing to deregulation, insurers, reinsurers, and financial institutions are progressively expanding into larger financial organizations by aggressively marketing products, services, and solutions in each other's traditional areas of expertise (Kane, 1995).

Consequently, it is not unusual to see banks and securities firms offering insurance-related products and services and attempting to resolve risk management problems frequently associated with insurance hazards. For example, pensions, long-term health care/disability coverage, and life insurance are becoming more commonplace offerings from commercial banks, while investment banks are increasingly taking on risks related to political unpredictability, natural disasters, and other factors. On the other hand, insurance and reinsurers actively manage a range of financial risks, including credit and market risks, and offer banking and investing services (Viswanathan & Cummins, 2003).

SUMMARY

- This chapter presents methods for optimizing enterprise value by implementing efficient risk management practices, emphasizing the crucial importance of the decision framework.
- The chapter examines many factors to be considered within the decision framework, including replacement, abandonment, and the detailed evaluation of costs and benefits. Real-life situations shed light on the practical consequences of strategic decisions.
- It explores the fluctuations in market cycles and examines the factors that influence insurance pricing. It also highlights the distinction between "hard" and "soft" markets, emphasizing the importance of adapting risk management strategies.
- The exploration involves acquiring additional risk capacity, which includes implementing diversification methods and increasing risk tolerance. It is strongly urged to apply this information in practical situations to ensure risk management techniques align with the objectives. It offers a comprehensive analysis of risk management drivers, providing valuable insights crucial for enhancing organizational resilience and optimizing value.

MULTIPLE CHOICE QUESTIONS

1. **What is the primary focus of this chapter on risk management drivers?**
   a. Profit Maximizing shareholder returns
   b. Enhancing organizational resilience
   c. Minimizing operational costs
   d. Expanding market share
2. **In the decision framework discussed, what components are considered for strategic risk management choices?**
   a. Replacement, abandonment, and market share
   b. Risk financing, diversification, and market analysis
   c. Replacement, abandonment, and costs and benefits assessment
   d. Marketing, pricing, and revenue generation
3. **What distinguishes "hard" markets from "soft" markets in the context of market cycles?**
   a. Hard markets have lower premiums, while soft markets have higher premiums
   b. Hard markets are characterized by increased capacity, while soft markets have reduced capacity
   c. Hard markets are associated with decreased competition, while soft markets exhibit intense competition

   d. Hard markets involve more stringent regulations, while soft markets have relaxed regulatory conditions.

4. Why is accessing new risk capacity important for organizations?

   a. To minimize risk exposure
   b. To enhance organizational flexibility
   c. To reduce regulatory compliance
   d. To optimize short-term profits

5. What does diversifying credit risk in intermediary relationships involve?

   a Minimizing credit exposure
   b. Expanding credit limits
   c. Assessing and mitigating risks associated with intermediary engagements
   d. Ignoring credit considerations

REVIEW QUESTIONS

1. What are the key components of the decision framework discussed in the chapter, and how do they contribute to strategic risk management choices?
2. Explain the distinctions between "hard" and "soft" markets in the context of market cycles. How should organizations adapt their risk management strategies in response to these market conditions?
3. Discuss the importance of accessing new risk capacity for organizations. Provide examples of strategies for diversifying credit risk and expanding risk tolerance.
4. In what ways does the chapter emphasize the adaptive nature of risk management in coping with market cycles? Provide practical examples to illustrate these concepts.

Answers to Multiple Questions

1. (b)   2. (c)   3. (b)   4. (b)   5. (c)

REFERENCES

1. Alff, G., (2002). Returning from a deep soft market and the largest catastrophe in history. *Risk Management*, *49*(1), 18.
2. Bachrach, P., & Baratz, M. S., (1963). Decisions and nondecisions: An analytical framework. *American Political Science Review*, *57*(3), 632–642.
3. Barth, J. R., (1989). Thrift deregulation and federal deposit insurance. *Journal of Financial Services Research*, *2*(3), 231–259.
4. Benston, G. J., (1992). The purpose of capital for institutions with government-insured deposits. *Journal of Financial Services Research*, *5*, 369–384.

5. Bodenheimer, T., & Grumbach, K., (1992). Financing universal health insurance: Taxes, premiums, and the lessons of social insurance. *Journal of Health Politics, Policy, and Law*, *17*(3), 439–462.
6. Bohnert, A., Gatzert, N., Hoyt, R. E., & Lechner, P., (2019). The drivers and value of enterprise risk management: Evidence from ERM ratings. *The European Journal of Finance*, *25*(3), 234–255.
7. Boyer, M. M., (2000). Insurance taxation and insurance fraud. *Journal of Public Economic Theory*, *2*(1), 101–134.
8. Boyer, M. M., (2001). Mitigating insurance fraud: Lump-sum awards, premium subsidies, and indemnity taxes. *Journal of Risk and Insurance, 1*(1), 403–435.
9. Bromiley, P., McShane, M., Nair, A., & Rustambekov, E., (2015). Enterprise risk management: Review, critique, and research directions. *Long Range Planning*, *48*(4), 265–276.
10. Chernew, M., Cutler, D. M., & Keenan, P. S., (2005). Increasing health insurance costs and the decline in insurance coverage. *Health Services Research*, *40*(4), 1021–1039.
11. Churchill, C., (2007). Insuring the low-income market: Challenges and solutions for commercial insurers. *The Geneva Papers on Risk and Insurance-Issues and Practice*, *32*, 401–412.
12. Cohen, M. S., (2015). Governance as the driver of culture change and risk management. *Journal of Risk Management in Financial Institutions*, *8*(4), 347–357.
13. Cole, S., (2015). Overcoming barriers to microinsurance adoption: Evidence from the field. *The Geneva Papers on Risk and Insurance-Issues and Practice*, *40*, 720–740.
14. Cummins, J. D., (1991). Statistical and financial models of insurance pricing and the insurance firm. *The Journal of Risk and Insurance*, *58*(2), 261–302.
15. Delis, M. D., Hasan, I., & Tsionas, E. G., (2014). The risk of financial intermediaries. *Journal of Banking & Finance*, *44*, 1–12.
16. Demidenko, E., & McNutt, P., (2010). The ethics of enterprise risk management as a key component of corporate governance. *International Journal of Social Economics*, *37*(10), 802–815.
17. Embrechts, P., (2000). Actuarial versus financial pricing of insurance. *The Journal of Risk Finance*, *1*(4), 17–26.
18. Emms, P., Haberman, S., & Savoulli, I., (2007). Optimal strategies for pricing general insurance. *Insurance: Mathematics and Economics*, *40*(1), 15–34.
19. Furneaux, B., & Rieser, L., (2022). User motivation in application abandonment: A four-drives model. *International Journal of Electronic Commerce*, *26*(1), 49–89.
20. Gold, S. M., Enck, P., Hasselmann, H., Friede, T., Hegerl, U., Mohr, D. C., & Otte, C., (2017). Control conditions for randomized trials of behavioral interventions in psychiatry: A decision framework. *The Lancet Psychiatry*, *4*(9), 725–732.
21. Greenspan, A., (2006). A framework for making a better decision. *Research Review*, *13*(1), 1.
22. Gruber, J., (2002). Taxes and health insurance. *Tax Policy and the Economy*, *16*, 37–66.

23. Hall, J., & Solomatine, D., (2008). A framework for uncertainty analysis in flood risk management decisions. *International Journal of River Basin Management*, *6*(2), 85–98.
24. Harclerode, M. A., Macbeth, T. W., Miller, M. E., Gurr, C. J., & Myers, T. S., (2016). Early decision framework for integrating sustainable risk management for complex remediation sites: Drivers, barriers, and performance metrics. *Journal of Environmental Management*, *184*, 57–66.
25. Harrington, S. E., & Niehaus, G., (2003). Capital, corporate income taxes, and catastrophe insurance. *Journal of Financial Intermediation*, *12*(4), 365–389.
26. Howe, K. M., & McCabe, G. M., (1983). On optimal asset abandonment and replacement. *Journal of Financial and Quantitative Analysis*, *18*(3), 295–305.
27. Hoyt, R. E., & Liebenberg, A. P., (2011). The value of enterprise risk management. *Journal of Risk and Insurance*, *78*(4), 795–822.
28. Hudin, N. S., & Hamid, A. B. A., (2014). Drivers to the implementation of risk management practices: A conceptual framework. *Journal of Advanced Management Science, 2*(3), 163–169.
29. Ibragimov, R., Jaffee, D., & Walden, J., (2011). Diversification disasters. *Journal of Financial Economics*, *99*(2), 333–348.
30. Infante, L., Piermattei, S., Santioni, R., & Sorvillo, B., (2020). Diversifying away risks through derivatives: An analysis of the Italian banking system. *Economia Politica*, *37*, 621–657.
31. Jackson, D., Moberg, O., Stenevik, D. E. M., Kane, F., & Hareide, H., (2018). The drivers of sea lice management policies and how best to integrate them into a risk management strategy: An ecosystem approach to sea lice management. *Journal of Fish Diseases*, *41*(6), 927–933.
32. Kane, E. J., (1995). Three paradigms for the role of capitalization requirements in insured financial institutions. *Journal of Banking & Finance*, *19*(3–4), 431–459.
33. Kimbrough, R. L., & Componation, P. J., (2009). The relationship between organizational culture and enterprise risk management. *Engineering Management Journal*, *21*(2), 1–20.
34. Klein, R. W., Phillips, R. D., & Shiu, W., (2002). The capital structure of firms subject to price regulation: Evidence from the insurance industry. *Journal of Financial Services Research*, *21*, 79–100.
35. Laeven, R. J., & Goovaerts, M. J., (2008). Premium calculation and insurance pricing. *Encyclopedia of Quantitative Risk Analysis and Assessment*, *3*, 1302–1314.
36. Lai, F. W., (2010). Shareholders value creation through enterprise risk management. *International Journal of Business Research, 10*(1).
37. Lai, F. W., Azizan, N. A., & Samad, M. F., (2010). A theoretical appraisal of value maximizing enterprise risk management. *International Journal of Accounting Information Science and Leadership*, *3*(6), 23–41.
38. Li, X., (2019). Research on financial risk control and prevention from the perspective of enterprise value maximization. In: *1st International Symposium on Economic*

Development and Management Innovation (EDMI 2019) (Vol. 1, No, 1, pp. 530–536). Atlantis Press.

39. Liberti, J. M., & Petersen, M. A., (2019). Information: Hard and soft. *Review of Corporate Finance Studies*, *8*(1), 1–41.
40. Lindholm, M., Richman, R., Tsanakas, A., & Wüthrich, M. V., (2022). Discrimination-free insurance pricing. *ASTIN Bulletin: The Journal of the IAA*, *52*(1), 55–89.
41. Luke, R., & Heyns, G. J., (2014). Reducing risky driver behavior through the implementation of a driver risk management system. *Journal of Transport and Supply Chain Management*, *8*(1), 1–10.
42. Manab, N. A., Kassim, I., & Hussin, M. R., (2010). Enterprise-wide risk management (EWRM) practices: Between corporate governance compliance and value. *International Review of Business Research Papers*, *6*(2), 239–252.
43. Mendeloff, J., (1993). Overcoming barriers to better regulation. *Law & Social Inquiry*, *18*(4), 711–729.
44. Merisalu, J., Sundell, J., & Rosén, L., (2021). A framework for risk-based cost–benefit analysis for decision support on hydrogeological risks in underground construction. *Geosciences*, *11*(2), 82.
45. Meza, I., Rezaei, E. E., Siebert, S., Ghazaryan, G., Nouri, H., Dubovyk, O., & Hagenlocher, M., (2021). Drought risk for agricultural systems in South Africa: Drivers, spatial patterns, and implications for drought risk management. *Science of the Total Environment*, *799*, 149505.
46. Miloš, S. D., Kožul, A., & Pecina, E., (2017). Managers' support–a key driver behind enterprise risk management maturity. *Zagreb International Review of Economics & Business*, *20*(SCI), 25–39.
47. Nocco, B. W., & Stulz, R. M., (2006). Enterprise risk management: Theory and practice. *Journal of Applied Corporate Finance*, *18*(4), 8–20.
48. Parry, I. W. H., (2005). Is pay-as-you-drive insurance a better way to reduce gasoline than gasoline taxes? *American Economic Review*, *95*(2), 288–293.
49. Parvin, Jr. A. J., & Beruvides, M. G., (2021). Optimizing the abandonment of a technological innovation. *Systems*, *9*(2), 27.
50. Peterson, N. D., (2012). Developing climate adaptation: The intersection of climate research and development programs in index insurance. *Development and Change*, *43*(2), 557–584.
51. Pritchard, T., & DeBoer, L., (1995). The effect of taxes and insurance costs on automobile registrations in the United States. *Public Finance Quarterly*, *23*(3), 283–304.
52. Raju, G. K., Gurumurthi, K., & Domike, R., (2016). Benefit-risk analysis for decision-making: An approach. *Clinical Pharmacology & Therapeutics*, *100*(6), 654–671.
53. Rao, A., (2009). Implementation of enterprise risk management (ERM) tools–a case study. *Academy of Accounting and Financial Studies Journal*, *13*(2), 87–103.
54. Renault, B. Y., Agumba, J. N., & Balogun, O. A., (2016). Drivers for and obstacles

to enterprise risk management in construction firms: A literature review. *Procedia Engineering*, *164*, 402–408.

55. Schanze, J., (2006). Flood risk management–a basic framework. In: *Flood Risk Management: Hazards, Vulnerability and Mitigation Measures* (Vol. 1, No. 1. pp. 1–20). Springer Netherlands.
56. Schiller, F., & Prpich, G., (2014). Learning to organize risk management in organizations: What future for enterprise risk management? *Journal of Risk Research*, *17*(8), 999–1017.
57. Schwarcz, D., (2013). Transparency opaque: Understanding the lack of transparency in insurance consumer protection. *UCLA L. Rev.*, *61*, 394.
58. Segal, S., (2006). Value-based enterprise risk management: The key to unlocking ERM potential. *Corporate Finance Review*, *10*(4), 16.
59. Stanford, R. H., Nag, A., Mapel, D. W., Lee, T. A., Rosiello, R., Vekeman, F., & Schatz, M., (2016). Validation of a new risk measure for chronic obstructive pulmonary disease exacerbation using health insurance claims data. *Annals of the American Thoracic Society*, *13*(7), 1067–1075.
60. Tadesse, M. A., Shiferaw, B. A., & Erenstein, O., (2015). Weather index insurance for managing drought risk in smallholder agriculture: Lessons and policy implications for sub-Saharan Africa. *Agricultural and Food Economics*, *3*(1), 1–21.
61. Tahir, I. M., & Razali, A. R., (2011). The relationship between enterprise risk management (ERM) and firm value: Evidence from Malaysian public listed companies. *International Journal of Economics and Management Sciences*, *1*(2), 32–41.
62. Tesselaar, M., Botzen, W. W., & Aerts, J. C., (2020). Impacts of climate change and remote natural catastrophes on EU flood insurance markets: An analysis of soft and hard reinsurance markets for flood coverage. *Atmosphere*, *11*(2), 146.
63. Viswanathan, K. S., & Cummins, J. D., (2003). Ownership structure changes in the insurance industry: An analysis of demutualization. *Journal of Risk and Insurance*, *70*(3), 401–437.
64. Weaver, C. P., Lempert, R. J., Brown, C., Hall, J. A., Revell, D., & Sarewitz, D., (2013). Improving the contribution of climate model information to decision making: The value and demands of robust decision frameworks. *Wiley Interdisciplinary Reviews: Climate Change*, *4*(1), 39–60.
65. Winter, R. A., (1988). The liability crisis and the dynamics of competitive insurance markets. *Yale J. on Reg.*, *5*, 455.
66. Winton, A., (1997). Competition among financial intermediaries when diversification matters. *Journal of Financial Intermediation*, *6*(4), 307–346.
67. Young, V. R., & Zariphopoulou, T., (2002). Pricing dynamic insurance risks using the principle of equivalent utility. *Scandinavian Actuarial Journal*, *2002*(4), 246–279.
68. Yow, S., & Sherris, M., (2008). Enterprise risk management, insurer value maximization, and market frictions. *ASTIN Bulletin: The Journal of the IAA*, *38*(1), 293–339.
69. Zaring, D., (2018). The federal deregulation of insurance. *Tex. L. Rev.*, *97*, 125.

CHAPTER 6

Linking Insurance and Mitigation to Manage Natural Disaster Risk

LEARNING OBJECTIVES

After studying this chapter, you will be able to:

1. To understand the challenges insurers face in managing natural disaster risks while maintaining solvency.
2. To explore the interplay between insurance practices and proactive risk mitigation efforts.
3. To recognize the pivotal role of building codes in shaping insurance practices related to natural disaster risk.
4. To analyze diverse strategies, including incentives and regulations, for encouraging risk reduction.
5. To identify future research directions linking insurance and mitigation for natural disaster risk.

INTRODUCTORY EXAMPLE

Consider a world where EcoGuard Insure, a leading insurance entity, stands at the forefront of addressing the intensifying challenges posed by natural disasters. In this imagined scenario, communities insured by EcoGuard Insure find themselves grappling with the heightened risks associated with an evolving climate. As we embark on this exploration, envision how EcoGuard Insure strategically intertwines insurance practices with proactive Risk Mitigation Measures (RMMs) to tackle the growing threat. Imagine policyholders incentivized to embrace resilient practices, all while the foundational influence of building codes shapes the landscape of coverage terms and premiums. In this imagined narrative, EcoGuard Insure navigates the delicate balance between financial viability and a steadfast commitment to managing and mitigating the impact of natural disasters.

UNIT INTRODUCTION

The insurance sector is now fully aware of its susceptibility to possible losses resulting from natural disasters. When Hurricane Andrew hit Florida's coast in August 1992, insurance companies paid more than $15 billion in losses. The entire insured damage may have been close to $50 billion if the storm had followed a more northerly path and struck Miami Beach and downtown. The Northridge earthquake in southern California resulted in more than $12 billion in insured damage. If a comparable earthquake had struck central Los Angeles, the insured amount might have exceeded $50 billion. A significant earthquake in central Tokyo might have cost more than $800 billion (Kunreuther, 1996).

The corporations now understand that to lower their chances of insolvency due to future catastrophic events, they will need to use risk mitigation measures or RMMs. For instance, research conducted after Hurricane Andrew revealed that if construction rules had been followed, 25% of the catastrophe's $15 billion in insured damage might have been avoided (Insurance Research Council and Insurance Institute for Property Loss Reduction, 1995). Early in the 1990s, a group of insurers established the Insurance Institute for Property Loss Reduction (IIPLR) (Smolka, 2006). An independent, nonprofit organization has conducted studies and research to promote steps that lessen the number of fatalities, injuries, property damage, and financial losses caused by natural disasters. It is currently known as the Institute for Business and Home Safety (IBHS). In the vehicle industry, insurers established the Institute for Highway Safety, whose main goal is to develop safer cars, paralleling their current strong interest in loss prevention strategies to lessen the damage caused by natural disasters (Kleindorfer & Kunreuther, 1999).

This chapter focuses on the circumstances in which insurers should use premium reductions to incentivize consumers to adopt cost-effective RMMs to lower their risk of insolvency and raise their projected profits in the future. When the predicted discounted benefits in the form of reduced losses surpass the measure's upfront cost, it is said to be a cost-effective risk mitigation measure (RMM) (Hodkin, 1991).

6.1. INSURERS CONCERN WITH INSOLVENCY

Learning Objectives

- To understand the indicators and factors leading to insurers' concerns with insolvency.
- To develop the ability to evaluate and apply risk mitigation strategies within the insurance industry.

The primary concern of insurers regarding mitigation is their potential insolvency due to future natural disasters. In 1982, Mayers and Smith used contemporary finance theory to refute the notion that insurers bear no risk of losses. Due to the potential difficulty for employees of an insurance company to find alternative employment in the event of bankruptcy, the insurer may opt to charge higher premiums for risks that carry the possibility of catastrophic losses, in order to offset this concern. In fact, property/ liability firms are willing to purchase reinsurance at premiums higher than their actuarial risks, as they are risk averse (Leadbetter & Dibra, 2008).

Figure 6.1. Diagram showing the importance of assessing insolvency risk. (Source: Hesham, Creative Commons License)

Additionally, insurers will be motivated to reduce their risk of insolvency to the extent that they have accrued franchise value, which they can only recover through continued operations. According to research, managers of mutual insurance companies ought to have more latitude than stock insurers when it comes to advancing the security of their businesses. Indeed, stock insurance company owners with limited capitalization and low franchise values could be incentivized to take on excessive risk (Barniv & Hathorn, 1997).

In an insurance company, Stone proposed that an underwriter deciding how much to charge for a premium would first try to maintain the probability of insolvency below a certain level (q*).

Figure 6.2. Diagram showing the importance of insurance. (Source: Canara, Creative Commons License)

An insurer seeks to take this action in order to enhance its capacity to establish higher rates and, consequently, increase cash flow. To be more precise, let's consider that the insurer possesses a portfolio of N policies, which may potentially result in a loss of L. The underwriter will then propose a premium P to ensure that the likelihood of insolvency is lower than q*. Empirical examinations of their pricing decisions indicate that underwriters desire to charge higher premiums for a given portfolio of risks when faced with risks that have more uncertain losses or greater ambiguity. This issue becomes particularly severe for closely connected losses, such as earthquake plans offered in a specific area of California (Schack, 1981).

A rule that aims to maintain the probability of insolvency below q* explicitly recognizes the role of risk in the decision-making process, as well as the role that mitigation strategies and reinsurance can play in reducing these concerns (Surminski, 2014).

6.2. LINKING MITIGATION WITH INSURANCE

Learning Objectives

- To understand the intricate linkage between risk mitigation strategies and insurance mechanisms.
- To understand the strategic alignment of risk mitigation measures with insurance solutions.

The choice of consumers to invest in loss prevention or RMMs has been extensively studied. Suppose the premium savings are significant enough to balance the additional expenses of investing in the loss prevention measure. In that case, those with insurance coverage will wish to invest in mitigation measures. What kind of premium incentives will insurers want to offer to their policyholders to entice them to switch to RMMs is the question that this inquiry attempts to answer. The insurer's surplus, the rate structure, and the policyholder's and insurer's concerns about insolvency all play a role in the decision (Linnerooth et al., 2019).

Figure 6.3. Representation of risk mitigation types. (Source: Michael, Creative Commons License)

Consider an insurance company attempting to determine the appropriate level of coverage to offer against the risk of earthquakes. The utilization of productive instances provides the opportunity to demonstrate how loss prevention can influence insurers' decision-making and the resulting trade-offs between profitability and insolvency. Initially, let us examine a large insurer with a substantial surplus in its current risk portfolio, which reduces the likelihood of insolvency to a level below q* (Davila et al., 2014).

Remember

Tax breaks as incentives for risk mitigation are not only about reducing financial burdens but also aligning with broader economic goals. Some regions offer tax incentives for green building practices, highlighting the interconnectedness of environmental sustainability and disaster resilience.

Consequently, the primary objective of encouraging policyholders to implement mitigation measures is to enhance the company's profitability. At present, the insurer must decide between promoting policyholders to adopt risk-reducing measures or purchasing reinsurance to minimize the amount of money paid out following a catastrophic event (Botzen et al., 2019).

Integrating mitigation with insurance represents a strategic risk management approach aimed at motivating policyholders to implement measures that reduce losses, benefiting both insurers and insured parties. Mitigation measures, commonly referred to as Risk Mitigation Measures (RMMs), encompass proactive steps taken to decrease the magnitude or probability of potential risks. Policyholders who actively engage in risk reduction enhance their safety and reduce the overall risk exposure for insurance firms (Kunreuther & Michel, 2013).

Insurance firms can cultivate a culture of awareness and risk reduction by providing premium incentives to policyholders who use efficient ways to reduce losses. These incentives include lower insurance premiums, decreased deductibles, or more coverage benefits. For example, a house installing a security system or a business implementing fire prevention measures may qualify for reduced insurance prices (Kunreuther, 1997).

6.3. ROLE OF BUILDING CODES

Learning Objectives

- Examine the significance of virtual memory security in preventing memory-based attacks.
- Explore access control mechanisms within the file system.
- Analyze authentication methods, such as password-based authentication.

Building codes have a significant impact on insurance practices, particularly when it comes to managing the risk of natural disasters. An important factor to consider is the impact of building codes on the assessment of risk and underwriting criteria. Insurers depend on these codes as essential standards when assessing and underwriting risks linked to different properties. Adhering to building codes plays a vital role in defining the conditions of coverage, establishing insurance premiums, and assessing overall insurability (Henderson & Ginger, 2008).

Building codes are fundamental in determining insurance procedures for the risks of natural disasters. They impact evaluating risk, developing strategies to prevent losses, recovering after disasters, complying with legal requirements, enhancing community resilience, and making data-based decisions. Together, these factors contribute to a complete and flexible approach to risk management in the insurance sector.

6.3.1. Building Code as Function Instrument

Moreover, building codes function as efficient instruments in encouraging the implementation of measures to prevent and mitigate losses. Insurers frequently encourage policyholders to keep up with these regulations by providing premium discounts. Adhering to these rules and implementing Risk Mitigation Measures (RMMs) helps ensure successful loss prevention, thereby decreasing the probability of claims and lowering potential losses (Enker & Morrison, 2020).

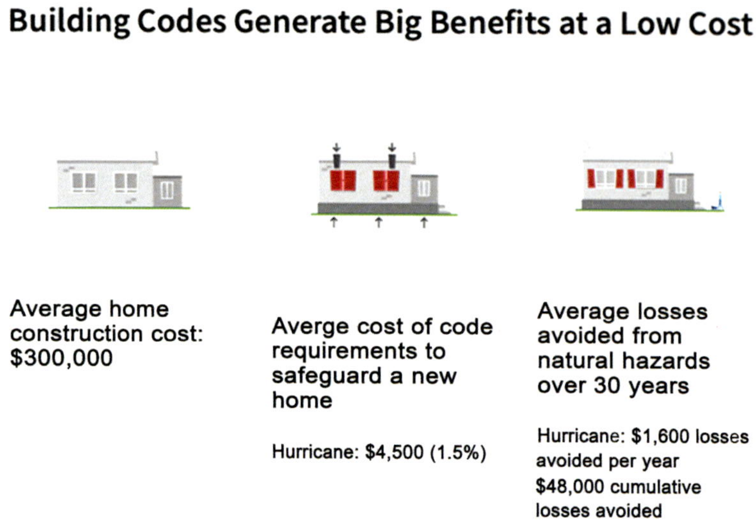

Figure 6.4. Illustration of building codes that generate big benefits at low cost. (Source: Bob Rehak, Creative Commons License)

6.3.2. Building Codes in Construction Process

Building codes play a crucial role in the reconstruction process during the post-disaster recovery phase. Insurance companies take into account compliance with building codes when a property is being rebuilt, which impacts the coverage terms and premiums for properties undergoing reconstruction. This highlights the importance of codes, not only in preventing future disasters but also in shaping the insurance landscape after catastrophic events (Listokin & Hattis, 2005).

From a legal perspective, building codes serve as more than just guidelines; they are mandatory regulations for construction. Insurance companies may require policyholders to adhere to local building codes in order to maintain the validity of their insurance policies. Failure to comply with these codes could potentially affect the validity of insurance coverage (Theckethil, 2006).

During the claims processing stage, insurance companies take compliance with building codes into consideration, including both the initial regulations and any subsequent revisions. The settlement amount is influenced by adherence to the codes, particularly if the property has been constructed or renovated according to current building standards.

6.3.3. Building Codes in Mitigating Risk

Furthermore, building codes play a crucial role in mitigating risks for individual properties and the entire community. Insurers have the opportunity to recognize and incentivize communities that collectively invest in complying with building codes. The shared commitment to ensuring safety and minimizing risks can potentially reduce insurance costs for property owners in specific areas (Colwell & Yavas, 1992).

6.4. MITIGATION THROUGH INCENTIVES AND REGULATIONS

Learning Objectives

- To understand the impact of incentives and regulations in fostering risk mitigation strategies.
- To develop the skills to design and implement mitigation initiatives through incentives and regulations.

Implementing mitigation measures, such as offering incentives and enforcing regulations, is a widely used method in various industries to minimize the impact of potential risks, especially in the case of natural disasters. This approach involves providing incentives to encourage individuals and organizations to voluntarily adopt risk mitigation strategies and establishing regulatory frameworks to ensure compliance. Here, we will examine in detail how the process of promoting mitigation through incentives and regulations operates (Ohrn, 2023).

PRACTICE PROBLEM

Consider a coastal region that is susceptible to storm surges and hurricanes. I propose a strategy that effectively integrates insurance practices with Risk Mitigation Measures (RMMs) to minimize the impact of storm-related damages.

SOLUTIONS TO PRACTICE PROBLEM

Introduce a Coastal Resilience Program where insurance premiums are linked to the implementation of specific storm mitigation measures. Policyholders who invest in storm-resistant building materials, elevated foundations, and comprehensive evacuation plans receive discounted premiums. This not only encourages individual risk reduction but also contributes to building a more resilient coastal community.

6.4.1. Incentives for Proactive Risk Mitigation

Offering financial incentives is an effective method to motivate individuals and corporations to willingly implement mitigation measures. Insurers can provide policyholders with lower premium rates if they minimize their vulnerability to potential risks. These incentives are tangible benefits that encourage stakeholders to invest in steps that improve their ability to withstand potential risks.

6.4.2. Tax Breaks and Credits

Governments can encourage mitigation efforts by providing tax incentives or credits to individuals and businesses that adopt preventive measures (Figure 6.5). This strategy promotes adherence and aligns with broader economic objectives, fostering resilience among communities (Enker & Morrison, 2017).

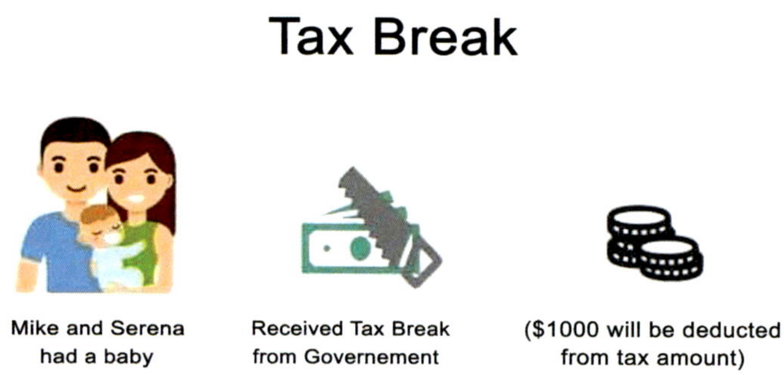

Figure 6.5. Illustration of tax break. (Source: Ashish, Creative Commons License)

6.4.3. Public Awareness Campaigns

It is essential to increase awareness about the advantages of risk mitigation. Public awareness programs educate individuals and communities on the significance of implementing preventive measures. These campaigns might emphasize the possible rewards and long-term benefits of investing in mitigation measures (Figure 6.6).

Figure 6.6. Representation of insurance benefit in disaster risk management. (Source: Barry Sheehan, Creative Commons License)

6.4.4. Regulatory Framework for Building Codes

Regulations are essential in establishing fundamental criteria for reducing risks. Building regulations provide mandatory criteria for construction to ensure that structures can withstand natural disasters. Ensuring compliance with regulations is a crucial requirement in the construction and maintenance of buildings, as it contributes to creating a safer built environment (Kim et al., 2016).

6.4.5. Insurance Requirements

Requiring specific amounts of insurance coverage can serve as an additional regulatory mechanism. Authorities may mandate property owners in certain areas or with specific types of buildings to have adequate insurance coverage. This ensures financial security and incentivizes property owners to prioritize risk mitigation (Plummer, 2004).

6.5. FUTURE RESEARCH DIRECTIONS

Learning Objectives

- To understand future research directions:
- To explore the connection between mitigation and insurance.

This chapter has proposed methods for integrating mitigation with insurance and other policy instruments to decrease potential damage caused by natural disasters in the future. Future research should prioritize enhancing risk estimation methods and defining the parameters of cost-effective mitigation techniques (Sagar et al., 2020).

6.5.1. Improving Estimates of Risk

Insurers will benefit from improved estimates of the risk associated with catastrophes in two ways. By obtaining more accurate data on the probability and impact of catastrophes, insurance companies can enhance their ability to determine premiums and tailor their portfolios to mitigate the risk of insolvency. The improved data should enable them to more precisely assess their need for protection through reinsurance or capital market instruments. Additionally, obtaining more precise risk data reduces the information asymmetry between insurers and other capital providers. Investors are more likely to provide additional funds when their confidence in the risk assessments of insured losses caused by natural catastrophes increases (MacLeod et al., 2015).

6.5.2. Encouraging Adoption of Cost-Effective Mitigation Measures

Identifying the specific cost-effective mitigation techniques that may be implemented in both new and existing structures and determining how they can be integrated into a risk management program is necessary (Figure 6.7). Insurers, builders, and financial institutions can collaborate effectively to integrate these safeguards into construction rules and offer property owners suitable incentives for implementing them (Rabechini et al., 2013).

Figure 6.7. Risk mitigation measures. (Source: Gayatri, Creative Commons License)

6.5.3. Project Impact

Project Impact aims to accomplish the objective of minimizing losses by establishing a community-driven collaboration with essential participants from the corporate sector, non-profit groups, and local, state, and federal governments. Before doing anything else, the community must thoroughly assess its susceptibility to natural disasters and pinpoint its weaknesses concerning those threats. Subsequently, it is essential to identify and prioritize steps to reduce risks and engage in mitigation operations. The local leaders must gain support for these measures and effectively promote their achievements to secure ongoing collaboration and support (Carvalho & Rabechini, 2015).

Keyword

RMM: Risk Mitigation Measures (RMM) are proactive strategies and interventions implemented to minimize the potential impact of risks. These measures encompass a spectrum of actions designed to reduce the likelihood of adverse events or mitigate their consequences. RMM can include preventive measures, contingency planning, and resilience-building initiatives across various domains such as finance, cybersecurity, and natural disaster preparedness. The overarching objective is to enhance an entity's ability to anticipate, manage, and mitigate risks effectively, thereby safeguarding against potential threats and fostering a more resilient and secure environment.

SUMMARY

- This chapter explores insurers' concerns over the probable insolvency among the rising risks of catastrophic disasters.
- This chapter examines the intricate task that insurers confront in maintaining solvency while still guaranteeing sufficient coverage in light of the increasing risks posed by natural disasters.
- Within this chapter, the symbiotic relationship between insurance practices and proactive risk mitigation efforts takes center stage.
- This chapter thoroughly analyzes how insurers incentivize policyholders to adopt Risk Mitigation Measures (RMMs), forming a crucial link between insurance premiums and collective disaster resilience efforts.
- The foundational role of building codes in shaping insurance practices related to natural disaster risk is a central theme in this chapter. The chapter underscores their significance in determining coverage terms and premiums by examining the influence of building codes on risk assessment, loss prevention, and post-disaster recovery.
- This chapter identifies future research directions, paving the way for ongoing scholarly inquiries into areas such as technological integration, innovative incentives, and the development of comprehensive risk management frameworks.
- Within the confines of this chapter, the discussion sets the stage for advancing the understanding and application of effective strategies in managing natural disaster risks within the insurance domain.

MULTIPLE CHOICE QUESTIONS

1. **What is a significant concern for insurers in terms of insolvency?**
   a. Building code enforcement
   b. Loss prevention incentives
   c. Policyholder compliance
   d. Future research directions
2. **How do insurers often encourage policyholders to invest in mitigation measures?**
   a. Ignoring building codes
   b. Legal compliance
   c. Increasing premiums
   d. Offering tax breaks
3. **What is the primary role of building codes in the context of natural disaster risk management?**
   a. Enforcement of insurance policies
   b. Regulatory barriers

c. Safety standards

d. Tax incentives

4. What is a common incentive for individuals and businesses to adopt preventive measures against natural disasters?

a. Increasing insurance premiums

b. Tax breaks and credits

c. Overregulation

d. Non-compliance penalties

REVIEW QUESTIONS

1. How do insurers address insolvency concerns while promoting policyholder compliance with risk mitigation measures?
2. What role do Risk Mitigation Measures (RMMs) play in the strategic link between insurance and proactive risk mitigation?
3. Discuss the pivotal role of building codes in influencing insurance decisions and enhancing community resilience in the face of natural disasters.
4. Explore the effectiveness of incentives and regulations in encouraging individuals and businesses to adopt preventive measures for mitigating natural disaster risks.

Answers to Multiple Questions

1. (c) 2. (d) 3. (c) 4. (b)

REFERENCES

1. Artzner, P., (1999). Application of coherent risk measures to capital requirements in insurance. *North American Actuarial Journal*, *3*(2), 11–25.
2. BarNiv, R., & Hathorn, J., (1997). The merger or insolvency alternative in the insurance industry. *Journal of Risk and Insurance*, 89–113.
3. Botzen, W. W., Kunreuther, H., & Michel-Kerjan, E., (2019). Protecting against disaster risks: Why insurance and prevention may be complements. *Journal of Risk and Uncertainty*, *59*, 151–169.
4. Carvalho, M. M. D., & Rabechini, Jr. R., (2015). Impact of risk management on project performance: The importance of soft skills. *International Journal of Production Research*, *53*(2), 321–340.
5. Colwell, P. F., & Yavaş, A., (1992). The value of building codes. *Real Estate Economics*, *20*(4), 501–517.
6. Cooper, R., & Ross, T. W., (2002). Bank runs: Deposit insurance and capital requirements. *International Economic Review*, *43*(1), 55–72.

7. Enker, R. A., & Morrison, G. M., (2017). Analysis of the transition effects of building codes and regulations on the emergence of a low carbon residential building sector. *Energy and Buildings*, *156*, 40–50.

8. Enker, R. A., & Morrison, G. M., (2020). The potential contribution of building codes to climate change response policies for the built environment. *Energy Efficiency*, *13*(4), 789–807.

9. Henderson, D., & Ginger, J., (2008). Role of building codes and construction standards in windstorm disaster mitigation. *Australian Journal of Emergency Management, The*, *23*(2), 40–46.

10. Hodkin, A., (1991). Insurer insolvency: Problems & solutions. *Hofstra L. Rev.*, *20*, 727.

11. Kim, J. J., Rogers, A. M., Ballem, N., & Schirmer, B., (2016). ASMBS updated position statement on insurance mandated preoperative weight loss requirements. *Surgery for Obesity and Related Diseases*, *12*(5), 955–959.

12. Kleindorfer, P. R., & Kunreuther, H., (1999). The complementary roles of mitigation and insurance in managing catastrophic risks. *Risk Analysis*, *19*(4), 727–738.

13. Kunreuther, H., & Michel-Kerjan, E., (2013). Managing catastrophic risks through redesigned insurance: Challenges and opportunities. *Handbook of Insurance*, *1*(1), 517–546.

14. Kunreuther, H., (1996). Mitigating disaster losses through insurance. *Journal of Risk and Uncertainty*, *12*, 171–187.

15. Kunreuther, H., (1997). Rethinking society's management of catastrophic risks. *The Geneva Papers on Risk and Insurance-Issues and Practice*, *22*, 151–176.

16. Kunreuther, H., (2006). Disaster mitigation and insurance: Learning from Katrina. *The Annals of the American Academy of Political and Social Science*, *604*(1), 208–227.

17. Leadbetter, D., & Dibra, S., (2008). Why insurers fail: The dynamics of property and casualty insurance insolvency in Canada. *The Geneva Papers on Risk and Insurance-Issues and Practice*, *33*, 464–488.

18. Linnerooth-Bayer, J., Surminski, S., Bouwer, L. M., Noy, I., & Mechler, R., (2019). Insurance as a response to loss and damage? *Loss and Damage from Climate Change: Concepts, Methods and Policy Options*, *1*(1), 483–512.

19. Listokin, D., & Hattis, D. B., (2005). Building codes and housing. *Cityscape, 1*, 21–67.

20. Love, K. M., Mehaffey, J. H., Safavian, D., Schirmer, B., Malin, S. K., Hallowell, P. T., & Kirby, J. L., (2017). Bariatric surgery insurance requirements independently predict surgery dropout. *Surgery for Obesity and Related Diseases*, *13*(5), 871–876.

21. MacLeod, M., Eory, V., Gruère, G., & Lankoski, J., (2015). *Cost-Effectiveness of Greenhouse Gas Mitigation Measures for Agriculture: A Literature Review, 1*(1), 1–20.

22. Newell, R. G., Jaffe, A. B., & Stavins, R. N., (2006). The effects of economic and policy incentives on carbon mitigation technologies. *Energy Economics*, *28*(5, 6), 563–578.

23. Ohrn, E., (2023). Corporate tax breaks and executive compensation. *American Economic Journal: Economic Policy*, *15*(3), 215–255.

24. Plummer, M., (2004). Improved estimates of floating absolute risk. *Statistics in Medicine*, *23*(1), 93–104.

25. Rabechini, Jr. R., & Monteiro De, C. M., (2013). Understanding the impact of project risk management on project performance: An empirical study. *Journal of Technology Management & Innovation*, *8*, 1–6.

26. Raz, T., Shenhar, A. J., & Dvir, D., (2002). Risk management, project success, and technological uncertainty. *R&D Management*, *32*(2), 101–109.

27. Sagar, S., Stamatiadis, N., Wright, S., & Green, E., (2020). Use of codes data to improve estimates of at-fault risk for elderly drivers. *Accident Analysis & Prevention*, *144*, 105637.

28. Schack, D. P., (1981). Reinsurance and insurer insolvency: The problem of direct recovery by the original insured or injured claimant. *UCLA L. Rev.*, *29*, 872.

29. Smolka, A., (2006). Natural disasters and the challenge of extreme events: Risk management from an insurance perspective. *Philosophical Transactions of the Royal Society A: Mathematical, Physical and Engineering Sciences*, *364*(1845), 2147–2165.

30. Surminski, S., (2014). The role of insurance in reducing direct risk: The case of flood insurance. *International Review of Environmental and Resource Economics*, *7*(3, 4), 241–278.

31. Theckethil, R., (2006). Building codes: A regulatory mechanism for reducing the vulnerability of urban areas. *Journal of Security Education*, *1*(4), 95–106.

32. Vaughan, E., & Turner, J., (2013). The value and impact of building codes. *Environmental and Energy Study Institute White Paper*, *20*, 501–517.

CHAPTER

7

Exploring Diverse Insurance Products

LEARNING OBJECTIVES

After studying this chapter, you will be able to:

1. To understand the role of diverse insurance products in comprehensive financial planning.
2. To analyze the specific risks addressed by each insurance type.
3. To evaluate the economic implications and societal impact of government-backed social insurance programs.
4. To examine the interconnectedness of various insurance products to create robust risk management strategies.
5. To explore potential innovations and adaptations in insurance products to address emerging risks and societal changes.

INTRODUCTORY EXAMPLE

Let's consider a common scenario to understand the importance of insurance. Meet Sarah, a working professional with a family to support. Sarah values the security of her loved ones and wants to ensure they are financially protected in case something unexpected happens. She decides to explore life insurance, a product designed to provide a financial safety net for her family if she were to pass away.

Now, let's imagine another situation where Sarah faces an unforeseen health issue requiring extensive medical treatment. Health insurance steps in, covering many of her medical expenses and reducing the financial strain on her family during a challenging time.

In a third scenario, Sarah experiences a temporary disability due to an accident, making it challenging for her to work. Disability income insurance becomes crucial, offering a steady income stream to help cover her living expenses until she can get back on her feet.

These examples highlight how different insurance products can play a vital role in protecting individuals and families from various life challenges, providing financial support and peace of mind in times of need.

UNIT INTRODUCTION

This chapter examines many insurance products specifically created to provide economic assistance during life's uncertainties. Consider life insurance to safeguard the family's financial well-being during their demise. Health insurance provides financial coverage for medical expenses during periods of illness or injury, while disability income insurance offers a monetary safety net for individuals unable to work. Property and casualty insurance assists in situations where accidents or damage occur, such as goods (Gustafsson et al., 2009).

Social insurance functions as a collective safeguard that encompasses the entire community. It aids in aging, securing employment after joblessness, or confronting obstacles such as handicaps. The reader will also examine the idea of old-age insurance, which guarantees a secure financial future as one age. Unemployment insurance provides financial assistance to unemployed individuals, giving relief throughout the job transition (Gatzert & Schmeiser, 2013).

As individuals browse various insurance policies, they may observe how these products interact, forming a comprehensive safety net that enhances financial stability and provides reassurance in a world characterized by uncertainties. Gaining comprehension of these diverse insurance alternatives enables individuals and communities to make well-informed choices, guaranteeing safeguards and assistance during times of utmost necessity (Schlag, 2003).

7.1. LIFE INSURANCE

Learning Objectives

- To understand the concepts underlying life insurance.
- To understand the different types of life insurance policies and their respective features.
- To analyze the factors influencing life insurance premiums, including age, health, and coverage amount.
- Evaluate the significance of underwriting in the life insurance application process.
- Explore the role of life insurance in financial planning, including its impact on beneficiaries and overall risk management.

Life insurance is an essential financial instrument that provides a safety net for individuals and their families (Figure 7.1). It involves paying regular premiums in exchange for a one-time death benefit payment to beneficiaries upon the insured person's death. Various forms of life insurance, such as term, whole, and universal life insurance, offer individuals the flexibility to customize their coverage based on their specific needs. Factors considered during the underwriting process include the insured individual's age, health condition, and lifestyle, all of which impact the insurance premium rates. Beneficiary designations allow policyholders to explicitly designate recipients. Overall, life insurance plays a crucial role in financial planning as it ensures financial security and addresses various responsibilities in the event of the policyholder's demise (Baumgardner, 1991).

Life insurance is renowned for its flexibility in accommodating various possibilities and requirements, making it a versatile financial instrument. An important feature is the inclusion of flexible coverage durations, which cater to immediate needs through term life insurance and provide lifelong security with whole life plans. These alternatives accommodate the ever-changing nature of individual circumstances, ensuring that policyholders can adjust their coverage to match various life phases and financial objectives (Goddeeris, 1984).

Life insurance provides additional support for the changing financial responsibilities that individuals encounter. For example, policies can be designed to specifically cover mortgage payments, education expenses, or provide income replacement in the case of the policyholder's death. The flexibility makes life insurance an essential component of a well-rounded financial plan (Mantis & Farmer, 1968).

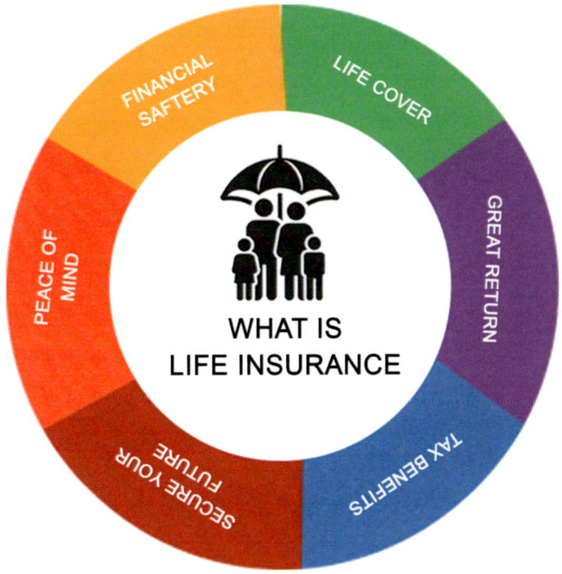

Figure 7.1. Diagram of life insurance. (Source: Rakesh, Creative Commons License)

Did you know?

The idea of social insurance can be traced back to ancient Rome. Roman soldiers contributed to a fund to provide financial assistance in the event of injury, showcasing early elements of collective risk-sharing.

7.1.1. Possibilities and Needs in Life Insurance

Furthermore, life insurance plays a vital role in estate planning. It can streamline the transfer of wealth to heirs, offer liquidity to cover estate taxes, and ensure financial continuity for recipients. This approach emphasizes the significance of life insurance, not just in safeguarding against unexpected events and promoting long-term financial stability, but also in planning for one's legacy (Lewis, 1989).

Life insurance is a versatile solution that caters to various needs, rather than being a one-size-fits-all option. It is a versatile and crucial tool that individuals can use to manage their financial commitments in the short term and establish a long-lasting legacy.

7.1.2. Types of Life Insurance

Life insurance policies can be broadly categorized as term or cash-value life insurance. Term insurance offers short-term coverage, but cash-value life insurance includes a savings element and builds cash values (Browne & Kim, 1993).

7.1.2.1. Term Insurance

Term insurance possesses various fundamental attributes. Initially, the protection period is transitory, such as 1, 5, 10, 20, or 30 years. If the policy is not renewed, the protection will expire at the end of the period. Term insurance contracts typically have the option to be renewed, allowing for additional periods of coverage without requiring proof of insurability. The premium is raised on each renewal date and is determined by the insured's attained age (Diacon et al., 2002).

The renewal provision serves to safeguard the insurability of the insured. Term insurance policies commonly possess the feature of convertibility, allowing the policyholder to exchange the term policy for cash-value coverage without requiring any proof of insurability. There are two approaches for converting a term policy. The insured's attained age determines the premium charged under the attained age approach at the conversion time. When purchasing the term insurance, the insured's age determines the premium charged under the original age method. Many insurers that provide the original-age method stipulate that the conversion must occur within a specific timeframe, typically five years, starting from the date the term insurance was issued (Ewold, 1991).

7.1.2.2. Whole Life Insurance

If the policyholder desires lifetime protection, term insurance is not feasible because the coverage is temporary, and the premiums are prohibitive in cost at older ages. On the other hand, whole life insurance is a type of policy—a cash value component—that offers lifetime coverage. Whole life insurance is also known as ordinary life insurance. Upon the insured's death, an agreed-upon sum is paid out to a specified beneficiary without regard to the timing of the death (Babbel, 1985).

7.1.2.3. Endowment Insurance

Endowment insurance is a conventional type of life insurance. It provides a payout equal to the insurance coverage if the insured person passes away during a specific period. If the insured person lives until the end of the endowment period, the insurance coverage amount is given to the policyholder at that time. For example, let's consider Stephanie, who is 25 years old and acquires a 20-year endowment policy. If Stephanie passes away at any point throughout the 20-year duration, the designated beneficiary will receive the face amount specified in the policy. On the other hand, if Stephanie remains alive until the end of the designated period, she will be paid the face amount specified (Sain & Selimovic, 2013).

7.1.3. Contract Theory of Life Insurance

The contract theory of life insurance serves as the basis for the legal and financial structure that regulates the connection between the insurer and the policyholder. A life insurance policy is a contractual agreement between two parties, defining the terms, conditions, and duties.

The contract theory comprises various fundamental components. The primary principle to consider is the notion of utmost good faith, often known as "uberrimae fidei," which entails that both parties must honestly reveal all pertinent information. The insured gives precise information regarding their health, lifestyle, and other relevant aspects. At the same time, the insurer responds by providing clear and open information regarding the terms and conditions of the insurance (Farsaci, 2012).

The agreement clearly outlines the precise rights and obligations of each person involved. Policyholders agree to make regular premium payments in return for the insurer's commitment to give a death benefit to beneficiaries upon the insured person's death. This contractual agreement provides financial security for the beneficiaries and adds to the overall risk management system for individuals and the insurance sector.

The contract theory includes the principle of indemnity, which states that the insurance will only compensate the policyholder for the specific financial loss resulting from covered events. Life insurance contracts deviate from standard indemnity principles by providing a predetermined sum (the death benefit) instead of compensating for specific financial losses (Huda, 2017).

In addition, the contract theory acknowledges the concept of insurable interest, which guarantees that the policyholder has a valid financial stake in the life of the insured individual. This measure prohibits individuals from obtaining life insurance policies on the lives of unrelated individuals, thereby reducing the risk of adverse incentives.

The contract theory of life insurance offers a legally and ethically binding framework that regulates the interaction between insurance companies and policyholders. This idea promotes confidence within the insurance sector by maintaining the integrity and trustworthiness of life insurance contracts through the principles of good faith, transparency, and fair dealing (Van der, 1970).

7.2. HEALTH INSURANCE

Learning Objectives

- To understand the functions of health insurance in the context of healthcare management:
- To analyze the impact of health insurance coverage on access to medical services and preventive care.
- To evaluate the role of health insurance in mitigating financial risks associated with medical expenses and promoting overall well-being.

One essential financial tool for easing the financial strain of medical bills is health insurance. Individuals pay premiums collectively under the principle of risk pooling, accumulating a fund that can be used for medical emergencies (Figure 7.2). Prescription drugs, hospitalization, outpatient treatment, and preventative care are just a few of the services these policies cover. Policyholders pay the regular premiums and any cost-sharing options, such as copayments and deductibles (Levy & Meltzer, 2008).

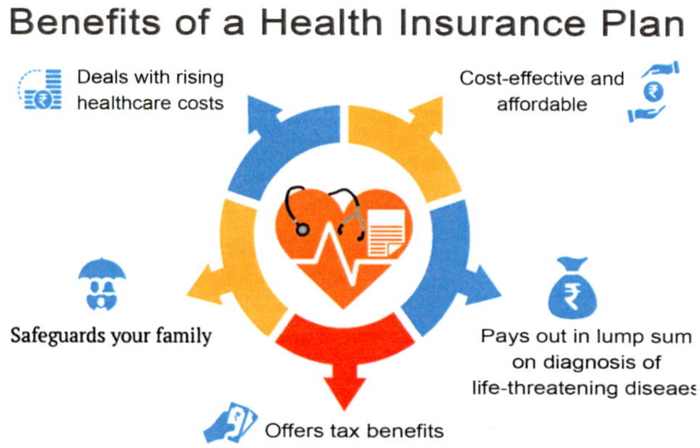

Figure 7.2. Illustration of health insurance plan benefits. (Source: Anuj, Creative Commons License)

To provide more affordable care, health insurance plans frequently operate within networks of healthcare providers. This promotes the utilization of in-network services, which often include wellness check-ups and preventive measures aimed at reducing serious health issues and associated expenses. Certain populations are covered by government-sponsored programs such as Medicaid and Medicare, which complement private health insurance. Regulatory frameworks ensure consumer protection and fair practices. Overall, health insurance is crucial for promoting financial stability, timely access to healthcare, and public health, as it safeguards individuals and families from the overwhelming costs of medical services and treatments (Gruber, 2000).

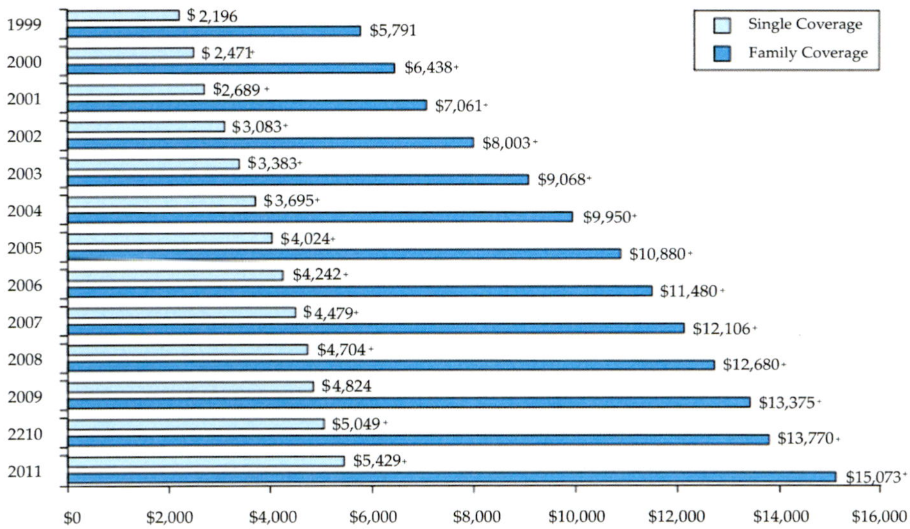

Figure 7.3. Depiction of average annual premiums for single and family coverage. (Source: George, Creative Commons License)

Remember

The insurance industry has embraced technology with innovations like telematics in auto insurance, where driving behavior is monitored to determine premiums. This tech-driven approach aims to reward safe driving habits.

7.2.1. Individual Medical Expense Insurance

Employer-sponsored group plans provide coverage for the majority of individuals under 65 who have private health insurance. However, individual medical expense insurance is also essential for providing financial stability to families and individuals who are not part of a group plan.

Individual protection is necessary for various situations, such as workers who quit, are laid off, or retire early. Additionally, many unemployed individuals require individual insurance while they are between jobs. College students also reach the age of 26 and lose their eligibility for coverage under their parents' plans. Furthermore, there is a significant portion of the population under 65 who are not employed and require individual protection.

Individual medical expense insurance offers protection against covered medical expenses resulting from illness or accidents. Customers have the option to choose from different policy options with varying premiums, coinsurance percentages, copayments, and deductibles (Browne & Doerpinghaus, 1993). Nowadays, many individual medical expense policies offer the following features:

a) Major medical benefits

b) The broad range of benefits
c) Calendar-year deductible
d) Coinsurance and copayments
e) Annual out-of-pocket limits
f) Exclusions

7.2.2. Long-term Care Insurance

A specific type of insurance known as long-term care insurance (LTCI) is designed to assist with the financial burden of long-term care needed for chronic illnesses, impairments, or age-related issues (Figure 7.4). The purpose of this insurance is to provide policyholders with financial support for various services, including adult day care, home healthcare, assisted living facilities, and nursing home care (Walls & Dowler, 2015).

One of the primary objectives of long-term care insurance is to protect individuals and their families from the high costs associated with long-term care services. As people live longer, the need for long-term care is more likely to arise, making this insurance increasingly important for individuals who are planning their finances.

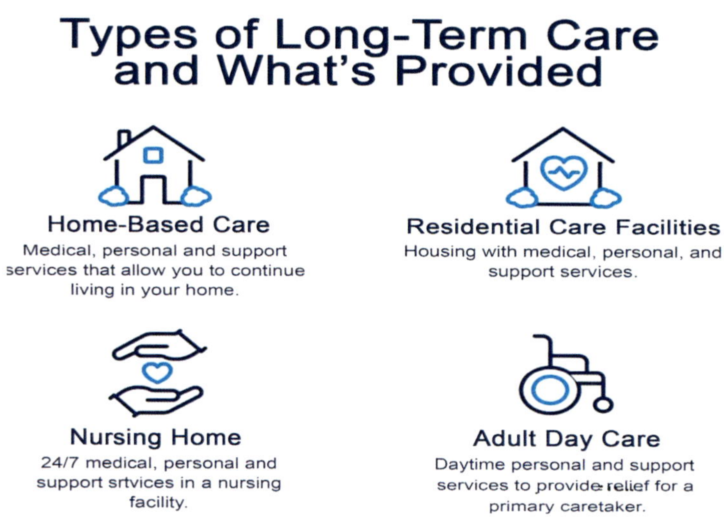

Figure 7.4. Diagram of long-term care insurance. (Source: Ramsey, Creative Commons License)

Long-term care insurance policies typically offer a daily or monthly benefit amount, and policyholders have the flexibility to choose the duration of the benefit and the waiting period before it takes effect, known as the elimination period. With these options, individuals can customize their insurance to meet their specific needs and financial constraints (Autor & Duggan, 2007).

Given the restrictions of other healthcare insurance, such as Medicare, which may not cover extended custodial care, this type of insurance is particularly advantageous. Medicaid covers long-term care, but not everyone is eligible as eligibility is means-tested.

A few examples of the variables that affect the cost of long-term care insurance are the policyholder's age, health, level of coverage, and elimination period selection. Because premiums are typically lower for younger customers, it is crucial to make early plans for long-term care needs (Hoem et al., 1971).

Long-term care insurance significantly reduces the potential financial obligations associated with extended care services. It allows individuals to protect their financial security and have control over the available care options as they age. Including long-term care insurance in comprehensive financial planning provides an added layer of security and peace of mind for individuals and their families facing the uncertainties of long-term care demands (Munch & Smallwood, 1981).

7.2.3. Group Disability Income Insurance

Employees with group disability-income insurance receive cash benefits weekly or monthly in the event of an accident or illness. There are two fundamental kinds of plans:

a) Short-term plans; and
b) Long-term plans.

7.2.3.1. Short-Term Plans

Many firms provide short-term plans that offer disability payments for relatively short durations, typically between 13 and 52 weeks. Most short-term plans have a maximum benefit payment period of 13 or 26 weeks. In addition, while accidents are usually covered from the first day of disability, most plans have a short elimination period for illness, which can range from one to seven days. Some plans have elimination periods that apply to both illnesses and accidents (Esho et al., 2004).

Certain plans do not have an elimination period, especially when the worker is hospitalized. The elimination period serves to reduce frivolous claims, control costs, and discourage feigning illness and excessive absenteeism.

7.2.3.2. Long Term Insurance

Many employers also offer long-term plans, which provide benefits for extended periods of time, typically from two years to age 65. However, benefits are only provided for a limited duration if the disability occurs after the age of 65. For instance, if the employee is below 60 years old at the time of disability, the maximum benefit period under one disability insurer's plan is until age 65 (Mayers & Smith, 1988).

Nevertheless, if a worker who is 66 years old becomes disabled, the maximum payment period is only 21 months. To determine the extent of disability, a dual definition is commonly applied. If individuals are unable to perform all the essential tasks associated with their work, they are classified as disabled for the initial two years. Even after two years, if the individuals are still considered incapable of performing any job for which they are qualified based on their education, experience, and training, they will continue to be classified as disabled. Additionally, long-term plans typically cover both occupational and nonoccupational injuries, in contrast to short-term policies.

7.3. PROPERTY AND CASUALTY INSURANCE

Learning Objectives

- To understand the purposes of property and casualty insurance.
- To differentiate between various types of property and casualty insurance coverages.
- To analyze the factors influencing property and casualty insurance premiums and policy terms.

Property and casualty (P&C) insurance is a broad category of insurance that encompasses various coverage options aimed at protecting individuals, companies, and organizations from financial losses caused by liability or property damage. This category includes policies for homes, cars, businesses, and other valuable assets (Figure 7.5).

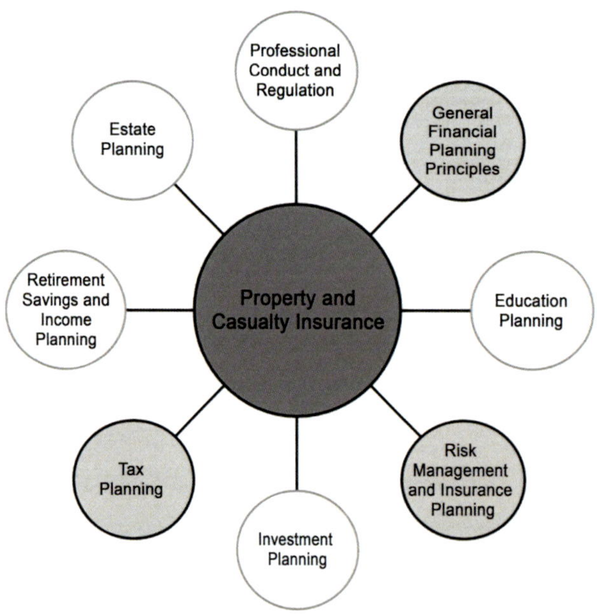

Figure 7.5. Diagram of property and causality insurance. (Source: Derek, Creative Commons License)

Property insurance provides coverage for the financial consequences resulting from physical loss or damage to assets. This may include coverage for residential properties, commercial structures, personal belongings, and other valuable properties. In the event of risks such as fire, theft, vandalism, and natural disasters, these policies may offer financial compensation to policyholders for repairing, replacing, or rebuilding damaged property (Serpa & Krishnan, 2017).

Casualty insurance, conversely, is primarily a liability coverage. It protects people or companies from the financial fallout of being found legally responsible for property damage or injuries to third parties. Auto liability, general liability for enterprises, and professional liability (errors and omissions) for certain professions are common forms of casualty insurance.

7.3.1. Automobile Insurance

Auto insurance is one of the most popular types of P&C insurance because it covers drivers and their automobiles. It usually covers liability for property damage, bodily injury, and optional coverages like collision and comprehensive.

7.3.2. Business Insurance

Business insurance, specifically property and liability insurance, is essential for organizations to manage risks and safeguard assets (Figure 7.6). While liability insurance pays for court costs and dispute damages, commercial property insurance protects structures, machinery, and inventory (Abraham, 2012).

Figure 7.6. Illustration of different types of business insurance. (Source: Amanda Cameron, Creative Commons License)

7.3.3. Specialized Coverages

P&C insurance also includes specialty coverages, including renters, homeowners, and inland marine insurance (which covers commodities in transit) and umbrella insurance, which extends liability coverage beyond the boundaries of regular plans.

7.3.4. Underwriting and Premiums

Assessing risks related to the insured property or liabilities involves underwriting for property and casualty insurance, considering elements including construction, location, and safety precautions. These risk assessments and the coverage levels the policyholder chooses are used to calculate premiums.

Due to its ability to offer financial protection against various risks, property and liability insurance is essential for risk management. This broad range of insurance guarantees that people and companies can financially recover from unforeseen circumstances, including property damage, liability claims, and other insured losses (Taylor, 1986).

7.4. SOCIAL INSURANCE

Learning Objectives

- To understand the objectives of social insurance as a governmental risk management strategy.
- To evaluate the ethical considerations associated with government-backed social insurance programs.
- To recognize the role of social insurance in addressing social risks such as unemployment, disability, and old age.

A government-backed program known as social insurance shields individuals and families from certain social risks, such as old age, disability, and unemployment, by providing financial support. Both employers and employees contribute to social insurance, creating a shared fund that assists individuals facing unfavorable life circumstances. The objective of programs like Social Security in the United States is to ensure a basic level of economic security and social welfare for citizens (Feldstein, 2005). Social insurance programs are crucial for several reasons:

a) Social insurance programs aim to address complex societal issues that impact the majority or all of society and require direct government intervention. For instance, during the Great Depression in the 1930s, the government took direct action to combat economic instability, leading to the establishment of the Social Security program.

b) Some risks cannot be adequately covered by private insurance, making social insurance schemes essential. Unemployment, for example, does not fully meet the criteria for insurable risks, making it challenging to obtain private insurance coverage. However, state unemployment insurance schemes can provide protection against the risk of unemployment (Chetty & Finklestein, 2013).

c) Social insurance schemes provide the population with a foundation of financial security. Most individuals benefit from financial protection offered by social insurance programs, safeguarding them against the long-term financial consequences of unemployment, old age, occupational and non-occupational disability, and premature death.

The social insurance systems in the United States are unique from other government insurance programs in several ways:

i. They are compulsory programs.
ii. They provide a floor of income.
iii. They emphasize social adequacy rather than individual equity.
iv. The benefits are loosely related to earnings.
v. The benefits are prescribed by law.
vi. There is no means test.
vii. Full funding is unnecessary.
viii. They are financially self-supporting.

PRACTICE PROBLEM

Sarah, a 30-year-old individual, is considering purchasing life insurance to provide financial security for her family in the event of her demise. She wants a policy that covers both her outstanding mortgage and additional funds for her children's education. Sarah is generally healthy and leads a non-risky lifestyle. How can she estimate an appropriate coverage amount for her life insurance policy?

SOLUTIONS TO PRACTICE PROBLEM

To calculate an appropriate coverage amount, Sarah can consider her outstanding mortgage, estimated future education costs for her children, and potential additional funds to support her family's lifestyle. For the mortgage, she can sum the remaining balance. For education, she can estimate the future costs based on the current age of her children, factoring in inflation. Adding these amounts and considering any additional funds needed will help Sarah arrive at a comprehensive coverage amount.

7.4.1. Old Age, Survivors, and Disability Insurance

The most significant social insurance program in the US is called Old-Age, Survivors, and Disability Insurance (OASDI), or Social Security. The Social Security Act of 1935 led to the passage of Social Security legislation. About one in six people receive a monthly cash benefit, while over nine out of 10 workers are employed in jobs covered by Social Security (Altmeyer, 1949).

Currently, Social Security covers almost all employees in the private sector. Coverage is mandatory for federal civilian employees hired after 1983 as well. Additionally, a voluntary agreement between the federal and state governments may provide coverage for employees of state and municipal governments. Most employees of local and state governments are now covered (Edwards et al., 2015).

7.4.1.1. Determination of Insured Status

Benefits cannot be received for the family unless a particular quantity of work in the covered job has been credited. Throughout the year, credits can be gained at any moment. For 2013, for every $1160 in covered earnings, one will receive one credit, often known as a quarter of coverage. Each year, a maximum of four credits may be obtained. As average incomes climb across the nation every year, so will the amount of covered earnings needed to receive one credit (Dey & Flinn, 2005). To qualify for the different advantages, one must become insured. There are three types of insured status:

i. Fully Insured
ii. Currently Insured
iii. Disability Insured

7.4.2. Unemployment Insurance

The Federal and state unemployment insurance programs provide weekly cash payments to employees who are involuntarily unemployed. Each state has its own unique program for unemployment insurance. The unemployment insurance provisions of the Social Security Act of 1935 gave rise to various state schemes (Hopenhayn & Nicolini, 1997). The primary goals of unemployment insurance are as follows:

i. Provide cash income during involuntary unemployment
ii. Assist unemployed workers in finding jobs
iii. Encourage employers to stabilize employment
iv. Help stabilize the economy

During short-term involuntary unemployment, unemployed workers receive weekly cash benefits, which help them maintain their financial security. A secondary goal is to assist jobless individuals in securing employment; recipients of benefits must register for jobs at nearby employment offices, where staff members provide support in finding suitable positions. Encouraging employers to use experience ratings to stabilize employment is the third goal. Lastly, during recessions, unemployment benefits contribute to economic stabilization (Schmieder & Von, 2016).

Most nonprofit organizations, state and municipal governments, and private businesses are eligible for unemployment compensation. If a private company employs one or more people for at least 20 weeks in a calendar year (or the year before) or pays wages of at least $1500 in a calendar quarter of that year, it is subject to the federal unemployment tax (Acemoglu & Shimer, 1999).

Unemployment insurance benefits are also provided for most positions held by state and municipal governments. On the other hand, state and local governments have the option to reimburse the system for the benefits provided to government employees instead of paying the federal unemployment tax (Moffitt & Nicholson, 1982).

Furthermore, a nonprofit organization is eligible if it is compassionate, educational, or religious and employs four or more people for at least one day in each of the twenty distinct weeks in the current or previous year. A nonprofit organization may choose to reimburse the states for benefits received or pay the unemployment tax (Meyer, 1995).

7.5. WORKERS COMPENSATION

Learning Objectives

- To understand the legal foundations of workers' compensation.
- To grasp the primary objective of workers' compensation insurance.

Workers' compensation is a social insurance policy that provides medical care, financial support, and rehabilitation services to employees who experience illnesses or injuries as a result of work-related accidents or diseases (Figure 7.7). The benefits play a crucial role in mitigating the financial instability that may arise from a job-related disability (Dionne & St-Michel, 1991).

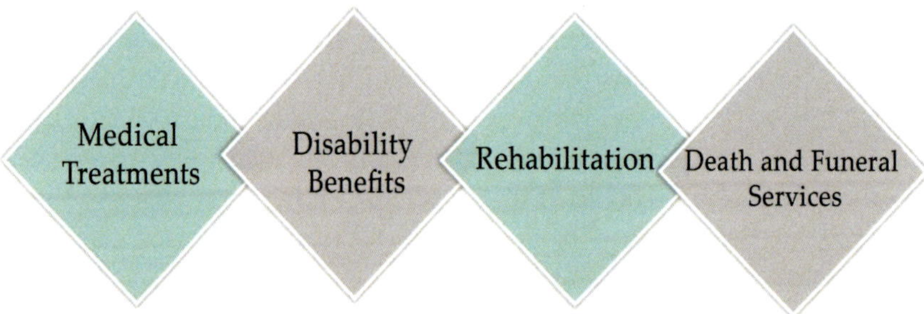

Figure 7.7. Representation of benefits offered by workers compensation insurance. (Source: Niti Gupta, Creative Commons License)

Before employees injured at work could be awarded damages, they had to file a lawsuit against their employers and demonstrate that their employers were negligent under the common law of industrial accidents, which dates back to 1837. However, a company may be able to defend against worker injury lawsuits using three common law defenses:

a) Contributory negligence doctrine;

b) Fellow-servant doctrine;

c) Assumption-of-risk doctrine.

If an injured worker had any role in causing the harm, they could not sue their employer for damages under the contributory negligence doctrine. If a fellow worker's negligence caused harm, the injured worker was not entitled to compensation under the fellow-servant doctrine. Furthermore, if the injured worker chose to work in a certain occupation despite being aware of the inherent risks, they would not be eligible for benefits under the assumption-of-risk concept. Due to the severe common law, comparatively few disabled workers were able to obtain sufficient compensation for their injuries (Guyton, 1999).

The next phase in workers' compensation was the enactment of employer liability laws between 1885 and 1910. This legislation strengthened the legal position of injured workers, diminished the effectiveness of common law defenses, and required that companies create safe working conditions for their staff. However, before receiving compensation for their injuries, injured workers had to file a lawsuit against their employers and demonstrate fault. Eventually, to address the issue of work-related accidents, the states implemented workers' compensation legislation. The federal government passed a worker's compensation law covering certain federal employees in 1908, and most states had enacted comparable legislation by 1920. Nowadays, workers' compensation laws exist in every state.

The foundational idea of workers' compensation is liability without fault. Regardless of fault, the employer is fully accountable for any illnesses or injuries employees incur. Workers who are disabled are compensated for their injuries according to a legally established benefits schedule. Employees do not have to file a lawsuit against their employers to receive benefits. The laws require that benefits be paid to disabled workers as soon as possible, without regard to fault, and with the least amount of formality possible. Consequently, normal production costs include the costs of workers' compensation benefits, which are regarded as a typical cost of production (Lippel, 2007).

State workers' compensation laws have several basic objectives:

a) Broad coverage of employees for job-related accidents and diseases;
b) Substantial protection against the loss of income;
c) Sufficient medical care and rehabilitation services;
d) Encouragement of safety;
e) Reduction in litigation.

Giving employees comprehensive coverage for illnesses and accidents related to their jobs is one of the main goals. That is, the great majority of professions or illnesses and accidents related to the job should be covered by workers' compensation regulations.

Providing strong protection against income loss is the second goal. To maintain the disabled worker's prior quality of life, the cash payments are intended to replace a significant percentage of their lost income (Strunin & Bolden, 2004).

The third goal is to ensure that injured workers receive adequate medical treatment and rehabilitation services. Under workers' compensation regulations, employers must cover hospital, surgery, and other medical expenses injured workers pay. Additionally, the laws offer disabled workers rehabilitation assistance to help them return to productive jobs.

Lastly, workers' compensation regulations aim to lower the number of lawsuits. Disabled workers receive payments immediately and do not need to file lawsuits against their employers. The goal is to avoid paying lawyers' fees and lengthy, costly trials and appeals (Lippel, 2012).

SUMMARY

- When investigating various insurance policies, readers delve into an extensive range of coverage alternatives to handle different aspects of life's uncertainties. A vital part of financial planning, life insurance provides beneficiaries with security during the policyholder's passing, providing a safety net of funds during hard times.
- Health insurance, the cornerstone of healthcare administration, facilitates prompt access to treatments and preventive care by navigating the intricacies of medical costs.
- Disability income insurance plays a major role in reducing the financial burden of disability by giving people replacement income if they cannot work.
- A collective safety net against social risks such as unemployment, disability, and old age is the goal of social insurance initiatives such as Social Security. Property and casualty insurance protects against unanticipated damages and liabilities, protecting homes, vehicles, and businesses.
- In addition, unemployment insurance and old age insurance are specifically designed to handle the financial difficulties brought on by aging populations and unstable employment. While unemployment insurance offers a temporary income buffer for people facing job loss, old age insurance aims to assure a stable financial future for seniors.
- Workers' compensation, a vital aspect of employee protection, provides financial support and medical benefits to workers injured.
- This exploration unveils the multifaceted landscape of insurance products, each designed to cater to specific needs and mitigate diverse risks in the intricate tapestry of life. Together, these insurance offerings foster financial resilience and societal well-being in the face of unforeseen challenges.

MULTIPLE CHOICE QUESTIONS

1. **What is the primary purpose of life insurance?**
   a. Provide income in retirement
   b. Navigate medical expenses
   c. Offer protection to beneficiaries in case of the policyholder's demise
   d. Safeguard against damages and liabilities
2. **Which insurance type takes center stage in mitigating the financial impact of disability?**
   a. Health insurance
   b. Old age insurance
   c. Disability income insurance
   d. Worker's compensation

3. **What does property and casualty insurance primarily safeguard against?**
   a. Unemployment
   b. Medical expenses
   c. Damage and liabilities
   d. Aging populations
4. **What does Social Insurance, exemplified by programs like Social Security, aim to create a collective safety net against?**
   a. Medical Expenses
   b. Old
   c. Unemployment
   d. Home damages
5. **Which insurance type is specifically designed to provide a temporary income buffer for individuals facing job loss?**
   a. Disability income insurance
   b. Health insurance
   c. Workers compensation
   d. Unemployment insurance

REVIEW QUESTIONS

1. Explore how different insurance products discussed in the chapter are interconnected in addressing comprehensive financial needs. Provide examples illustrating how a combination of insurance types can create a robust risk management strategy.
2. Investigate the government's role in social insurance, particularly programs like Social Security. Discuss the societal impact and ethical considerations of government-backed initiatives in providing a safety net for citizens.
3. Examine the economic implications of unemployment insurance. Evaluate how this type of insurance contributes to economic stability during periods of job loss and the potential challenges or criticisms associated with such programs.
4. Discuss the ethical issues surrounding workers' compensation.

Answers to Multiple Questions

1. (c) 2. (c) 3. (c) 4. (b) 5. (d)

REFERENCES

1. Abraham, K. S., (2012). Four conceptions of insurance. U. Pa. L. Rev., 161, 653.
2. Acemoglu, D., & Shimer, R., (1999). Efficient unemployment insurance. Journal of Political Economy, 107(5), 893–928.
3. Altmeyer, A. J., (1949). Old-age, survivors, and disability insurance. Social Security Bulletin, 12(4), 3.
4. Autor, D. H., & Duggan, M. G., (2007). Distinguishing income from substitution effects in disability insurance. American Economic Review, 97(2), 119–124.
5. Babbel, D. F., (1985). The price elasticity of demand for whole life insurance. The Journal of Finance, 40(1), 225–239.
6. Baumgardner, J. R., (1991). Hong, J. H., & Rios-Rull, J. V., (2012). Life insurance and household consumption. American Economic Review, 102(7), 3701–3730.
7. Brown, J. R., & Finkelstein, A., (2007). Why is the market for long-term care insurance so small? Journal of Public Economics, 91(10), 1967–1991.
8. Brown, J. R., & Finkelstein, A., (2009). The private market for long-term care insurance in the United States: A review of the evidence. Journal of Risk and Insurance, 76(1), 5–29.
9. Browne, M. J., & Doerpinghaus, H. I., (1993). Information asymmetries and adverse selection in the market for individual medical expense insurance. Journal of Risk and Insurance, 1(1), 300–312.
10. Browne, M. J., & Kim, K., (1993). An international analysis of life insurance demand. Journal of Risk and Insurance, 1(1), 616–634.
11. Butler, R. J., & Worrall, J. D., (1983). Workers' compensation: Benefit and injury claims rates in the seventies. The Review of Economics and Statistics, 1(1), 580–589.
12. Campbell, J. C., Ikegami, N., & Gibson, M. J., (2010). Lessons from public long-term care insurance in Germany and Japan. Health Affairs, 29(1), 87–95.
13. Çevrimli, M. B., Mat, B., Tekindal, M. A., & Günlü, A., (2022). Determination of risk factors in cattle and small ruminant livestock enterprises from the perspective of animal life insurance: A case study in Turkey. Arquivo Brasileiro de Medicina Veterinária e Zootecnia, 74, 21–32.
14. Chen, L., & Xu, X., (2020). Effect evaluation of the long-term care insurance (LTCI) system on the health care of the elderly: A review. Journal of Multidisciplinary Healthcare, 1(1), 863–875.
15. Chetty, R., & Finkelstein, A., (2013). Social insurance: Connecting theory to data. In: Handbook of Public Economics (Vol. 5, pp. 111–193). Elsevier.
16. Cutler, D. M., & Zeckhauser, R. J., (2000). The anatomy of health insurance. In: Handbook of Health Economics (Vol. 1, pp. 563–643). Elsevier.
17. Dey, M. S., & Flinn, C. J., (2005). An equilibrium model of health insurance provision and wage determination. Econometrica, 73(2), 571–627.
18. Dionne, G., & St-Michel, P., (1991). Workers' compensation and moral hazard. The Review of Economics and Statistics, 1(1), 236–244.

19. Edemekong, P. F., Annamaraju, P., & Haydel, M. J., (2018). Health Insurance Portability and Accountability Act, 1(1), 1–20.
20. Edwards, G., Martínez, G., & Contreras, J. P., (2015). An empirical analysis of possible reforms to the disability and survivors insurance in Chile. Journal of Population Ageing, 8, 279–302.
21. Ehrenberg, R. G., & Oaxaca, R. L., (1976). Unemployment insurance, duration of unemployment, and subsequent wage gain. The American Economic Review, 66(5), 754–766.
22. Esho, N., Kirievsky, A., Ward, D., & Zurbruegg, R., (2004). Law and the determinants of property-casualty insurance. Journal of Risk and Insurance, 71(2), 265–283.
23. Ewold, F., (1991). Insurance and risk. The Foucault Effect: Studies in Governmentality, 197210, 201–202.
24. Farsaci, B., (2012). Insurance contract: Historical and theoretical profiles from the perspective of European law. Ins. L. Rev., 38, 1–20.
25. Feldstein, M., (2005). Rethinking social insurance. American Economic Review, 95(1), 1–24.
26. Fischer, S., (1973). A life cycle model of life insurance purchases. International Economic Review, 1(1), 132–152.
27. Gatzert, N., & Schmeiser, H., (2013). New life insurance financial products. In: Handbook of Insurance (Vol. 1, No. 1, pp. 1061–1095). New York, NY: Springer New York.
28. Goddeeris, J. H., (1984). Medical insurance, technological change, and welfare. Economic Inquiry, 22(1), 56–67.
29. Gruber, J., (2000). Health insurance and the labor market. Handbook of Health Economics, 1, 645–706.
30. Gustafsson-Wright, E., Asfaw, A., & Van, D. G. J., (2009). Willingness to pay for health insurance: An analysis of the potential market for new low-cost health insurance products in Namibia. Social Science & Medicine, 69(9), 1351–1359.
31. Guyton, G. P., (1999). A brief history of workers' compensation. The Iowa Orthopedic Journal, 19, 106.
32. Hing, E., & Jensen, G. A., (1999). Health insurance portability and accountability act of 1996: Lessons from the states. Medical Care, 1(1), 692–705.
33. Hoem, J. M., Riis, J., & Sand, R., (1971). Disability income benefits in group life insurance. Scandinavian Actuarial Journal, 1971(3, 4), 190–203.
34. Hoffman, C., & Paradise, J., (2008). Health insurance and access to health care in the United States. Annals of the New York Academy of Sciences, 1136(1), 149–160.
35. Holmlund, B., (1998). Unemployment insurance in theory and practice. Scandinavian Journal of Economics, 100(1), 113–141.
36. Hopenhayn, H. A., & Nicolini, J. P., (1997). Optimal unemployment insurance. Journal of Political Economy, 105(2), 412–438.

37. Huda, M. K., (2017). Good faith in life insurance contract by Indonesian court. Hasanuddin Law Review, 3(1), 49–58.

38. Landais, C., & Spinnewijn, J., (2021). The value of unemployment insurance. The Review of Economic Studies, 88(6), 3041–3085.

39. Levy, H., & Meltzer, D., (2008). The impact of health insurance on health. Annu. Rev. Public Health, 29, 399–409.

40. Lewis, F. D., (1989). Dependents and the demand for life insurance. The American Economic Review, 79(3), 452–467.

41. Lippel, K., (2007). Workers describe the effect of the workers' compensation process on their health: A Quebec study. International Journal of Law and Psychiatry, 30(4, 5), 427–443.

42. Lippel, K., (2012). Preserving workers' dignity in workers' compensation systems: An international perspective. American Journal of Industrial Medicine, 55(6), 519–536.

43. Mantis, G., & Farmer, R. N., (1968). Demand for life insurance. Journal of Risk and Insurance, 1(1), 247–256.

44. Mayers, D., & Smith, Jr. C. W., (1988). Ownership structure across lines of property-casualty insurance. The Journal of Law and Economics, 31(2), 351–378.

45. McCluskey, M. T., (1997). The illusion of efficiency in workers compensation reform. Rutgers L. Rev., 50, 657.

46. Meyer, B. D., (1995). Lessons from the US unemployment insurance experiments. Journal of Economic Literature, 33(1), 91–131.

47. Moffitt, R., & Nicholson, W., (1982). The effect of unemployment insurance on unemployment: The case of federal supplemental benefits. The Review of Economics and Statistics, 1(1), 1–11.

48. Munch, P., & Smallwood, D., (1981). Theory of solvency regulation in the property and casualty insurance industry. In: Studies in Public Regulation (Vol. 1, No. 1, pp. 119–180). The MIT Press.

49. Osei, A. B., & Agyemang, S., (2017). Analyzing the influence of health insurance status on peoples' health seeking behavior in rural Ghana. Journal of Tropical Medicine, 1(1), 1–20.

50. Quinlan, M., & Mayhew, C., (1999). Precarious employment and workers' compensation. International Journal of Law and Psychiatry, 22(5, 6), 491–520.

51. Sain, Z., & Selimovic, J., (2013). Endowment life insurance. UTMS Journal of Economics, 4(2), 175–186.

52. Schlag, C. H., (2003). Determinants of demand for life insurance products-theoretical concepts and empirical evidence. Swiss Re Economic Research & Consulting, 8(9), 1–20.

53. Schmieder, J. F., & Von, W. T., (2016). The effects of unemployment insurance benefits: New evidence and interpretation. Annual Review of Economics, 8, 547–581.

54. Serpa, J. C., & Krishnan, H., (2017). The strategic role of business insurance. Management Science, 63(2), 384–404.

55. Sommers, B. D., Gawande, A. A., & Baicker, K., (2017). Health insurance coverage and health—What the recent evidence tells us. N Engl. J. Med., 377(6), 586–593.
56. Stone, D. A., (1993). The struggle for the soul of health insurance. Journal of Health Politics, Policy, and Law, 18(2), 287–317.
57. Strunin, L., & Boden, L. I., (2004). The workers' compensation system: Worker friend or foe? American Journal of Industrial Medicine, 45(4), 338–345.
58. Taylor, G. C., (1986). Underwriting strategy in a competitive insurance environment. Insurance: Mathematics and Economics, 5(1), 59–77.
59. Van, D. M. S. W. J., (1970). The concept of insurance and the insurance contract. Comparative and International Law Journal of Southern Africa, 3(2), 149–167.
60. Walls, R. T., & Dowler, D. L., (2015). Disability and income. Rehabilitation Counseling Bulletin, 58(3), 146–153.

CHAPTER

8

Trends and Challenges in Risk Management and Insurance

LEARNING OBJECTIVES

After studying this chapter, you will be able to:

1. To understand emerging trends in risk management through technological innovations.
2. To analyze the impact of globalization on insurance practices worldwide.
3. To comprehend the implications of regulatory and compliance changes in the insurance industry.
4. To explore future trends in insurance products.
5. To develop strategies for addressing future challenges in the field of risk management.

INTRODUCTORY EXAMPLE

Consider a scenario where CyberGuardInsure, a multinational insurance firm, leverages cutting-edge artificial intelligence (AI) algorithms for real-time risk evaluation. This technological breakthrough not only enhances the efficiency of risk management but also exemplifies current industry trends. By employing advanced AI, CyberGuardInsure proactively identifies potential risks, swiftly analyzes vast datasets, and implements dynamic risk mitigation strategies. This proactive use of AI aids in eliminating uncertainties and swiftly responding to emerging challenges, showcasing the interconnected dynamics of technology progress, globalization, regulatory shifts, and proactive risk management in the evolving insurance sector.

UNIT INTRODUCTION

This chapter thoroughly examines risk management in the insurance industry. The analysis includes an examination of developing trends, technical improvements, the worldwide influence on insurance practices, legislative modifications, and the prediction of future barriers. The chapter seeks to provide a comprehensive grasp of the dynamic forces that influence risk management strategies by conducting a thorough analysis of these elements (Munich, 2005).

In risk management, the objective is not to completely eradicate the variability of future events but rather to manage the variability of such outcomes. It is impossible for a company to come out ahead financially if all risks are completely removed. It is possible for individuals working for an organization to lie somewhere on the spectrum between being risk averse and being risk takers. When it comes to this spectrum, there is frequently a balance that is in accordance with the objectives of the company.

Over the course of the investigation, the incorporation of real-world examples and academic insights serves to shed light on fundamental ideas, which in turn makes it easier to get a comprehensive understanding of the ever-changing dynamics that are present within the insurance sector (Njegomir & Marovic, 2012).

8.1. TECHNOLOGY INNOVATIONS IN RISK MANAGEMENT

Learning Objectives

- To understand the impact of artificial intelligence and machine learning on enhancing risk assessment.
- To explore the integration of emerging technologies in developing proactive risk mitigation strategies.

Effective risk management is essential for enterprises to navigate uncertainties and sustain resilience in a world that is becoming increasingly complex and interconnected. The risks and challenges that businesses encounter change along with the business environment. Emerging technologies are transforming risk management approaches in a significant manner to address these issues (Nughrahanti, 2023).

Risk management offers a wide range of career options, from more technical roles to more strategic positions. Technical roles have attracted the interest of many MSBA students. For instance, risk analysts utilize data to forecast the likelihood of specific events, such as flash fires or opioid usage. Moreover, opportunities have arisen in the insurtech sector, which leverages technology to enhance the effectiveness and efficiency of the insurance industry. Addressing the common challenge of reducing administrative expenses through technology is a key focus for insurtech companies, with the ultimate goal of making insurance more accessible to everyone. Many MBA students expressed interest in pursuing careers as brokers or risk managers in strategic positions. The primary distinction between a risk manager and a broker is that the former acts as a mediator, establishing relationships with various businesses, while the latter works within a single company, advising staff members on viable opportunities and potential risks (Mishchenko et al., 2021).

Insurance offered at the point of sale that reduces risks inherent in goods or services is known as embedded insurance. Examples include home insurance provided by Zillow, renters' insurance offered at the time of lease signing, and insurance offered by Tesla at the time of automobile purchase. Companies such as Tesla, which gather data on driver behavior to improve their predictions and estimates for auto insurance, may benefit from embedded insurance. Businesses that provide embedded insurance may have problems protecting proprietary data and maintaining data privacy (Ali et al., 2017).

Did you know?

In the food industry, there have been instances where companies insure the taste testers' palates. This ensures that if a taster loses their ability to taste due to illness or injury, the company is compensated for the potential impact on product quality.

8.1.1. Evolution of Technology in Risk Management

Traditional risk management techniques have undergone a paradigm shift due to technological advancements. The industry has transitioned from conventional actuarial approaches to sophisticated data analytics, utilizing technology to identify, evaluate, and manage risks with unprecedented precision. This development highlights the constant interaction between technology and risk management techniques (Nikolova et al., 2015).

Risk management has its origins in conventional actuarial techniques, which rely on historical data and statistical models to assess and mitigate risks. While these methodologies laid the groundwork for risk assessment, they were limited in their ability to handle the increasing complexity and interconnectedness of risks in the modern environment.

In the latter half of the 20th century, there was a shift towards greater emphasis on quantitative methods. The growing importance of financial models and mathematical frameworks has empowered risk managers to accurately identify and quantify risks. This period marked a significant departure from relying solely on past information, prioritizing a forward-looking and data-driven perspective (Bowers & Khorakian, 2014).

The pivotal moment in risk management occurred when technology was incorporated into conventional methodologies. The introduction of computers and advanced software has made it possible to handle large amounts of data, giving risk experts the ability to assess information immediately. This integration enabled a more agile and adaptable approach to risk assessment.

The emergence of data analytics in the 21st century marked a significant milestone in the evolution of risk management. Organizations were able to utilize big data analytics to effectively utilize massive and diverse datasets, revealing previously elusive patterns and relationships. Data analysis has become a fundamental aspect of successful risk management methods, since it allows for the identification of practical and useful information (Culp, 2008).

The current risk management landscape is defined by the widespread impact of artificial intelligence (AI) and machine learning (ML). These technologies have introduced an era of predictive modeling, allowing risk experts to predict potential risks with exceptional precision. The AI and ML technologies improve decision-making processes and support a proactive approach to risk management through their adaptive learning capabilities.

Organizations are already embracing comprehensive risk management frameworks to address the growing intricacy of risks. These frameworks encompass a wide range of risks, such as financial, operational, strategic, and developing risks. Technology is crucial in combining various data sources, allowing for a complete understanding of possible risks and possibilities (Hansen et al., 2007).

8.1.2. Artificial Intelligence and Machine Learning

Artificial Intelligence (AI) and Machine Learning (ML) play a crucial role in combating fraud in the insurance sector. These technologies employ advanced algorithms to detect abnormal patterns indicative of fraudulent activities. By continuously analyzing historical data, AI systems can effectively adapt to evolving fraudulent strategies, providing insurers with a powerful tool to mitigate financial losses.

The integration of AI and ML technologies empowers insurers to deliver highly personalized consumer experiences. By analyzing consumer data, preferences, and behaviors, insurers can tailor insurance policies to meet individual needs. This not only enhances customer satisfaction but also fosters greater client loyalty and retention (Zia & Kalia, 2022).

However, the incorporation of AI and ML in the insurance sector requires careful consideration of ethical implications and the implementation of measures to address bias. As these technologies heavily rely on historical data, they are susceptible to perpetuating existing biases. Insurers must establish procedures that ensure fairness, transparency, and accountability in their AI and ML systems.

Furthermore, regulatory compliance in the insurance industry demands a proactive approach due to the utilization of AI and ML. Ensuring the transparency of algorithms is essential to meet regulatory obligations. Insurers must strike a delicate balance by leveraging sophisticated technologies while providing clear justifications for their actions, in accordance with regulatory requirements (Biju et al., 2023).

8.1.3. Big Data Analytics

The emergence of big data analytics has transformed risk management approaches by facilitating instantaneous processing and analysis of extensive and varied datasets. This skill not only expedites decision-making processes but also offers a more nuanced comprehension of intricate risk variables. The application of big data analytics enables a proactive and adaptable approach to risk assessment.

The huge quantity of data produced by enterprises presents both advantageous prospects and complex obstacles in risk management. Big data analytics empowers firms to derive important insights from both structured and unstructured data sources. Through the analysis of data patterns and correlations, companies can proactively identify potential risks, evaluate their consequences, and develop suitable measures to mitigate those risks. Big data analytics improves risk forecasting abilities, enabling firms to make well-informed decisions and optimize their risk management processes (Dicuonzo et al., 2019) (Figure 8.1).

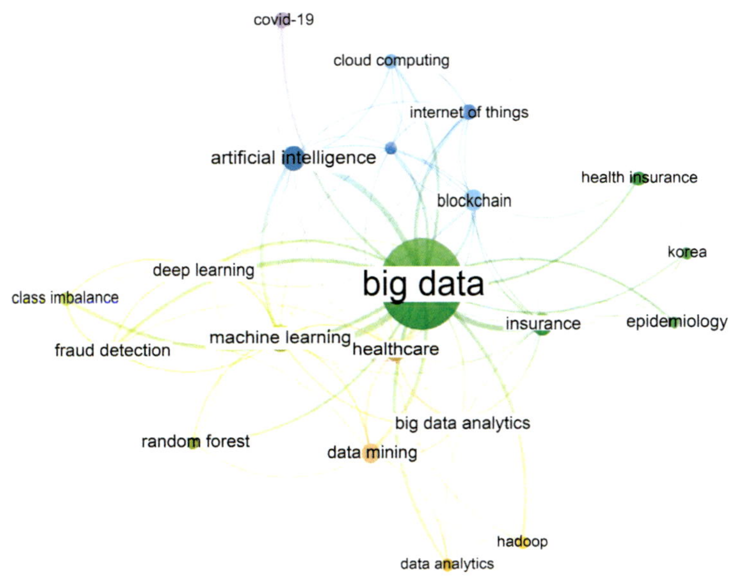

Figure 8.1. Representation of big data in the insurance industry. (Source: Nejla Ellili, Creative Commons License)

Big Data Analytics offers a strong foundation for predictive modeling in the field of risk management. Insurers can achieve a higher level of accuracy in risk prediction by utilizing extensive datasets that include historical, real-time, and external data sources. This proactive approach enables the timely implementation of risk mitigation solutions, aligning with the industry's growing demand for forward-thinking risk management (Berthele, 2018).

Big Data Analytics allows risk managers to gain immediate insights, facilitating flexible decision-making processes. In a dynamic and unpredictable environment, the ability to analyze and interpret data in real time enhances the industry's capability to effectively address emerging threats. This capability becomes even more crucial considering the development of global issues.

Big Data Analytics empowers insurers to go beyond generic techniques, ushering in an era of personalized products and tailored solutions. By analyzing detailed data on consumer behavior, preferences, and risk profiles, insurers can create customized insurance policies. This trend aligns with the industry's shift towards increased customization and a focus on consumer needs (Araz et al., 2020).

Big Data Analytics is crucial in managing cyber risks since they constantly change and develop. Insurers can improve their ability to detect and understand cybersecurity risks by consistently monitoring and analyzing large volumes of relevant data. This enables businesses to proactively address cyber risks, which is crucial considering the increasing frequency and complexity of cyber-attacks (Senousy et al., 2018).

Big Data Analytics enables insurers to provide openness and accountability, hence facilitating strong regulatory compliance. Regulatory authorities are increasingly requiring detailed information about insurers' risk management strategies, and the use of Big Data Analytics allows for thorough reporting. Nevertheless, this pattern also presents a difficulty in terms of maneuvering intricate regulatory environments and guaranteeing adherence across several countries.

Remember

After the tragic events of September 11, 2001, there was a surge in the demand for terrorism insurance. This event significantly impacted the insurance industry, leading to the development of new products to address emerging risks.

8.1.4. Block Chain Technology

The advent of blockchain technology has proven to be a revolutionary influence, especially in domains such as fraud mitigation and transaction visibility. The decentralized and unchangeable nature of blockchain guarantees the establishment of secure and transparent networks, thereby minimizing the occurrence of fraudulent acts. The implementation of blockchain technology in risk management enhances the overall reliability of procedures, fostering confidence and responsibility (Pagano et al., 2019).

The defining characteristic of blockchain is its ability to establish trust and transparency in a decentralized manner. Smart contracts, which are automatically executed upon meeting predetermined conditions, enhance the efficiency of insurance contracts. This trend aligns with the industry's increasing focus on transparent and trust-based partnerships, creating a more responsible and reliable risk management environment (Tarr, 2018) (Figure 8.2).

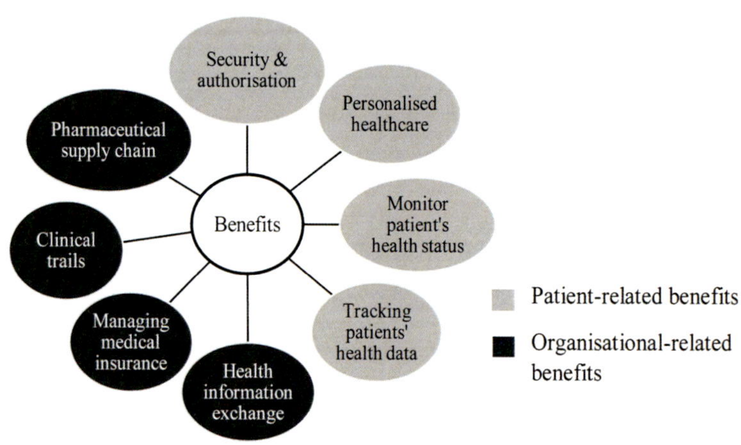

Figure 8.2. Diagram of blockchain technology benefits in health industry. (Source: Israa, Creative Commons License)

Blockchain enhances the efficiency of claims processing by establishing an immutable and transparent log of transactions. Smart contracts enable the automatic settlement of claims, thereby decreasing administrative workload and eliminating delays.

Blockchain is becoming a prominent trend in claims management, revolutionizing the existing practices in response to the industry's demand for quicker and more effective processes (Popovic et al., 2020).

The cryptographic features of blockchain enhance security in the storing and processing of data and transactions. This not only mitigates the likelihood of data breaches but also enhances fraud prevention mechanisms. The immutability of the Blockchain ledger ensures a tamper-resistant record, thereby improving the industry's capacity to combat fraudulent actions. This is particularly important given the always increasing cyber risks (Brophy, 2020).

The rise of interoperability and industry collaboration is driven by Blockchain's ability to establish a shared and secure ledger that can be accessed by numerous parties. This promotes cooperation among insurers, reinsurers, and other parties involved, simplifying procedures, and minimizing unnecessary repetition. Nevertheless, the task of obtaining extensive collaboration within the industry presents a difficulty, necessitating the establishment of standards and coordinated endeavors throughout the sector (Amponsah et al., 2021).

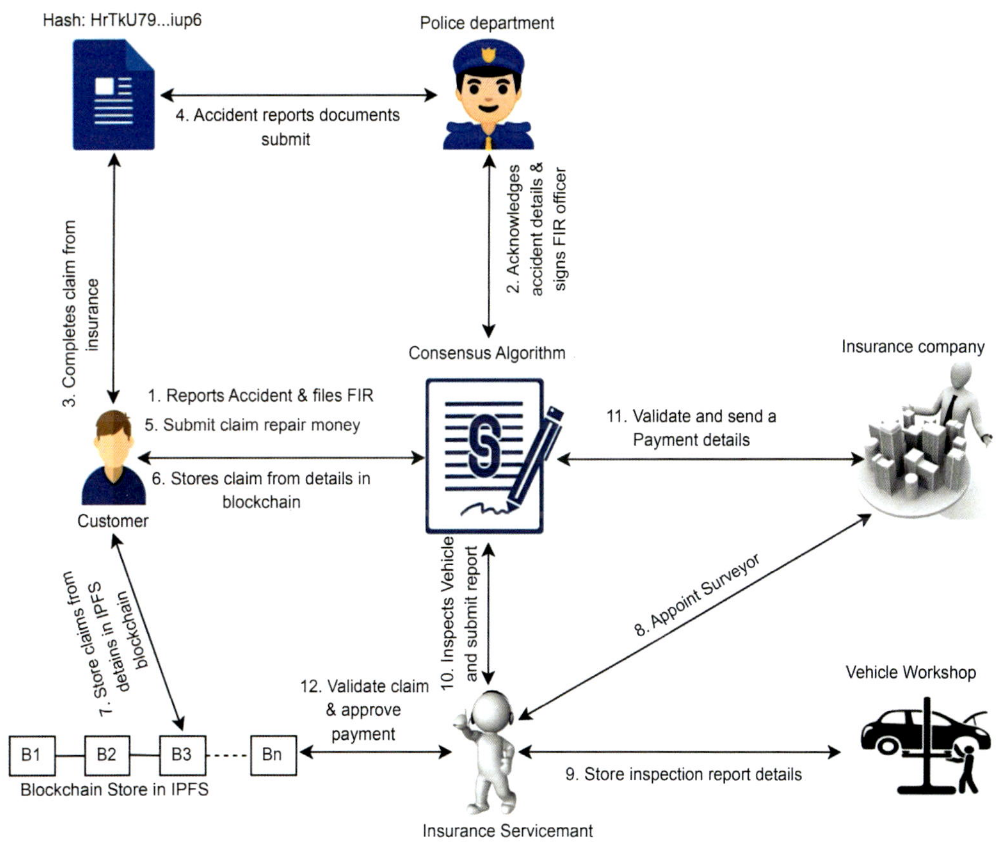

Figure 8.3. Illustration of vehicle insurance framework based on blockchain technology. (Source: Vincent Charles, Creative Commons License

Blockchain enables the process of converting assets and insurance products into tokens, which enables the possibility of dividing ownership into smaller fractions and conducting trade. This trend adds liquidity to historically illiquid assets and offers creative opportunities in establishing and trading insurance-linked instruments. Nevertheless, the presence of regulatory obstacles and the necessity for a strong legal structure for tokenized assets persist as obstacles that must be resolved (Figure 8.3).

Smart contracts, implemented on Blockchain, provide automatic adherence to predetermined laws and regulations. This not only decreases the probability of human errors but also guarantees compliance with regulatory requirements. The current shift in the industry towards automated compliance is in line with the urgent need to navigate through a regulatory landscape that is becoming more and more intricate (Gatteschi et al., 2018).

The decentralized nature of blockchain technology enables individuals to exert enhanced control over their data and identities. This phenomenon addresses the increasing apprehensions over data privacy and security by empowering individuals with greater ownership and authority over their personal information. Nevertheless, it is crucial to carefully deliberate the problems pertaining to legal frameworks and the establishment of standards for decentralized identity management (Shetty et al., 2022).

8.1.5. Cyber Risk Management

The increasing and complex range of potential risks in the digital realm requires a concentrated emphasis on the management of cyber risks. Technological advancements in this field encompass the creation of sophisticated cybersecurity tools, threat intelligence systems, and proactive methods to protect critical information. The ongoing development of these technologies is essential to ensure the ability of enterprises to withstand rapidly changing cyber-attacks (Figure 8.4).

Figure 8.4. Diagram of cybersecurity risk management plan. (Source: Meeba, Creative Commons License)

Considering the widespread adoption of digitalization and networked systems, cybersecurity has emerged as a crucial component of risk management (Figure 8.5). Organizations are confronted with a growing number of risks stemming from cyber assaults, data breaches, and vulnerabilities in information security. Deploying resilient cybersecurity protocols is crucial in safeguarding confidential data, proprietary assets, and client records. Advanced cybersecurity technologies, including threat intelligence, encryption, and behavioral analytics, play a crucial role in detecting and reducing cyber hazards (Kosub, 2015).

Figure 8.5. Examples of risk management in cybersecurity. (Source: Meeba, Creative Commons License)

8.2. IMPACT OF GLOBALIZATION ON INSURANCE PRACTICES

Learning Objectives

- To examine the implications of globalization on the insurance industry and its practices.
- To understand how cross-border risks and opportunities influence traditional models of risk assessment.
- To explore the role of emerging markets in shaping the dynamics of insurance practices on a global scale.
- To examine the implications of globalization on the insurance industry and its practices.
- To understand how cross-border risks and opportunities influence traditional models of risk assessment.
- To explore the role of emerging markets in shaping the dynamics of insurance practices on a global scale.

The advent of globalization has had a significant impact on the insurance industry, leading to the emergence of a new era characterized by interconnected markets, diverse risks, and a changing regulatory landscape. This impact is evident in various aspects of the insurance industry, shaping corporate strategy, risk assessments, and client interactions.

One important outcome of globalization on insurance practices is the expansion of risk horizons. Insurers now face a wider range of risks originating from different geographical regions and industries. The expanded scope of potential risks necessitates a more sophisticated approach to risk evaluation, as insurance companies must navigate the diverse cultural, economic, and regulatory differences across international borders (Olasehinde & Balcilar, 2020).

Furthermore, the process of globalization has accelerated the growth of international firms, resulting in an increased demand for complex insurance solutions. Insurers must now develop plans that provide comprehensive coverage across various jurisdictions, taking into account differences in legislative frameworks, business practices, and geopolitical considerations. This phenomenon demonstrates the industry's ability to adapt to the evolving needs of multinational corporations operating in a complex and interconnected global environment.

The increased interdependence facilitated by globalization has made supply networks more complex and vulnerable to disturbances. Insurers are currently faced with the task of addressing the difficulties of reducing risks linked to worldwide supply chains, which encompass geopolitical conflicts, natural calamities, and political instability. The intricate nature of the situation highlights the significance of adopting a comprehensive risk management strategy that goes beyond conventional limitations (Labonte et al., 2011).

Furthermore, globalization has a significant influence on the regulatory environment. Insurers encounter the difficulty of complying with numerous regulatory systems in various nations, each with its own distinct set of compliance obligations. To successfully navigate this complex network of rules, one must possess a comprehensive comprehension of worldwide regulatory patterns and the capacity to adjust to changing compliance criteria.

PRACTICE PROBLEM

A traditional insurance company is considering implementing artificial intelligence (AI) and machine learning in its risk assessment process. Two potential benefits of adopting these technological innovations are improved accuracy in risk assessment and increased efficiency in processing large amounts of data. However, one challenge they might face is ensuring the privacy and security of sensitive customer information.

SOLUTIONS TO PRACTICE PROBLEM

Benefits:

Improved Accuracy: AI can analyze vast datasets to identify patterns, leading to more accurate risk assessments.

Efficiency Gains: Machine learning algorithms can automate routine tasks, reducing the time and resources needed for risk management.

Challenge:

Implementing new technologies may raise concerns about the security of sensitive customer data.

8.3. REGULATORY CHANGES AND COMPLIANCE CHANGES

Learning Objectives

- To analyze the evolving regulatory landscape and its impact on insurance practices.
- To understand the role of technological advancements in addressing compliance challenges within the insurance sector.

The focus is on regulatory changes and compliance dynamics in risk management and insurance, among rising trends and future problems.

8.3.1. Evolving Regulatory Frameworks

The risk management and insurance sector encounters a changing set of regulatory frameworks that adapt to dynamic economic, technical, and geopolitical changes. Insurers must keep up with changing compliance requirements as regulatory bodies adjust to new risks. This tendency highlights the industry's requirement for adaptability in negotiating regulatory modifications and aggressively tackling rising compliance obstacles (Morgan & Soin, 2018).

8.3.2. Technology Integration and Regulatory Compliance

The incorporation of technology in risk management adds an additional level of intricacy to regulatory compliance. Insurers are using modern technologies like artificial intelligence and big data analytics. Regulatory agencies have the responsibility of upgrading frameworks to guarantee ethical use, data protection, and transparency. To successfully navigate this intersection, industry actors must synchronize technological innovation with the changing regulatory demands (Bamberger, 2009).

8.3.3. Globalization and Harmonization of Regulations

Amidst the growing trend of globalization, regulatory modifications frequently transcend national boundaries. The trend of harmonizing legislation across different jurisdictions is shaping the future of risk management and insurance. Insurers that operate in several locations must confront a variety of compliance regulations, which makes it necessary to adopt a strategic approach to maintain consistency and comply with global standards (Heinmiller & Woodrow, 2000).

8.3.4. Sustainable and ESG Compliance

The incorporation of Environmental, Social, and Governance (ESG) aspects into risk management procedures signifies an increasing focus on sustainable and ethical company behavior. Insurers are facing the difficulty of adapting their operations to meet the evolving sustainability standards as regulatory bodies are now including ESG concerns in compliance criteria (Khovrak, 2020).

8.3.5. Data Privacy and Consumer Protection

With the increasing importance of data in risk management, legal reforms are placing greater emphasis on data privacy and consumer protection. Adhering to data protection standards is crucial for preserving trust and credibility in a context where privacy concerns are intensified. Insurers are required to navigate an intricate framework of regulations, carefully managing the utilization of client data while ensuring privacy protections (Ohlhausen & Okuliar, 2015).

8.3.6. Insurtech and Regulatory Innovation

Insurtech disrupts conventional regulatory frameworks by introducing cutting-edge business models and technologies. Regulatory authorities are obligated to adjust to these technological changes, creating an atmosphere that promotes innovation while protecting consumer interests. Insurers need to adapt to the changing regulatory environment in order to take advantage of the benefits offered by Insurtech, while also ensuring that they comply with regulations (Stoeckli et al., 2018).

In response to the emergence of Insurtech, regulatory authorities are also undergoing innovative changes to accommodate the evolving environment. Regulatory innovation encompasses the creation of systems that promote innovation while guaranteeing consumer protection, financial stability, and adherence to current legislation. Regulatory sandboxes offer a controlled setting in which Insurtech startups can experiment and improve their products without adhering to all regulatory requirements. This facilitates the process of testing and learning. In addition, regulators are progressively adopting technology to improve their ability to monitor and enforce regulations. The partnership between Insurtech businesses and regulatory agencies is essential in attaining an equilibrium that fosters innovation, protects consumer interests, and upholds the stability of the insurance industry. Regulatory innovation will be essential in establishing a flexible and adaptable framework that promotes innovation and maintains the integrity of the insurance business, as the Insurtech wave continues to grow (Chatzara, 2020).

8.3.7. Compliance Automation and Regtech

The integration of Regulatory Technology (Regtech) is the future of risk management in regulatory compliance. Automation and digital technologies optimize compliance operations, improving both efficiency and accuracy. Insurers must adopt these technology innovations to fulfill compliance obligations and effectively handle and reduce emerging risks related to non-compliance (Freij, 2020).

8.4. FUTURE TRENDS IN INSURANCE PRODUCTS

Learning Objectives

- To explore emerging trends in insurance products, including the integration of artificial intelligence and machine learning.
- To understand the shift towards personalized insurance products tailored to individual behaviors and needs.
- To explore emerging trends in insurance products, including the integration of artificial intelligence and machine learning.
- To understand the shift towards personalized insurance products tailored to individual behaviors and needs.

It is crucial to thoroughly investigate the upcoming trends that are influencing the creation and provision of insurance products, considering the ongoing dynamic changes in the risk management and insurance market.

Keyword

IoT (Internet of Things): The Internet of Things (IoT) refers to a network of interconnected devices embedded with sensors and software, allowing them to exchange data and communicate over the internet. These devices, ranging from everyday objects to industrial machinery, collect and share information, enabling automation, remote monitoring, and data-driven decision-making. IoT aims to create a more efficient and connected world by facilitating seamless communication and interaction between physical objects.

8.4.1. Parametric Insurance Solutions

The rising use of parametric insurance solutions is a significant trend for insurance products in the future. These solutions provide coverage based on predetermined characteristics instead of traditional loss assessment, thanks to developments in data analytics and modeling. This change addresses issues with claim accuracy and efficiency by enabling quicker claim processing and increased transparency (Lin & Kwon, 2020).

8.4.2. Integration of IoT for Risk Management

In the future of insurance products, the Internet of Things (IoT) is expected to be crucial, especially for risk management. Real-time risk monitoring is made possible by the integration of IoT devices, such as wearable devices in health insurance or telematics in auto insurance. With the use of this information, insurers can create individualized risk evaluations and motivate policyholders to take precautionary measures (Fazio et al., 2014).

The overall operational efficiency of healthcare systems and risk management techniques are being greatly improved by the integration of the Internet of Things (IoT) (Figure 8.6). Using wearables with Internet of Things capabilities, including health trackers and smartwatches, for remote patient monitoring is one important use case. These devices are particularly helpful for managing chronic diseases since they continuously gather and transmit real-time patient data, enabling proactive healthcare treatments and the early diagnosis of potential health risks. Predictive maintenance for medical equipment is another crucial topic (Koduru et al., 2018).

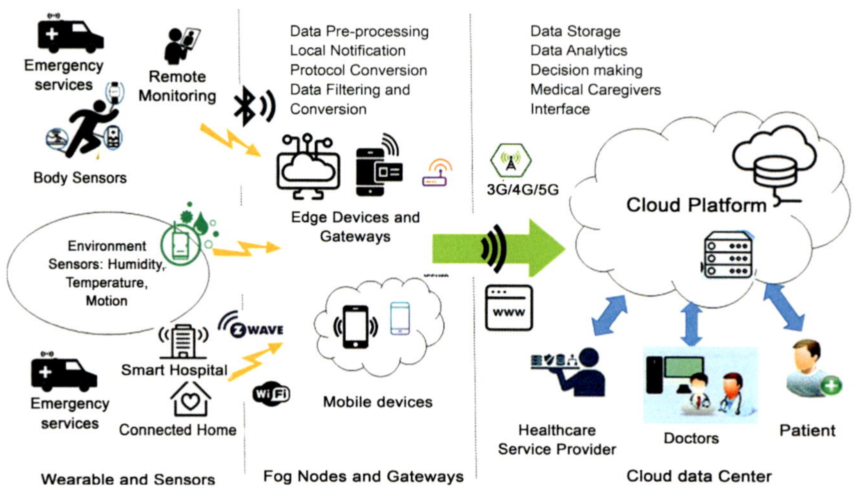

Figure 8.6. Diagram of integration of IoT for healthcare services. (Source: Dinesh, Creative Commons License)

IoT ensures the dependability and peak performance of vital equipment by detecting and resolving possible problems with medical devices before they result in breakdowns through real-time monitoring and predictive analytics. Furthermore, when utilizing IoT in the healthcare industry, data security and privacy must be prioritized. To protect sensitive patient data and reduce the risk of data breaches, strong security procedures and adherence to healthcare data protection laws are essential. IoT is also crucial for supply chain management as it monitors factors such as inventory levels and temperature. This ensures the timely replacement of medical supplies and reduces the likelihood of drug or vaccine deterioration.

Moreover, IoT-powered smart sensors can monitor hand hygiene compliance and facilitate efficient contact tracing during outbreaks, both of which enhance infection control and create a safer hospital environment. Despite the numerous advantages, the seamless and secure integration of IoT in healthcare systems requires addressing issues such as interoperability, data security concerns, and regulatory compliance complexity (Christofilou & Chatzara, 2019).

8.4.3. Eco-system Driven Insurance Models

It is anticipated that future insurance products will adopt ecosystem-driven strategies in place of more conventional coverage models. Partnerships between insurers and other service providers might result in all-encompassing solutions that go beyond simple financial protection. To handle growing risks holistically, insurance products could be combined with wellness initiatives or smart home technologies (Figure 8.7).

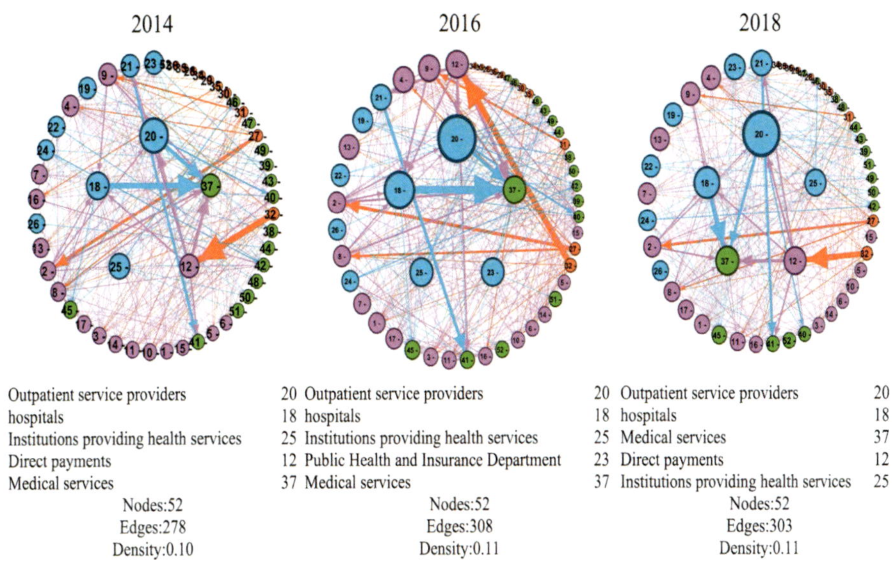

Figure 8.7. Diagram of network of elements of health insurance ecosystem in the NHA. (Source: Rohaneh, Creative Commons License)

This model's emphasis on collaborations and partnerships is one of its main characteristics. To build interconnected ecosystems, insurers collaborate with technology firms, healthcare providers, and other service providers. Health insurers might, for instance, work with telemedicine platforms or creators of wellness apps to provide policyholders with comprehensive healthcare options. These ecosystems' interconnection improves policyholder value propositions and opens new revenue streams for insurers (Baumgartner, 2007).

Furthermore, a customer-centric approach is a common feature of ecosystem-driven models. Insurers can address more facets of their clients' life and build enduring relationships and consumer loyalty by offering a wide range of services beyond standard insurance coverage. For example, home automation, financial planning, and health and wellness services might all be part of an insurance ecosystem.

These models provide great potential, but they also come with difficulties, especially when it comes to data security, privacy, and building strong partnerships amongst many stakeholders. Nevertheless, ecosystem-driven insurance models offer a potential path forward for the insurance sector as long as insurers keep up with evolving client expectations and make use of technology breakthroughs. They could reshape the conventional insurance landscape, generating greater value for policyholders and advancing an integrated, customer-focused approach to risk management (Zeier et al., 2022).

8.4.4. Personalized and On-Demand Coverage

Insurance products of the future are expected to become more flexible and individualized. Thanks to advancements in data analytics, insurers now have the ability to offer personalized products by tailoring coverage to each individual's risk profile. Additionally, on-demand insurance models provide policyholders with greater control and the ability to adapt to changing risk environments, as coverage can be activated or deactivated as needed.

For instance, telematics in auto insurance enables real-time tracking of driving habits, allowing insurers to offer customized rates based on actual behavior rather than statistical averages. Similarly, health insurers can utilize data from wearable devices to develop personalized wellness programs that encourage policyholders to lead healthier lives. Digital platforms enable on-demand coverage, granting customers the freedom and affordability to activate or deactivate coverage as required. This flexible approach aligns well with the evolving expectations of modern customers who seek prompt access to services and tailored solutions.

Future insurance products should be more tailored, efficient, and responsive to the diverse needs of policyholders, as long as the insurance industry continues to embrace these trends (Bosomworth et al., 2017).

8.5. ADDRESSING FUTURE CHALLENGES IN RISK MANAGEMENT

Learning Objectives

- To understand emerging trends and technologies shaping future challenges in risk management
- To develop strategic skills in designing and implementing adaptive risk management frameworks

To effectively navigate the ever-changing world of risk management and insurance, it is crucial to adopt proactive approaches and embrace new trends. The integration of cutting-edge technologies such as big data analytics, machine learning, and artificial intelligence should be prioritized in the sector.

i. Cyber risk preparedness becomes paramount, necessitating sophisticated incident response strategies and threat detection systems to safeguard sensitive data and maintain customer confidence.

ii. Efficient governance and regulatory compliance require staying abreast of evolving legislation and promoting transparent reporting.

iii. In order to align insurers with sustainable practices, it is imperative to incorporate Environmental, Social, and Governance (ESG) factors into risk assessments and underwriting procedures (Martin & Halachmi, 2012).

iv. The insurance sector must also develop innovative insurance products and integrate climate risk assessments to address the challenges posed by climate change.

v. Enhancing talent diversity and expertise, particularly in the fields of data analytics and emerging technologies, improves the industry's ability to tackle complex problems.

vi. The industry's resilience in the face of uncertainty is further strengthened by robust pandemic preparedness, customer-centric innovation, and a commitment to openness.

These strategic efforts lay the foundation for overcoming challenges and establishing long-term sustainability as the risk management and insurance landscape continues to evolve (Lamberti et al., 2018).

SUMMARY

- Technological innovations in risk management are shaping the future of the insurance industry, with a focus on leveraging artificial intelligence and machine learning for more accurate and predictive risk assessments.
- Globalization has introduced new dynamics, with cross-border risks challenging traditional methods of evaluating and mitigating risks. Emerging markets play a significant role in reshaping insurance practices, demanding flexibility and responsiveness.
- Regulatory changes and compliance challenges underscore the need for a dynamic and adaptable risk management framework. The evolving regulatory landscape, coupled with advancements in technology, requires insurance professionals to stay vigilant and agile in their approach to compliance.
- Future trends in insurance products point towards a more personalized approach, tailoring coverage to individual behaviors and needs. The adoption of blockchain technology ensures transparency and security in insurance transactions, fostering trust among stakeholders.
- Addressing future challenges in risk management involves not only fortifying cybersecurity measures but also enhancing data analytics capabilities. Proactive risk mitigation strategies, informed by advanced analytics, are crucial in navigating an increasingly complex risk landscape.
- Collaboration within the industry is key to overcoming challenges and standardizing best practices. By sharing information and collectively addressing issues such as data security and compliance, the insurance sector can create a more resilient and adaptive ecosystem.

MULTIPLE CHOICE QUESTIONS

1. **What is a key role of blockchain technology in insurance?**
   a. Transparent and secure transactions
   b. Enhancing taste buds
   c. Alien abduction coverage
   d. Insuring vocal cords
2. **Which historical practice contributed to the development of early risk management?**
   a. Coffeehouse discussions
   b. Tea ceremonies
   c. Bowling tournaments
   d. Jousting competitions
3. **What does Lloyd's of London have a reputation for underwriting?**
   a. Tastebuds
   b. Alien Abduction

c. Werewolf attacks

d. All of the above

4. Which event led to an increased demand for terrorism insurance in the insurance industry?

a. The invention of coffee

b. The moon landing

c. September 11, 2001

d. The discovery of new planet

5. How did globalization influence insurance practices?

a. Reduced need for cross-border risk assessment

b. Increased reliance on traditional assessment models

c. Elevated importance of emerging markets

d. Decreased interconnectedness in the industry

REVIEW QUESTIONS

1. Discuss the impact of technological innovations on risk management in the insurance industry. How are artificial intelligence and machine learning being utilized for risk assessment?
2. Examine the influence of globalization on insurance practices. How do cross-border risks and emerging markets shape the dynamics of the insurance industry globally?
3. Analyze the regulatory changes discussed in the chapter and their implications for risk management. How can the insurance sector adapt to evolving regulatory landscapes and compliance challenges?
4. Explore the phenomenon of Insurtech and its impact on traditional insurance models. What challenges and opportunities does the rise of Insurtech present to the industry?
5. Discuss the challenges associated with addressing cybersecurity in the context of risk management. How can the insurance industry enhance its cybersecurity measures to mitigate evolving cyber threats?

Answers to Multiple Questions

1(b) 2. (a) 3. (d) 4. (c) 5. (c)

REFERENCES

1. Abusaimeh, H., & Shkoukani, M., (2012). Survey of web application and internet security threats. *International Journal of Computer Science and Network Security, 12*(12), 67–76.

2. Aghav, S. A., & Bedi, R. R., (2014). An enhanced authentication protocol resistant to password stealing and reuse attack. *International Journal of Engineering Research, 3*(6), 1–20.
3. Alenezi, M., & Javed, Y., (2016). Open source web application security: A static analysis approach. In: *2016 International Conference on Engineering & MIS (ICEMIS)* (Vol. 1, No.1, pp. 1–5). IEEE.
4. Ali, S., Shahzad, S. K., & Javed, H., (2009). SQLIPA: An authentication mechanism against SQL injection. *European Journal of Scientific Research, 38*(4), 604–611.
5. Balasundaram, I., & Ramaraj, E., (2011). An authentication mechanism to prevent SQL injection attacks. *International Journal of Computer Applications, 19*(1), 123–127.
6. Bandhakavi, S., Bisht, P., Madhusudan, P., & Venkatakrishnan, V. N., (2007). CANDID: Preventing SQL injection attacks using dynamic candidate evaluations. In: *Proceedings of the 14th ACM Conference on Computer and Communications Security* (Vol. 1, No. 1, pp. 12–24).
7. Bhavani, A. B., (2013). *Cross-Site Scripting Attacks on Android WebView* (pp. 1–20). arXiv preprint arXiv:1304.7451.
8. Boyd, S. W., & Keromytis, A. D., (2004). SQLrand: Preventing SQL injection attacks. In: *Applied Cryptography and Network Security: Second International Conference, ACNS 2004, Yellow Mountain, China; Proceedings 2* (pp. 292–302). Springer Berlin Heidelberg.
9. Buehrer, G., Weide, B. W., & Sivilotti, P. A., (2005). Using parse tree validation to prevent SQL injection attacks. In: *Proceedings of the 5th International Workshop on Software Engineering and Middleware* (Vol. 1, No. 1, pp. 106–113).
10. Catal, C., Akbulut, A., Ekenoglu, E., & Alemdaroglu, M., (2017). Development of a software vulnerability prediction web service based on artificial neural networks. In: *Trends and Applications in Knowledge Discovery and Data Mining: PAKDD 2017 Workshops, MLSDA, BDM, DM-BPM Jeju, South Korea; Revised Selected Papers 21* (pp. 59–67). Springer International Publishing.
11. Curphey, M., & Arawo, R., (2006). Web application security assessment tools. *IEEE Security & Privacy, 4*(4), 32–41.
12. Dahse, J., & Holz, T., (2014). Static detection of {second-order} vulnerabilities in web applications. In: *23rd USENIX Security Symposium (USENIX Security 14)* (Vol. 1, No. 1, pp. 989–1003).
13. Dasmohapatra, S., & Priyadarshini, S. B. B., (2022). A comprehensive study on SQL injection attacks, their mode, detection, and prevention. In: *Proceedings of Second Doctoral Symposium on Computational Intelligence: DoSCI 2021* (pp. 617–632). Springer Singapore.
14. Deepa, G., & Thilagam, P. S., (2016). Securing web applications from injection and logic vulnerabilities: Approaches and challenges. *Information and Software Technology, 74*, 160–180.
15. Devi, S. M., & Geetha, M., (2013). OPass: Attractive presentation of user authentication protocol with resist to password reuse attacks. *International Journal of Computer*

Science and Mobile Computing, 8(2), 174–180.

16. Di Lucca, G. A., Fasolino, A. R., Mastoianni, M., & Tramontana, P., (2004). Identifying cross site scripting vulnerabilities in web applications. In: *Proceedings Sixth IEEE International Workshop on Web Site Evolution* (Vol. 1, No. 1, pp. 71–80). IEEE.
17. Fonseca, J., & Vieira, M., (2008). Mapping software faults with web security vulnerabilities. In: *2008 IEEE International Conference on Dependable Systems and Networks With FTCS and DCC (DSN)* (Vol. 1, No. 1, pp. 257–266). IEEE.
18. Garcia, V. H., Monroy, R., & Quintana, M., (2006). Web attack detection using ID3. In: *IFIP World Computer Congress, TC 12* (pp. 323–332). Boston, MA: Springer US.
19. Gollmann, D., (2008). Securing web applications. *Information Security Technical Report, 13*(1), 1–9.
20. Gupta, S., & Gupta, B. B., (2017). Cross-site scripting (XSS) attacks and defense mechanisms: Classification and state-of-the-art. *International Journal of System Assurance Engineering and Management, 8*, 512–530.
21. Halfond, W. G., Viegas, J., & Orso, A., (2006). A classification of SQL-injection attacks and countermeasures. In: *Proceedings of the IEEE International Symposium on Secure Software Engineering* (Vol. 1, pp. 13–15). IEEE.
22. Hydara, I., Sultan, A. B. M., Zulzalil, H., & Admodisastro, N., (2015). Current state of research on cross-site scripting (XSS)–A systematic literature review. *Information and Software Technology, 58*, 170–186.
23. Jovanovic, N., Kruegel, C., & Kirda, E., (2006). Pixy: A static analysis tool for detecting web application vulnerabilities. In: *2006 IEEE Symposium on Security and Privacy (S&P'06)* (pp. 6-pp). IEEE.
24. Kals, S., Kirda, E., Kruegel, C., & Jovanovic, N., (2006). Secubat: A web vulnerability scanner. In: *Proceedings of the 15th International Conference on World Wide Web* (Vol. 1, No. 1, pp. 247–256).
25. Kapodistria, H., Mitropoulos, S., & Douligeris, C., (2011). An advanced web attack detection and prevention tool. *Information Management & Computer Security, 19*(5), 280–299.
26. Kassim, M. M., & Sujitha, A., (2013). Procurepass: A user authentication protocol to resist password stealing and password reuse attack. In: *2013 International Symposium on Computational and Business Intelligence* (Vol. 1, No. 1, pp. 31–34). IEEE.
27. Kaur, P., & Kour, K. P., (2015). SQL injection: Study and augmentation. In: *2015 International Conference on Signal Processing, Computing and Control (ISPCC)* (Vol. 1, No. 1, pp. 102–107). IEEE.
28. Khalid, M. N., Farooq, H., Iqbal, M., Alam, M. T., & Rasheed, K., (2019). Predicting web vulnerabilities in web applications based on machine learning. In: *Intelligent Technologies and Applications: First International Conference, INTAP 2018, Bahawalpur, Pakistan, Revised Selected Papers 1* (pp. 473–484). Springer Singapore.
29. Kirda, E., Jovanovic, N., Kruegel, C., & Vigna, G., (2009). Client-side cross-site scripting protection. *Computers & Security, 28*(7), 592–604.

30. Kothari, N., Mahajan, R., Millstein, T., Govindan, R., & Musuvathi, M., (2011). Finding protocol manipulation attacks. In: *Proceedings of the ACM SIGCOMM 2011 Conference* (Vol. 1, No. 1, pp. 26–37).
31. Kour, H., & Sharma, L. S., (2016). Tracing out cross site scripting vulnerabilities in modern scripts. *International Journal of Advanced Networking and Applications, 7*(5), 2862.
32. Kumar, P., (2013). The multi-tier architecture for developing secure website with detection and prevention of SQL-injection attacks. *International Journal of Computer Applications, 62*(9), 1–20.
33. Kumar, S., Mahajan, R., Kumar, N., & Khatri, S. K., (2017). A study on web application security and detecting security vulnerabilities. In: *2017 6th International Conference on Reliability, Infocom Technologies and Optimization (Trends and Future Directions) (ICRITO)* (Vol. 1, No. 1, pp. 451–455). IEEE.
34. Lawal, M. A., Sultan, A. B. M., & Shakiru, A. O., (2016). Systematic literature review on SQL injection attack. *International Journal of Soft Computing, 11*(1), 26–35.
35. Li, X., & Xue, Y., (2011). *A Survey on Web Application Security* (Vol. 25, No. 5, pp. 1–14). Nashville, TN USA.
36. Li, X., & Xue, Y., (2013). LogicScope: Automatic discovery of logic vulnerabilities within web applications. In: *Proceedings of the 8th ACM SIGSAC Symposium on Information, Computer and Communications Security* (Vol. 1, No. 1, pp. 481–486).
37. Liang, J., Zhao, W., & Ye, W., (2017). Anomaly-based web attack detection: A deep learning approach. In: *Proceedings of the 2017 VI International Conference on Network, Communication and Computing* (Vol. 1, No. 1, pp. 80–85).
38. Medeiros, I., Neves, N., & Correia, M., (2016). DEKANT: A static analysis tool that learns to detect web application vulnerabilities. In: *Proceedings of the 25th International Symposium on Software Testing and Analysis* (Vol. 1, No. 1, pp. 1–11).
39. Medhane, M. H. A. S., (2013). Efficient solution for SQL injection attack detection and prevention. *International Journal of Soft Computing and Engineering (IJSCE), 3*, 396–398.
40. Nasereddin, M., ALKhamaiseh, A., Qasaimeh, M., & Al-Qassas, R., (2023). A systematic review of detection and prevention techniques of SQL injection attacks. *Information Security Journal: A Global Perspective, 32*(4), 252–265.
41. Nikose, B. V., Gupta, R., & Shrivastav, G., (2014). Preventing password reuse attack using authentication protocol. *IJRDET, 2*(2), 31.
42. Noman, M., Iqbal, M., & Manzoor, A., (2020). A survey on detection and prevention of web vulnerabilities. *International Journal of Advanced Computer Science and Applications, 11*(6), 1–20.
43. Priyanka, A. K., & Smruthi, S. S., (2020). WebApplication vulnerabilities: Exploitation and prevention. In: *2020 Second International Conference on Inventive Research in Computing Applications (ICIRCA)* (Vol. 1, No. 1, pp. 729–734). IEEE.
44. Rodríguez, G. E., Benavides, D. E., Torres, J., Flores, P., & Fuertes, W., (2018).

Cookie scout: An analytic model for prevention of cross-site scripting (XSS) using a cookie classifier. In: *Proceedings of the International Conference on Information Technology & Systems (ICITS 2018)* (Vol. 1, No. 1, pp. 497–507). Springer International Publishing.

45. Rudman, R. J., (2010). Framework to identify and manage risks in Web 2.0 applications. *African Journal of Business Management, 4*(15), 3251.
46. Sadeghian, A., Zamani, M., & Abdullah, S. M., (2013). A taxonomy of SQL injection attacks. In: *2013 International Conference on Informatics and Creative Multimedia* (Vol. 1, No. 1, pp. 269–273). IEEE.
47. Sadotra, P., & Sharma, C., (2017). SQL injection impact on web server and their risk mitigation policy implementation techniques: An ultimate solution to prevent computer network from illegal intrusion. *International Journal of Advanced Research in Computer Science, 8*(3), 1–20.
48. Sadqi, Y., & Maleh, Y., (2022). A systematic review and taxonomy of web applications threats. *Information Security Journal: A Global Perspective, 31*(1), 1–27.
49. Sarmah, U., Bhattacharyya, D. K., & Kalita, J. K., (2018). A survey of detection methods for XSS attacks. *Journal of Network and Computer Applications, 118*, 113–143.
50. Sasirekha, K., (2013). Users cell phone and short message service to prevent password stealing and password reuse attacks. In: *International Conference on Engineering and Technology* (Vol. 1, No. 1, p. 102).
51. Scholte, T., Balzarotti, D., & Kirda, E., (2012). Have things changed now? An empirical study on input validation vulnerabilities in web applications. *Computers & Security, 31*(3), 344–356.
52. Scholte, T., Robertson, W., Balzarotti, D., & Kirda, E., (2012). Preventing input validation vulnerabilities in web applications through automated type analysis. In: *2012 IEEE 36th Annual Computer Software and Applications Conference* (Vol. 1, No. 1, pp. 233–243). IEEE.
53. Shar, L. K., & Tan, H. B. K., (2012). Automated removal of cross site scripting vulnerabilities in web applications. *Information and Software Technology, 54*(5), 467–478.
54. Shar, L. K., & Tan, H. B. K., (2012). Defeating SQL injection. *Computer, 46*(3), 69–77.
55. Shrivastava, G., & Pathak, K., (2013). SQL injection attacks: Technique and prevention mechanism. *International Journal of Computer Applications, 69*(7), 1–20.
56. Spett, K., (2005). Cross-site scripting. *SPI Labs, 1*(1), 20.
57. Sudhodanan, A., Khodayari, S., & Caballero, J., (2019). Cross-origin state inference (COSI) attacks: Leaking web site states through XS-leaks. arXiv preprint arXiv:1908.02204, 1-20.
58. Sun, F., Xu, L., & Su, Z., (2011). Static detection of access control vulnerabilities in web applications. In: *20th USENIX Security Symposium (USENIX Security 11)* (Vol. 1, No. 1, pp. 1–20).
59. Sun, H. M., Chen, Y. H., & Lin, Y. H., (2011). oPass: A user authentication protocol

resistant to password stealing and password reuse attacks. *IEEE Transactions on Information Forensics and Security,* 7(2), 651–663.

60. Thomas, K., Pullman, J., Yeo, K., Raghunathan, A., Kelley, P. G., Invernizzi, L., & Bursztein, E., (2019). Protecting accounts from credential stuffing with password breach alerting. In: *28th USENIX Security Symposium (USENIX Security 19)* (Vol. 1, No. 1, pp. 1556–1571).
61. Tyagi, S., & Kumar, K., (2018). Evaluation of static web vulnerability analysis tools. In: *2018 Fifth International Conference on Parallel, Distributed and Grid Computing (PDGC)* (Vol. 1, No. 1, pp. 1–6). IEEE.
62. Vargas, S., Vera, M., & Rodriguez, J., (2019). Security strategy for vulnerabilities prevention in the development of web applications. In: *Journal of Physics: Conference Series* (Vol. 1414, No. 1, p. 12017). IOP Publishing.
63. Vogt, P., Nentwich, F., Jovanovic, N., Kirda, E., Kruegel, C., & Vigna, G., (2007). Cross site scripting prevention with dynamic data tainting and static analysis. In: *NDSS* (Vol. 2007, p. 12).
64. Wang, R., Xing, L., Wang, X., & Chen, S., (2013). Unauthorized origin crossing on mobile platforms: Threats and mitigation. In: *Proceedings of the 2013 ACM SIGSAC Conference on Computer & Communications Security* (Vol. 1, No. 1, pp. 635–646).
65. Wassermann, G., & Su, Z., (2008). Static detection of cross-site scripting vulnerabilities. In: *Proceedings of the 30th International Conference on Software Engineering* (Vol. 1, No. 1, pp. 171–180).
66. Wei, K., Muthuprasanna, M., & Kothari, S., (2006). Preventing SQL injection attacks in stored procedures. In: *Australian Software Engineering Conference (ASWEC'06)* (p. 8). IEEE.
67. Yeole, A. S., & Meshram, B. B., (2011). Analysis of different technique for detection of SQL injection. In: *Proceedings of the International Conference & Workshop on Emerging Trends in Technology* (Vol. 1, No. 1, pp. 963–966).

Index

D

E

Kolibri 360 GmbH
Ferdinand-Jühlke-Straße 7
99095 Erfurt, Deutschland
produktsicherheit@kolibri360.de